KU-430-134

THIS IS EUROPE

Ben Judah is a Franco-British author and journalist. He has reported from across Europe with his writing on politics and society featuring widely, including in *The New York Times*, *The Financial Times* and *Foreign Policy*. His first book, *Fragile Empire*, was published by Yale University Press in 2013. His second book, *This is London*, published by Picador, was shortlisted for the Baillie Gifford Prize 2016 and for the 2019 Ryszard Kapuscinski Award for Literary Reportage. He speaks English, French, Russian and Hebrew. He lives in New York City with his wife and cat.

Also by Ben Judah

FRAGILE EMPIRE

THIS IS LONDON

BEN JUDAH

THIS IS EUROPE

HOW WE LIVE NOW

PICADOR

First published 2023 by Picador
an imprint of Pan Macmillan
The Smithson, 6 Briset Street, London EC1M 5NR
EU representative: Macmillan Publishers Ireland Ltd, 1st Floor,
The Liffey Trust Centre, 117–126 Sheriff Street Upper,
Dublin 1, D01 YC43
Associated companies throughout the world
www.panmacmillan.com

ISBN 978-1-4472-7626-5

Copyright © Ben Judah 2023

The right of Ben Judah to be identified as the
author of this work has been asserted by him in accordance
with the Copyright, Designs and Patents Act 1988.

All rights reserved. No part of this publication may be reproduced,
stored in a retrieval system, or transmitted, in any form, or by any means
(electronic, mechanical, photocopying, recording or otherwise)
without the prior written permission of the publisher.

Pan Macmillan does not have any control over, or any responsibility for,
any author or third-party websites referred to in or on this book.

9 8 7 6 5 4 3 2 1

A CIP catalogue record for this book is available from the British Library.

Printed and bound by CPI Group (UK) Ltd, Croydon, CR0 4YY

This book is sold subject to the condition that it shall not, by way of
trade or otherwise, be lent, hired out, or otherwise circulated without
the publisher's prior consent in any form of binding or cover other than
that in which it is published and without a similar condition including
this condition being imposed on the subsequent purchaser.

Visit **www.picador.com** to read more about all our books
and to buy them. You will also find features, author interviews and
news of any author events, and you can sign up for e-newsletters
so that you're always first to hear about our new releases.

Dedication dedication dedication dedication.

CONTENTS

You live in a continent of seven hundred and forty-eight million people.

You catch glimpses of it. You fly. You drive. You work. You wake up somewhere else. You walk in a city where you can't speak the language. You find yourself in terminals, on beaches, in bus stations. You feel lost. You catch snapshots. You overhear things you can't understand. You sit wondering who these people are. Or where they are on the arc of life. You want what politicians and pundits and political scientists can't give you.

You want to listen. You want to know how we live now.

1 ROTTERDAM

First you see the lights.

Then you see the colours.

White. Orange. Red. A black horizon.

Coming closer. Tankers. Ferries. Containers.

Moving. Distant glows. Glints in single file.

Welcome to Rotterdam, radios control.

Pilot on the way to your vessel. Over.

The deck is freezing. The night wind bites his face. Jelle can hardly make out the waves in the dark water. *Prepare for pilot boarding. Over.*

'I'm the start of Europe.'

His small boat rocks in the spray.

The super container is so close now. A castle in the tide.

His heart beats faster. He gestures at his skipper. *We're almost there.*

'I meet them when all you can see of Europe is an orange glow.'

'Twelve miles out. The point they can go no further alone.'

The orders from the control tower are always the same.

Approaching vessel, they call.

Reduce your speed. Over.

Jelle checks the time: 5:07 a.m. It's not yet dawn.

The system has to keep moving. It can never stop.

'After this point there are too many ships. Too many currents. Too many obstacles for the ships to enter alone. So they send the pilots. We take them in.'

He's getting closer to the ship. He can practically touch it now. *Put your ladder out. Over.*

He's in his fifties now. He's got light hair and a clipped beard.

He looks tired but a smile of tense excitement creeps over his face.

You know this feeling if you're a harbour pilot.

You see the ladder coming down. You hear it clattering.

You know you're about to jump. Between one ship and another. Right over the water.

'Every time it happens like this, when we board. When it's summer, when it's daylight, when it's warm, you just step over.'

You hardly notice it. You forget it.

Another moment that flashes past in the sun.

'But when it's bad weather, when it's dark, when the waves are rolling, when it's surging, when it's raining, it's something else. You feel nerves . . . you actually feel tense. Before you step. Especially at night.'

The ladder comes down from the vessel.

He raises his eyes. It's like a huge metal wall.

His face is wet from streaking rain. He feels the wind pushing.

You know this feeling too.

You're tense to make that jump.

Then Jelle has to climb as fast as he can.

Everything races in his mind.

'You think: *This is the moment. This is the moment.*'

'Then you make that step.'

You're tense because the waves could fall away beneath you, then surge back – when you're on that ladder. You're tense because the waves could pull the boats apart, then slam them together – when you're on that ladder. Because they can crush you, they can pull you anywhere. You take a chance when you grab that ladder.

When you make that jump.

'You see the water rushing and the waves, and you have to hold on. You can see the water rushing in the night and the deck lights and the water is black, just black. You see nothing. Just the face of the water and the spray, and you're scared.'

'Because you want to go home again.'

His gloves grab the bars.

He pulls up. He's thinking, *Shit, this is rough today.*

'I've got to go as fast as I can.'

He feels the ladder blown by the wind.

He's tense because accidents happen. Not often, but they have. Once or twice a year they fall. Once, the pilot boat got flipped over by huge waves they never expected and suddenly they found themselves stuck underneath it. Banging on the hull.

Doing anything to get out.

This is in his mind as he jumps.

It's not too bad today. The rain's not too heavy.

Once or twice Jelle has slipped. Hanging on with one hand.

'Then you're dangling in between. You forget everything. You just focus. You just climb. You just do it. Then the guy on the ship grabs you. But that moment, it goes too fast, too quickly, for you to feel anything.'

Then you wave to the guys in the boat below.

'Thanks a lot, see you next time.'

Everybody's got to get back to work.

And then he makes his wet way to the bridge.

It's dark tonight. Only a few lights glowing from the machines. There are a lot of people on the bridge but Jelle makes straight for the captain.

Hello, he says. *Good morning.*

Welcome to Rotterdam.

He always does this on purpose. They think he's a guest on their vessel.

But really, they are guests in Rotterdam.

Welcome to Europoort.

And then he gets to work.

There's a tear on the horizon, a pink light, a pale dawn, as he takes the controls.

It's just rain today. But when the weather is at its worst, they suspend the jump.

The little boats are grounded. And they go in by helicopter.

You can't stop working. There are 30,000 ships a year here.

Someone has to pilot most of them: that's 440 million tonnes. They fly when the waves are over two and a half metres high. When they are higher than ceiling height. When they throw themselves at you with the force of speeding cars.

The helicopter flies in and hovers over the supertanker in the storm. There is so much at stake. So much on them. You have to get a pilot there if it is physically possible.

They tell them it's all worth hundreds of millions.

Jelle looks out. The hoist operator is trying to find a place to land. The wind, the worst of it, keeps pressing against the chopper, shaking it, buffeting it, rattling it. The waves lashing against the vessel. He feels like an onboarding pirate.

Because the wind can get so bad, it can sway the chopper so much, crews panic. They think that chopper is about to crash and they rush outside in what look like moon suits, crinkly, aluminium, reflective fire suits, trembling and shaking with their long hoses pointed right at him. Their hearts pounding. They know fire could blow up the tanker.

'They are waiting and they're on deck. But when we get closer and it's allowed, we see a spot on the bridge wing and I think, *How about there*, so I don't need to walk so much, that's nice . . . *Let's hoist there.*'

The captain radios – *Permission granted.*

'The door opens and I come down like a teabag on a single string.'

Into this world of force and water.

Into this world of waves and wind and the beating rotor.

'But all I think when I land on the deck is, *Is my security harness disconnected? Is my bag disconnected?* Because I can hardly think with the rain and the noise. And if I make one mistake it will pull me up. Dangling. Half attached.'

It's all good. Jelle gives a thumbs-up.

And the chopper soars up and away.

It's not been like that today. It's time to stop thinking about it. Now it's time to work.

The ship needs to get to Rotterdam. There's a time slot. A rush.

'Sometimes I'll walk into the bridge and they'll laugh and they've taken pictures. But sometimes the captain will be really angry and yell . . . *We wanted you to hoist over there! We thought the chopper was much too close!*'

But the Rotterdam pilots will always be firm then.

'We know what we're doing.'

Thinking, if you don't like it this way you can turn around.

Now the job begins. He'd got to know them over the years. Thousands of ships. Thousands of captains. And there are patterns to them which he could see. With the Indian captains and the Indian crews it is always procedure, procedure. Running through the checklist. *Pilot, are we sticking to the procedure?* They would be so committed to the procedure sometimes they would ask: *Mr Pilot, do we encounter any other vessels today?*

They would be surrounded by other vessels.

Coal barges. Incoming ferries. Orange gas tankers.

Nah, he'd say, *today you're the only one.*

The Indian first mate would start writing and then suddenly flinch.

Mr Pilot, are you making jokes?

The old-style Russian captains, with those old-style Russian crews, on those old-style Russian ships, now, they were the worst. No jokes. No small talk. No humour. You came onboard. They barely greeted you. If you were lucky a Russian officer might grunt.

Coffee?

Sure, he'd nod.

Then they'd grab whatever mug they found in the cabin, shove three fingers in to give it a quick manual scrub before plonking it down in front of him.

'With the old-style Russians it's always the same. They ignore me.'

'I ignore them back.'

That way it would drag on. Three hours. Alone.

But the young ones, they were different. Modern Russian captains with modern Russian crews on modern Russian ships.

You weren't so alone.

'But even then, the Russian captains are not very popular with us.'

Now the Germans, those were his favourites.

Because they got excited. When the tension started building. When super containers were coming in. When speed was building. When they got close to the limit.

		Name	Ship	Nationality
	7737	DELFIN, ULYSSES	PLAIN PALMS	FILIPINO
	7738	AEJI, L ANGELO	PLAIN PALAIS	FILIPINO
	7739	Ji Jin ping	PLAIN PALAIS	FILIPINO
	7740	WANG SHI HUA	HE HUA HAI	CHIAN
	7741	zhang song	He HuA HAI	CHIAN
	7742	ZHAO PING	He HuA HAI	CHIAN
	7743	WU MAI Bin	43 HUA HAI	CHINA
	7744	zhanghaiming	HE HUA HAI	CHINA
	7745	Parthasarathi Sikdar	HE Hua Hai	China
	7746	G. BALASUBRAMANI	MV FALCON BAY	INDIA
	7747	V. JAWTHIVEL	MV FALCON BAY	INDIA
		DINSDAG	12 maart	2019
	7748	Arpit Prashant	MV Falconbay	Indian
	7749	Neeraj Kumar	MV Falconbay	Indian
	7750	Partho Sikdhar	MV Falcon Bay	Indian
		WOENSDAG	13 maart	2019
	7751	Aharsh	HARVEST FROST	INDIN
	7752	Dileep sworn	HARVEST frost	indian
	7753	Surender Singh	Harvest Frost	Indian
	7754	Khalssi Kiran	HARVEST FROST	INDIAN
	7755	Dmitry Sokolov	Harvest Frost	Russian
	7756	Sudheep . cm	HARVEST FROST	INDIAN
	7757	SWESH SUPRY KC	HARVEST FROST	INDIAN
	7758	Tandel Pragnesh	Falcon Bay	INDIAN
	7759	Tandel Dharmesh	Falcon Bay	INDIAN
	7760	TANMAY	Falcon Bay	INDIAN
	7761	G BALASUBRAMANI	FALCON BAY	INDIAN
	7762	V SAUTHIVEL	FALCON BAY	INDIAN
	7763	JOSEPH Pius	FALCON BAY	INDIAN
		Donderdag	14 maart	2019
	7764	AHARSH	HARVEST FROST	INDIAN
	7765	Shimon. M J	Harvest Frost	INDIAN
	7766	Cheeketi Pandseban	,,	INDIAN
	7767	BHANUDADA PRATAP	DL,	Indian

They'd start shouting.

Faster. Faster. Ropes.

'They're our favourites because they are just like the Dutch.'

But with the Chinese it was very different. They were very polite. They were welcoming. They wore these long green jackets. But they never listened.

'First you say what to do. *Throw the ropes like that.* That kind of thing. Then they say, *Yes. Yes, we'll do it.* Then they do their own plan.'

It always worked the same way. Rank was very important on a Chinese vessel. From captain to crew the jump was immense. When something urgently, right now, needed to get done you had to find the right man. And when you'd find him and say, *This is how we do it in Rotterdam,* he'd say, *Yes,* nod and then ignore you completely with his Chinese plan.

'You've just got to adjust. Each time they say yes and do it differently.'

There were lots of things he didn't understand on a Chinese ship.

It was one of those today.

Is this really all they eat for breakfast? Jelle wonders, glancing around.

Just a pear? Or is that just what the Chinese gave me? What is the captain shouting about in such a loud voice to the mate? And what is suddenly so funny?

Jelle will be at the controls.

Check this. Check that.

'The job is simple, really. Approach and dock.'

The tug-boats will be there now. Ready to assist. The berthmen will give him the signal. They're ready. The first ropes are tied. Then you begin to see it.

The chimneys. The windmills. The blinking red.

You get closer still. You breathe a bit easier.

Now it takes about an hour.

Houses. Landing bays.

'The beginning of Europe.'

And then, over them, those huge machines.

Whirring. Jolting. Humming. Working.

It's dawn running smoothly.

Then he has time to think. About his family. About himself.

His father was a welder, he could make anything. His brother captains a tug-boat. He was eighteen when he first went out to sea. It crushed him. The loneliness. On the banana boat to the Caribbean. Back and forth to Newport near Cardiff. Odd pallets crawling with spiders. But he would never forget what it was like at night.

'That first time you go out on the night watch your heart skips faster.'

That memory kept coming back to him.

'You look starboard from the bridge and you see the captain's cabin and you see he's drawn his curtains. He's trusting me.'

And now you have it. You have command. The ship is yours.

'You can look outside. You can see the ocean, which is endless. You feel something. Something deep inside you. But then I remember that I'm not here on a sailing boat. That I'm on a commercial vessel. You've got to go from A to B.'

'And it's a business and you're not free.'

'It's a prison, actually.'

At night, that was when the worst accidents happened. You can't let a thing slip. Even here. He remembers that night in the South China Sea, the voices around him. It sends him shivers to think about it even now. That moment on the Shell supertanker when suddenly – *clack, clack, clack* – the green lights of Chinese fishermen in tiny bobbing craft went off around him.

Alert. Everywhere around the tanker.

'They want their fish to come closer, you see . . . so they turn their lights on. They don't have any communications to warn us where they are. So you only see them when you see them. It makes your heart skip a beat.'

It comes back with a chill.

That feeling, when he was in trouble, when he was piloting one of the biggest machines ever built – so immense, it takes a huge effort even to turn – that exact moment when he felt cold nerves. A supertanker can't just zigzag between the fishermen.

'It's too late, too late, you think.'

'But there's a way, there's always a way.'

And then you find it.

But that was years ago and this is Rotterdam.

The control tower calls.

All clear. Ready for you at Europoort.

And it begins.

What's the tide?

What's the wind? What happens if we turn?

The radio commands are coming in.

Traffic. Vessels.

Starboard side.

Rudder port twenty.

The sun blaring bright now.

You turn at the Hook of Holland. You enter the wide mouth of the River Maas where everything flows. Then you turn again to the Maasvlakte, that vast artificial claw of land where the Europoort is. You use the sightlines. One crane. Then another crane.

And you dock.

You have to get it right. Exactly parallel. Focus, otherwise you'll hit the cranes with 300,000 tonnes. And they'll fall like dominoes.

'One mistake and it's a disaster.'

The boatmen come in. The ropes are thrown. There is a rush and clamour onboard. Men are yelling. Then with a thud it's done.

'Nobody claps. Nobody cheers. It's not like you've arrived in the Canary Islands on a package holiday. Only if you've been through gale-force winds will the captain turn and say to you: *Thank you so much, Mr Pilot . . . I really appreciate you being here.*'

It's time to go home.

Jelle looks at himself in the mirror.

Thinking: *It's not an easy job.*

He feels the week building up on him.

The way it works is a rota between the pilots. Each one moving up like the penny falls until it is his turn. Seven days on. Seven days off. But they can call you, at any time, in those seven days. And the rule is fixed. Only eight hours of fixed home rest between each job. They can call you at three in the morning, or three in the afternoon.

'When you're wide awake and they still haven't called, it's the worst.'

That's when you woke up early. And then they don't call. Lunch. Afternoon. Gone. And you'll still be waiting at home. Your energy dipping.

'It's difficult to sleep in advance.'

It's then Jelle begins to feel a low feeling of dread. That's happening now. Evening is coming. They're going to call him. He knows it. They could call at any moment. But they haven't.

He knows he's got to force himself to sleep.

'But I just can't at 7 p.m. when I'm not tired.'

Jelle lies staring at the ceiling. Thinking.

'Thinking: *Shit. I can't sleep. I can't sleep.*'

Settling like an irritant. Unable to catch it. To let go. Feeling more and more tense and tense because he's tired and there is no room for mistakes but it's still so hard to sleep. Knowing they're going to call him. And when they call him it could be midnight.

'And they'll ring me and be like, *All right, we've got a container vessel, a large vessel, a small vessel. It's coming to Rotterdam, coming to Europoort.*'

Then the phone finally rings.

Jelle leaves. He drives. Across that flat, simple land, once reclaimed from the sea. But he can already feel it. Tiredness, like weights, inside him.

An hour later he's at the pilot station.

'We have no way of knowing in advance how busy it's going to be.'

And he can tell from the rain, it is going to be rough.

'You become more exhausted. You become more and more tired through the night. And at 9 a.m. you think . . . *Oh fuck, I really want to sleep.*'

'It's like you're completely spent.'

Jelle is on the bridge when it hits.

Twelve kilometres out there at sea.

I'm feeling so tired, he sighs.

I've got to focus. I'll focus.

This is when accidents happen.

The rain is starting to lash.

'That's the worst part of the job.'

Jelle tries to focus. He can always focus. The controls are going smoothly.

It's one of those storms when the excitement still gets him. When he remembers how much he loves this: when the weather gets tough, when he makes that jump, when he pushes close to the limit. It's one of those nights he feels a thrill.

Yet something else hangs over him tonight.

'Sometimes I get this feeling.'

'That I'm carrying rubbish.'

Jelle turns and behind him sees the stacked cargo deck.

Hundreds of them.

'And then I think I'm on this huge cargo ship carrying 10,000 containers. And then I suddenly think . . . *What rubbish is actually in these containers?* Toys. TVs. Chairs. Tables. Bicycles. Shampoo. Only rubbish. Plastic American or Chinese rubbish.'

It's one of those nights, when Jelle is piloting in, between the hulking cargoes of those metallic giants, and in the distance he can see the port like a city of coiled lights, like a space station, like a semiconductor.

And as it glows, he thinks.

'I've got this feeling that sixty per cent of the containers are filled with rubbish. Europe is just eating shit. Everyone is risking their life . . . and I just think half of this is filled with rubbish. Just poisoning the world.'

He looks out.

He knows it doesn't stop there.

There are the distribution centres, the warehouses, the pipelines. The barges and the trucks. The lines wrapping and packing. The men with parcels knocking on doors at first light. This system of maximum efficiency that creates maximum waste.

'I catch myself and think: *This is one of the biggest machines in the world full of more than 300,000 tonnes of cargo and most people don't know it exists and that we exist.* They don't think about how any of this exists. That I exist.'

Jelle looks at the machines and it's a strange feeling of love.

'This is the mouth of Europe. We're feeding the mouth of Europe. Full of little parcels. Filling it with little pieces of crap.'

2 BALOGA

He woke up gasping and crossed himself. Pulling himself out of nothingness in the lorry cabin. His head was killing him. Like his brain wasn't working right. He coughed: a thick, horrible cough, foul-tasting and full of acid. His eyes stung.

The dashboard blinked 11 a.m.

Fuck. He'd been set to get the hell out of here at 4 a.m.: the orders, the company, the schedules, the whole route – now it was all fucked.

He could hardly focus: he was dizzy, he realized.

Ionut coughed some more and covered his eyes; for a moment it felt like the cabin was swaying.

What the – with a bash he grabbed the door and began to yell when he saw what they'd done. The entire front hood of the lorry had been lifted up: round the back it had been ripped open and emptied. The work of a knife. His goods were gone.

The only things left were the order papers flapping on the ground.

It had been a professional job.

'That's when I realized they'd gassed me.'

Those loose papers told him what he'd lost: perfumes – expensive French perfumes. For a moment he just stood there. A beefy man in a hoodie and glasses with a thick neck and a forty-something face. His head pounding. Not sure what to do. Then he snapped out of it.

Muttering thanks that he was still here.

'They'd hit me with sleeping gas.'

Then it all came back to him: the loading bay yesterday, those French Arabs that had made him dawdle and delay, who kept on telling him they weren't done, the crates weren't ready, no, he couldn't go. By the time the packing was done it was too late,

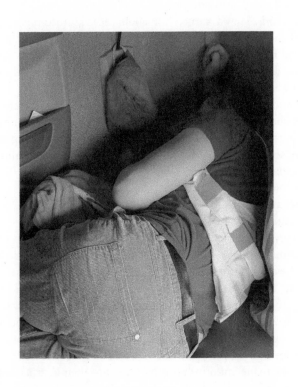

he was exhausted and he parked close by in one of the streets. There were lorries everywhere. Full of the usual boys: Poles, Lithuanians, Hungarians, the lot, and a ton of other Romanians.

'It was another immigrant-infested area.'

Yes, he thought, his head pounding, his eyes scratching, *it must have been those Arabs. That must have been why they were making me wait. They were tricking me. They wanted me to park here and not make it the hell out of Paris into a proper secure bay.*

Bastards. They'd warned him about these Moroccan gangs. He'd heard about this a lot at pit stops all over Europe. Old truckers had warned him that this was how they liked to operate, with sleeping gas. And now they'd done it to him. Knocked out cold.

It was such an easy thing to do, really.

Ionut could almost see them doing it as he stood there. One, or maybe two of them, lifting up the hood. One press – that hiss – them spraying the gas into the air vent. His face slumping to side, when, seconds later, it seeped out of the heating. Putting him out.

Nothing, he swore, *can stop a professional.*

It took minutes to call the police.

Then it was painfully slow.

'Some filthy careless cops came over.'

They took him in for paperwork.

Ionut struggled to make himself understood: but they only shrugged and used a bit of English, a language they more or less shared. Then they disappeared. He could still feel the gas: his eyes were still scratchy, his thoughts were heavy and slow and kept on getting lost in themselves. He wasn't quite sure where he was or how to get back. They wouldn't just leave him here. *Would they? Yes*, they'd take him back. *That was right. They had to.* It was an hour before the uniforms returned: *Get out* – their instructions were clear. This is a police station not a taxi company.

It felt like something burst inside.

Who the fuck cares about a Romanian lorry driver?

'My mind was so clouded and I was so furious I just set off walking. I swear I was cursing the country, my job and everything around. But I realized nothing will change.'

He put the key in the ignition and drove.

These were the kind of things that happened.

He'd switch the music on and wonder how it had come to this. Forty years old. The lorry. The road out of Cluj. The road out of Transylvania. This was not who he had wanted to be.

'I wanted to be a singer. I really like singing.'

That was never an option for him, he knew.

Not for a boy from that village called Baloga.

'I was really fascinated by synth-pop . . .'

'But it's all gone, my voice included.'

It was a long time ago. Ionut never sang any more.

Often, he wasn't sure why, he'd think of his eighteenth birthday.

He could see himself clearly. He'd planned to work on the farms all summer. Haymaking, harvesting – that kind of thing. Then throw a big party at the village restaurant. The farm girls were pretty. He remembered that very clearly: exceptionally pretty. Ionut kept thinking about them when he bought some blue jeans and booked the restaurant. Then his luck crapped out. Two days before, his farmer boss disappeared. That scumbag left Romania. Left without paying him and all his other workers. Even there in the cabin he could still feel the burn: from calling person to person saying the party's off.

Yes, he'd think, *I'm not a lucky guy.*

He'd chuckle. In the end his party had just been him, three buddies and a bottle of Perfect Lemon vodka.

Then he'd sigh. Ionut could see all those faces now. They'd all gone.

That's my whole generation, he'd think. *Migrants.*

You leave for two, three, four months, when you leave.

You get to know those motorways.

Autostrada A1. M5-ös Autópálya.

You know how they feel.

The first week was always the worst. Everything hit him again, on the way to Rotterdam. How small the cabin was. How much his back hurt. How much noise there was: the engine, that constant groaning, that trembling sound as the lorries hurtled past you.

You lose your appetite.

You can hardly face it in the cabin. You can't sleep. You keep lying there, on that thin trucker's mattress over the seats, that feeling you're not quite safe, never leaving you.

'Every time, I'm off into this same shit.'

Pile-ups. Coordinators yelling. Phoning him. Orders: *More, fast, get to the depot.*

Superiors giving him a piece of their mind: *Too late, too slow. Sprechen sie Deutsch? Get there faster.* Fleshy-faced men who never cared about you and only about how much money they were making out of the company. Ionut would only nod.

They know how bad it is, he'd think.

They just don't give a shit.

Then something would come over him, like a rhythm.

The same thing over and over again: endless dual carriageways, perpetual warehouses, more perimeter fences. The same colours. Concrete. Dark tarmac. Metallic grey. Corrugated green. Endless passing cars. The same low panic. The same feeling: always knowing exactly where you were on the GPS and feeling nowhere at the same time. The same thoughts.

This is what killed my marriage.

The distance: it got into everything.

It had got between them.

Ionut was left with two kids he never saw, and for every three months on the road he sent so much money back for them he hardly had any left when he set back off for home.

I'm picking up more debt than I can earn.

The same pattern. Until his heart sank that it was change day.

When the company made you swap cabins.

You flinch before you open those doors.

You know when it hits you. That smell.

Ionut couldn't even describe it. That stench when someone's been living like an animal; when there's thick stains on the seats, mouldy bread bits everywhere, under the bed, in the fridge, smears round the doors and – *Is it piss?* – on the floor. Having flashbacks to the time he swapped with some German. Then vomited the instant he saw the cabin.

Oh, I know why.

Ionut would curse at the wheel.

I know why the fuck this happened. I know this guy would have cared if a Romanian trucker had left the cabin dirty for him. But a German leaving it dirty for a Romanian . . .

He'd smelt that guy for days.

Until finally, his nose numbed, or the smell began to fade.

There's one rule in Europe, thought Ionut. *Eastern Europeans are second rate. One rule for Brits, French and Germans; one rule for them. Everywhere, we're doing the dirty jobs.*

Everywhere, they were told not to complain.

Then it seemed to get easier. The second week, the third week, the fourth.

His days blurring into each other. His shift stretching out. Not the official nine: but ten, eleven, twelve hours. Until the street lamps started to glow and he'd see the German truck drivers turning off into the fancy car parks with restaurants and showers.

'Maybe if I were a German driver and paid like one I could afford to stop in one of those car parks. Or get myself a warm meal in a restaurant like a German driver . . . what's twenty euro for a German guy?'

Then he'd laugh at the wheel.

He might be in Stuttgart but he was still on a Cluj salary.

'That's the whole fucking point.'

The car parks he'd pull into were the ones where you didn't have to pay: where the drivers would piss by their wheels and shit in the bushes round the back, or else the Portaloos were full of worms.

The sound of rats scuttling and squeaking under their tyres.

They follow me everywhere, he'd think.

Those pit stops, no matter where, were full of conmen.

There were so many of them: guys out there who could swindle you out of your wallet or even your whole truck. The worst were the truckers with the shakes and those wide eyes. There were amphetamines everywhere on the road. He could tell them a mile off: the guys who took them so that they didn't have to slow down.

'I wish I was a priest. I should have listened to my mother when I was still young. But there's no chance now. It's too late.'

Those nights, he'd lie there and think.

He didn't want to talk to them. He didn't want to drink with them.

Whatever they had in those bottles.

'It's permanent stress . . . you wake up stressed and you go to sleep stressed. We're overwhelmed with back pains. You can hardly ever sleep. The tiredness and the stress just stack up on more tiredness and more stress. It's continual . . . your mind no longer perceives it as stress but your body does. It just gets worse over time.'

It was on nights like that he'd really feel it. This cabin was his whole world.

Thousands of miles. Fixed in one spot.

You woke up in the truck. You washed in the truck; slapping water on your face from a plastic bowl. That's where you ate, too. Warming some stew, or whatever you had, over a little gas stove. Or that's a dream, just what you'd like to do: he'd gone weeks eating only cold food.

'No matter what country in Europe it is, our conditions are the same.'

'You're overworked like a slave . . .'

'You just feel exploited eighty per cent of the time.'

He felt nothing when he reached Rotterdam.

The longest trips always seemed to end up there.

The bleeping terminals with the massive load–unload bays where the men in high-viz never let you wait, where they kept waving at you, *Get out, get out – time's up.*

It worked like a machine. One enormous machine.

I'm just a piece, he'd think, looking up.

Unload. Load. Reload.

The night made him nervous in Rotterdam: they said it was full of Turkish gangs and illegal Filipinos, runaway sailors, all sleeping in the other lorries parked illegally around him. Those were the nights when he struggled; when he wasn't sure if he was awake or asleep or trapped somewhere in between; when he kept being jolted by the same dreams, the ones he always had – the ones of never-ending bleeping, of reversing into the loading bay, or of suddenly hitting the brakes.

The mornings in that port were cold and damp. The kind that felt like it kneaded into your bones. Those mornings when he would wake up in the dark. The deliveries were scheduled early. The alarm was always trilling: 3:45 a.m. Ionut would wash himself in his trusty plastic bowl in the cabin, step outside to smoke a cigarette and then drive.

You know that air on the motorways.

You know the air that leaves you out of breath.

He'd breathe that for weeks. His thoughts would start to fog.

There've been so many accidents, he'd think.

Sometimes at the wheel he would think of the dead. So many drivers had died. So many of them in collisions. So many of them had heart attacks.

'Young drivers ranging from thirty to fifty years old, they just die . . . that's it.'

He'd think of the husband-and-wife crew that had been driving near Mulhouse. But he hated thinking about it. They'd been working in shifts. Right after the husband took the wheel something failed. Something was worn out. Exhausted. Not working any more. They didn't see a traffic column up ahead and rammed into it at 56 kilometres an hour.

The wife died on impact.

He'd think of the guy he knew who had a heart attack driving in Italy. How he never made it back to Romania. He thought about how devastated his wife was.

He could see her now.

'Your mind takes a proper toll in this job.'

The first time he almost crashed, Ionut was in Italy. He wasn't sure how it happened. How could you know when it happened? For a moment he just wasn't there: gone. He dozed off on the leftmost lane and when he woke up the lorry was hurtling several lanes off to the right. The noise of horns honking frantically hooting disaster from all sides.

'A fraction of a second. I blinked, I woke up . . . it scared my sleep off proper.'

It had been so quick.

'I have hundreds of other occasions where I actively had to dodge potential crashes, nutjobs driving too fast. You know how roads are.'

It happened once. In Romania. Some guy hit the brakes hard in front of him. It was too late. Crunching metal and screaming glass. He was hurtling. He felt a wrenching weight. Something was

buckling. His trailer was pulling him. Spinning him. The cabin was tumbling. Then he was turning over. The alarm was singing.

Then he was still.

'I did manage to get out in the end but the truck was wasted.'

He could still see himself in that ditch: punching to get out of the door and pull himself free. He thought about it often enough. *These were the kinds of things that happened to a truck driver.* Sometimes, when he was alone in the car park on Sundays, Ionut would stop. He would put his hands together and think of the road.

Then he would close his eyes, mumble and pray.

You know truckers are like sailors.

You're three months here. You're four months there.

You'll find lonely souls.

Ionut was divorced when he went on Cami's Facebook page. He wasn't supposed to be there. He cycled through her photos from start to finish, so he even saw what she was like when she was really young. Then he left a like. The light of the phone lit up his face. Then he left a comment.

'I don't know how it happened . . . nothing is coincidental in this world.'

Something surprising happened. Cami liked back. Ionut left another comment. She left another like.

Am I going too far? No, he decided, then sent the first private message.

hi :)

'Then slowly we began to message.'

how's your day?

Ionut couldn't believe it. Cami was a truck driver.

A real truck driver in flesh and blood.

'She said she wanted to start driving across Europe.'

That was when they started to call.

He told her about what had happened in Paris. He told her that, once, some other time, he'd gone into the city centre, then wandered the streets, but that he'd left sad, as it was so expensive there was no place for him there.

He told her that spring was his favourite season.

He told her of the flowers that sometimes grew by the side of the road.

He told her that he was a mountains guy; yes, that's who he was.

He told her about the Alps. That when he was driving that was what he looked forward to: the jagged cliffs, the roads that wound and turned, the mountains bared like gigantic teeth. Their peaks like some distant Valhalla. Ionut told her you needed your wits about you up there. You couldn't just be any old driver up there when the windscreen wipers beat back the powdery snow in the crystal light you got at the very end and the very beginning of the day. Ionut told her that was where he felt something, where his heart beat faster: when the white crust covered everything – when you lost sight of the road ahead.

She called him when he was in the parking lot and said she was divorced too.

'She was surprised that I got it, that I understood.'

'Because when you've been divorced you know how they've suffered too.'

They kept on calling.

He told her that he had been hurting. That he was lonely. He heard her voice down the telephone. It was all he wanted to hold on to, saying, *I understand, I've been hurting too.* He didn't want to hang up. *I understand,* she said, *I'm almost forty too.*

'We kept on calling for about three months . . . four months.'

He wouldn't feel so alone afterwards in the cabin.

He would lie there on the thin mattress thinking just one thing after these calls: *Maybe this is what love is. Maybe this is all that love is.*

'She understands me.'

'I never wanted anything more than this . . . just to be understood.'

They kept calling. He kept driving. His routes crossed Europe until he was back in Romania. Then he realized something. He looked at the GPS. He knew where Cami was. It made him tense. His stomach tingled. Their trucks were nearing.

hey I'm going to be in bucharest you wanna meet up???

He could barely focus on the road.

'When he finally met it was in a parking lot.'

Ionut parked the truck as neatly as he could.

Switched off the ignition and pulled out the key.

'I felt a lot of feelings right then . . . I felt butterflies in my stomach.'

There she was, standing there, brown eyes and black hair, between the lorries.

And that was when they kissed.

Things were different now. They worked together.

When Ionut drove, she would sleep; nine hours at the wheel and then they'd switch over. Then he would try and sleep as Cami drove. But he never could, properly.

She wasn't as tough as him after all these years. Cami had no resistance to tiredness at all. Her face would change when it hit her and she would have to lie down. Always, she would fall asleep instantly. But fifteen years in these cabins meant Ionut could hold out. He always wound up making dinner: buns, little stews, bits of meat he'd warm up on his old gas flame. Things to make it nice for Cami. Then he would pass out.

'I think we only endure this because the organism adapts . . . it has to.'

The truck was often still for less than five hours a night. It felt like snatches: what they had together. When they needed each other they would do it in the cabin. But there were weeks in a row where, from exhaustion, they wouldn't want it.

'It's relentless. It's continuous. It's one day like this after another.'

It wasn't always like this, but sometimes, he would feel it wearing into him.

'Our daily work stretches up to almost twenty hours, nine hours each, out of which you're left with less than five hours where you've got to wash, eat and sleep in the end. For months . . . We're mocked and made fun of with such conditions, treated like sub-humans.'

His mood would swing; it wasn't going well. Those were the moments when Cami would hold him and whisper to him. *You feel joyful and lucky when you realize you're alive . . . You're alive. You can consider yourself lucky you got through a working season without anything happening to you. You might not, my sweetheart. One day you might not.*

'That's what she always tells me.'

—

The jobs they got were mostly to England.

Thousands of miles of grey that stretched in front of the eye. The night glows and the stripes on the road were always the same. It felt like they were travelling in a tube, or going back on themselves; or, when they drove in darkness, like they were even underground. Sometimes you'd blink and without the GPS there'd be no way of knowing you weren't in exactly the same place.

The further he got from Romania the more worried he got for the truck.

'In terms of actual physical abuse, vandalization, or attacks on the driver, the dangerous country is France. But when it comes to mugging, robberies, merchandise theft or general thievery? It's England. That's the worst country in Europe. England is especially dangerous when it comes to losing trailers.'

The road that worried him the most was the M1. There were highwaymen there. Truckers had stepped into a service station outside Leeds only to find their load gone by the time they'd come out again. Hoods with knives had gone for some of the old drivers. There were Albanians in Britain; Poles, Romanians, the lot. There were so many of them. He couldn't believe it. He felt like there must be millions of them. It was as though the villages in Eastern Europe had emptied to fill all the towns that ran along the M1.

In England, he thought a lot about the thieves.

'Over the course of several years I've noticed the thieves are the transitional people. The immigrants. Natives don't do this stuff in Britain or France, or at least in very small percentages. It's the people from Africa, Afghanistan, Romania, Poland . . . people from those lands are the rogues.'

He hated seeing Romanians begging.

Ionut could never sleep on the M1 unless he was in secure parking. There were tricksters here: people who'd play you like a fiddle. He'd heard so many stories. All the truckers would share them. Like the one about the thieves dressed as policemen who'd bark something at you in English and before you'd understood they weren't coppers they'd made off with six pallets in a white van 'for inspection'.

He thought about this often when he was driving.

'Especially at night the chances that you run into a lot of thieves at the service stations or the car parks is very high. Say you innocently park by the side of the road off the motorway between London and Birmingham, you mark yourself out as an obvious victim. You'll just be a sitting duck for thieves. Absolutely nobody assures your safety. They can seize your truck whole.'

It was damp in England, at night, when he stepped out and smoked: his legs swollen and sore. They were like prisons, he thought, the lots they slept in when they were here. The company knew about the situation here. That's why it was all rimmed by perimeter fences and nasty barbed wire. Ionut would pull on his cigarette and breathe: everything was so tightly packed together it felt like creeping through a metal alley between the trucks. Urban glows would fill the darkness. He knew he was being watched: there were cameras everywhere. He'd glance up at them, thinking.

'I can't mock England, even though such things are happening. The country is beautiful, the natives are very calm, they're very understanding, patient with you . . . especially if you have some problems in traffic or you need some help or directions. The English will help you. However, if you ask an immigrant from Eastern Europe you might never get the help you seek. I know too well that many English natives sold a lot of their property in London and moved up north – fleeing the immigrant-infested areas. God forbid that immigrant situation ever gets out of hand there.'

'This situation baffles me. The immigrants are taken in as the workforce, cared for by England and in return they do their best to up the crime rate! Is that how they repay the country for taking them in and offering them work and proper living conditions?'

Then the time would come to leave.

They would see so many small towns by the side of the road and flash by so many trembling little houses staring right into the traffic. It didn't take long to leave England but he would wonder long afterwards what it would be like to live there. There was something so ordered, so calm, so polite about the English that he met there.

'You know what? Everyone condemns them for bouncing out of the EU . . . but it's the only country in Europe in which, if it wasn't for the immigrants, I'd like to live.'

—

Not every trip led to Britain, but all it seemed, led through Germany.

That was where his brother was. In Heilbronn on a turning off Autobahn 6; that was where that little flat was, with the little bed, which he could collapse into and where he could sleep like a little boy again. That was where he had memories too: like that party – oh he didn't want to forget it – they had thrown that summer. It has started just like that. A crazy thought. Ten or twelve truckers had started messaging.

Let's just do it, they said.

One of the lorries dropped a pin: then the flags got closer.

'It was a proper party to remember . . . nobody bothered us there.'

They were laughing and the hiss and flick of the beers was going and for a moment Ionut smiled. He felt something cool and good through him and for a moment he drank deeply. He listened: the women were gossiping, their voices rising and falling, the way they do when they are having fun, and the meat began to crackle and spit on the stove as that smell, the smell of home, filled his nose. They passed the vodka round. Things speeded up. He was telling stories, the gypsy jazz was playing, he was dancing.

The light turned a dark blue. The night was coming; the kind of summer night you get in Europe, where the breeze is cool and the warmth lingers from the day, when the swallows make it their home.

He could see Cami dancing.

'I'll never forget that night.'

They first heard about the virus when they were in Italy. The news in brief cut between the music. Then the company briefed them over the radio. *Attention*: they were near the infected areas. Ionut switched off the hip-hop and tuned into the news. They tried to listen on the road: what it was, how it was spreading in China. Now there were towns just behind them that had been closed. He couldn't follow. The Italian newscasters spoke so fast he could barely understand.

'As a driver . . . you're always on the periphery of anything that's happening, outside, isolated.'

He could feel the tension at the loading bays. High-viz men

were keeping their distance; wrapping scarves around their faces. Soon they were wearing masks. There was shouting. Voices were radioing in saying they didn't know what was happening.

Calls started coming.

'The panic seemed to grow worse and worse.'

Then everything stopped. The company was suspending operations: the job was cancelled – *Go back to Romania*. They drove back as the borders were closing. They drove as fast as they could. His eyes were tired. He was exhausted. They didn't stop.

They kept on going.

You know this feeling.

The last miles are always the hardest.

'That's when you start to break down, towards the end . . . there are so many layers of tiredness and stress stacked up onto each other that you no longer look after anything or care about anything but finishing the route. All those months of work; you're finished. You don't care about conditions any more, about how clean toilets are. You count your days like you are a few weeks away from being demobbed from military service.'

'Just waiting to get home.'

They had to get there. The night was falling. But he kept on driving.

'The night is always the same. You're more relaxed driving at night but the tiredness, the lack of concentration and the feeling you are slipping away make it worse. You can't even gather your thoughts or realize the freedom of the night. You don't have the time. You need to keep going.'

Cami was sleeping but Ionut kept driving. The music stopped. There was a jingle: it was 6 a.m. The light was turning. He could feel sleep pulling. He felt heavy: like a zombie, hardly alive. He slapped his face. He turned up the music. He put some spit on his eyelids. That always helped to keep him awake. He had to keep going.

Everything felt foggy: like he was driving in slow motion.

'Dawn is something I wouldn't wish for you to catch when you're driving. It's the worst part of the day and after a long night of driving . . . you're effectively terminated, worn out, tired beyond repair. Half your brain is already asleep. No matter the season, dawn isn't a pretty time of day.'

He felt empty. Dried out. He began to cough.

The light was here: the one that made everything seem hard.

The sky had turned pale. Ionut could see the moon rising: half-blue, like it was coming out of water. He felt something; he felt something strong. That he didn't want to do this any more.

He could feel it coming: washing over him like waves.

That moment we all feel in our turn: the feeling of defeat.

When we know the tide takes the last boats away.

The cabin trembled and he swerved as a lorry hurtled past him: close, much too close. He thought of Cami. He thought of his children. He could see their faces: for a moment he could feel them. It caught him by surprise: how much he always missed them.

He thought of Romania and then he thought of Baloga.

How he would give anything in the whole world to go back to his village. To live in a little house. To feel still. To hear the dogs barking in the morning. He thought of the castle overgrown with greenery and secrets. He thought of the *strigoi* – the troubled spirits they said rose from the grave, buried close by. And he thought of the smell he missed so much he could practically breathe it between the fumes and the diesel. The smell of his childhood. That smell that was always fresh: the long grass, the piles of hay, the bread baking, the air clear like water. He glanced back into the wing mirror and sighed.

Because that was all he wanted.

3 İSTANBUL

The Erasmus exchange had only just started in Amsterdam.

Sezen had butterflies in her stomach as she left her new dorm. There were some welcome drinks at the student bar to get to. And then she saw him. This very handsome boy in baggy jeans smoking under a tree.

It was a sudden volte.

What a good-looking guy, she thought.

Almost taken aback as she got closer.

Is he Australian? Is that the accent?

Most of the students somehow did, but this boy didn't look national. Just hot – very hot – with dark hair. But really smiley. And now she was so close she had to say something. He was looking at her now.

What am I going to say to him?

Sezen nervously pulled out her cigarettes.

That would work.

Do you have a light?

Then for a split second her nerves took over.

What if he doesn't understand my English?

The last person she'd talked to, back in the dorms, was from the UK and their accent was so strong she hadn't understood a single word.

What if he also speaks like that?

But the boy smiled and turned away from the guy next to him.

Was that German? Ah, yes, that's what he was speaking.

He was much better looking close up.

Hi, I'm Andi, he said. *What's your name?*

Him just looking at her made her tingle. Her heart was racing.

Her mind was now galloping into thoughts so fast she could hardly stop them.

I like this boy, she heard herself think.

This feels so crazy but I'd like him to smile at me for ever.

It was a sudden heady feeling. One she was now trying to keep a handle on.

My name's Sezen, she managed to grin. *I'm from Turkey.*

He was so handsome she could hardly look at him.

That's cool, said Andi. *I'm Austrian.*

Austria, she thought. He had to be from a country she knew nothing about. Mentally she only had some vague idea of a fancy Vienna and for the rest there was a total blank. They finished smoking, then he said, *Shall we go inside?*

It was as dark as a dive bar inside, lit with some green light. The tables were smoky and full, that night, of this cheerful, optimistic air, of hopes for a new term, in a new city, and Sezen spoke every language she knew.

How do you talk such good French?

What . . . you also have Italian?

Andi was sitting next to her and as the evening went on, they stopped speaking to everyone else – it was like the United Nations at that table, Germans chatting to Australians, Turks talking to Italians, Belgians teasing Americans – and she leaned closer in, until she could almost touch him, to be heard over the jokes and the music and the din, as he kept on asking questions.

Does he like me? she kept thinking. *Does he really?*

He was looking at her so intently and he was listening, really listening as she started to tell him everything; how she was from İzmir, how that's a very secular part of Turkey, how she'd gone to a French lycée, that's how she spoke French so well, how she loved novels, she had been carrying *My Name Is Red* by Orhan Pamuk around with her for days and what she really wanted was to be a lawyer with her own firm and her own office. This normally sent guys to sleep. But he was still looking at her, smiling.

It's all got so deep, she thought. *Like we're the only people here.*

They were ignoring the others now.

Then he said, *Do you want to come to this party?*

And she followed Andi out of the bar. They turned down long dark corridor after long dark corridor, across the brutalist campus, until she began to panic. Five, ten, fifteen minutes. It seemed to be taking much too long.

It's pitch black. Where's he taking me?

I'm into him but I don't know him.

Sezen's mind filled with stories of red-light districts and Amsterdam and terrible things that happened to women by the canals until there it was, the murmuring of a party, then the door.

Shall we smoke on the balcony?

Andi gestured where to go. And as they stepped into the laughter and the dancing; past Erasmus friends gesturing excitedly over their beers, through snatches of Spanish and Dutch and what was unmistakably an American, onto the balcony as someone turned up the music; she felt, for the first time that *this* – this sudden opening of the world – was what she had studied for. Then the track skipped. And as it did she felt a clear happiness rushing through her.

Andi was telling her why he'd chosen Amsterdam.

He was leaning so close to her, on the balustrade.

The whole empty complex beneath them.

I think he likes me, she thought, looking closer. There was almost a flicker of something in his eyes: excitement, joy, invitation, all of it. And then, a sudden movement. They kissed. Once. Then again. Like it was the most natural thing in the world. Something electric felt like it rushed down her spine.

Smile!

Some friend of Andi's came by and took a photo of them. The party got noisier and rowdier. There was some loud dance music now, until there was hardly any space left on the balcony. They were not the only couple now.

Andi broke away for a second to ask, *Do you want to come to the terrace in my block?*

There was nothing there but an old red sofa, out in the open, and that night they lay there, kissing and talking, under the cool September night, the kind that still feels gentle, before the leaves begin to fall.

You're way too good looking, said Sezen, looking at him, holding

him, wanting so strongly to see him, wanting not to forget this, her eyes focusing in that way somebody does when they want more than just to see you; they want to imprint you as a memory.

You've had this moment too.

You're so good looking I think you might be a bad boy.

Andi, laughed, tried to say no, but she continued.

I'll try and not fall in love with you.

She was caressing him, beaming.

Because I think you might break my heart.

And they kept kissing, until it was finally cold, somewhere deep in the night, still before the birds, and she said it was time for her to go home.

The next day Sezen woke up in surprise.

I'm kind of feeling in love, she thought, lying there, in the morning. It was like nothing she had ever felt before. She felt it all over her body. All across her mind – this longing, this obsession – *So this is what they call love.*

There was space for no other thoughts.

You know you really shouldn't fall for him.

There was much she had to do.

You don't know this guy.

She pulled herself up slightly in bed.

You're only setting yourself up to get hurt.

And then she got up for the day. But the feeling only got stronger as she went to the migration bureau and got her papers checked and her documents in order. *This is a surprise.* That night, she couldn't stop dreaming about Andi, on that sofa – *My Austrian boy* – who, she'd noticed, had written her name down as Cezanne in his phone – until she woke up again thinking, *I'm not going to wait for him, I'm not going to play Oh, the boys must text first – I'll do it.*

That was him. That was the right Facebook account.

And then she messaged him.

hey andi let's go out let's party :)))

That night they went into Amsterdam, the neon glinting on the canal, the city unfolding, like they were carried by some weightless happiness, as their little group found a place to dance, wound up in a chip shop, before laughing at every stop home on the night tram; the whole time Sezen finding it stranger and stranger, that they didn't like the same books, they didn't like the same movies and they didn't even like the same music but that she only liked him more and more.

'I'd never felt so joyous and careless and free.'

Then term really started, classes and lectures in the morning, those rolling evenings when the whole course was cooking for everyone else: the Poles making pierogi, the Italians making pasta and the Turks, they made dolma.

They kept seeing each other. They kept talking. Like they'd always known each other.

They kept texting each other.

how was your day :)

how was your class :)))

About a week later Andi called her.

Hey, can we meet?

He said it nervously.

I want to talk to you about something.

Immediately Sezen felt a chill.

The longer she waited, the more she worried.

He doesn't like me any more. That's it. He's coming to say he's not interested. I know, he's met somebody else. It's so embarrassing . . . I just wrote to my friend in İstanbul a whole stupid email about him.

Then he was at her door, his smile slightly tense.

Shall we go for a walk? he said.

And then they crossed the campus, chatting about everything, chatting about nothing, this feeling of doom swelling inside her, until the path took them into a small wood, which ran along a canal, where they found a bench.

Andi looked worried as he sat down.

Then he turned to her.

I wanted to tell you . . .

Then he paused.

It's like this . . . I talked to my best friend about you and he said . . . Bro, whaoh, I think you're in love, man . . . from the way you talk about this girl.

He paused for a moment.

And I thought about it and I think, I am . . . I'm in love.

Then he looked at her like everything depended on it.

Everything inside her was turning upside down.

You're so beautiful, he said. *It's like . . . when I was a little boy, I invented an imaginary French girlfriend to tell my friends about. I called her Jacqueline. And she had a little back fringe like you . . . you're her. You're my Jacqueline. I've found you.*

It was like the whole rest of the world had disappeared.

There was only the bench and them.

I love you too, said Sezen.

I'm her . . . I'm your Jacqueline.

And they started laughing.

Was it all a dream? Sezen thought, as she plodded along the street in İstanbul, weighed down by those thick law books she studied, her mind filled with bits of Amsterdam: that time Andi took her for sushi and his card bounced; that day they spent at the Van Gogh Museum; and all those nights. *Because I'm back here*, she thought, *in the suburbs*, as she fumbled for her headphones, *with the same songs one after another, the same old men smoking outside the same old shops, in the streets where I was before.*

Like none of it ever happened.

Sezen was almost home.

Almost at that point where, if you look over motorway, out towards that enormous bridge, past the mosque, you can see those green wooded hills sloping into the Bosphorus, all hidden villas and crooked paths, taking you onto a riviera which, five times a day, echoes with the call to prayer.

She hit shuffle on her bright pink iPod.

Then she heard it. A German rap song.

Andi had downloaded it.

No, it was all real.

A smile breaking over her face.

It all happened. It all happened to me.

Then it all came back again: those days when she had realized term was running out; that night she was crying, when they said, *No we don't want to break up*; that letter she wrote for him to read on the plane to Washington; the one that said, *We will make this work but also enjoy yourself*; that last kiss at Schiphol. It was always going to end. Their Erasmus was just one semester. And for him, the next one was in America.

And she was back in İstanbul.

Sezen, dreaming, unlocked her door.

You never realize how painful it is to miss someone.

You never expect to feel it in your body, in your heart.

It feels like I'm sick, she wrote in her diary.

I feel like there's no brightness without Andi.

That night she skyped him, like she did every night, but with this creeping sense it wasn't working; they weren't living the same life any more. They would be talking; her day would be ending, his would be starting. He would be pressed for time, she would be exhausted. Then she would start to feel his words meant nothing to her, Dupont Circle, Farragut North. That her words meant nothing to him, Boğaziçi University, Taksim Square.

Like he was in mist.

They skyped for months.

Through the winter and the spring, when the mist is thick over the Bosphorus in the morning, and the rain is cold; when you realize this is a Balkan city after all, and the fishermen look like a black and white photo on the shore.

They began to bicker.

To say things they didn't mean.

You don't love me. You just say you do!

Those mornings, on the bus to university, the teeming city crowding in on her, its traffic grinding to a halt, she'd suddenly know she had no idea what Andi was doing, where he was or who he was with. Blotting out everything else, she'd start to feel pain. The pain of jealousy, of uncertainty. The pain from manic racing thoughts.

He's going to meet somebody else.

He's in an international environment. There'll be girls from France, England, America there . . . really hot ones. And you're stuck here in İstanbul.

The colour would drain out of her days. Like she was aching for him.

You know those moments too.

You know those excruciating things you see in your mind.

I can see it, she'd mutter.

with you in Vienna would be
more than dreamy. I want to
have little dates. Whatever I
do with you is so much fun.
Come and take me in
your arms.

28.07.2010
My love,
We just talked on the phone. When
you're unhappy, I become sad too.
I want to cheer you up as much
as I can, I hope I manage it.
I missed you so much, I can't
take it anymore. I am counting
the days. 9 days left. In 9 days
I'll be in your arms. I watched
Elif Safak's speech the other day.
She just told what I hate most.
Being the representative of your
country. Well I won't develop it
in here, because I want to have
one of our nice conversations
about this issue. In Orhan
Pamuk's last book [It's called
the museum of innocence],
the guy keeps the girl's things

I can see what's going to happen to me.

Those evenings, on Skype, she'd start crying, she could hardly stop herself, as he told her about all the internships he'd applied to in İstanbul and how they'd all failed; then she'd explain again how she couldn't leave Turkey for at least two years if she ever wanted to actually qualify as a lawyer.

'Our financial situation was like this.'

'The idea that I could get on a plane and go to Washington. Or he could get on a plane and come here. It was just completely out of the question.'

I love you, she'd say.

I love you too, he'd say.

But I don't know how to get to you.

Sezen would cry some more, eat, then she would spend the night writing him letters – real, old-fashioned ones, which she would post – or coming up with presents like the time she covered one of those little tourist brochures to the city, the free ones which they leave in hotels, with Post-It notes of everywhere she'd take him.

I'm a great tour guide.

My price is just one kiss.

Imagining him on the ferry.

Imagining him in the places she loved.

But he didn't come. Andi needed an internship, he said. He was frantic with the idea he was graduating, that what he needed was a plan. Nothing he'd applied for had worked out in Turkey, he said. He hadn't even got a reply. He was going to apply in Washington and when he got one – he was telling her about it on Skype – she could hardly stop crying, even for a long, long time, after the call.

'The timeline had slipped out of sight.'

'I had no idea now when I would see him again.'

'I'd just failed. We'd just failed.'

The bus rides into university. The bickering calls.

The same scratching angst as she walked home: it all continued. About a month later Sezen was playing cards with her friend. The faster she threw them down, the more she was winning, until she had wiped them clean.

'They started to joke with me, *Watch out, Sezen; when you win in*

gambling, as we say in Turkish, *you lose in love.* They were teasing, *Look at that flush. Again? He's going to break up with you now.'*

Then it was time to go home.

That night they skyped.

We just can't make it work, Andi said.

Then he dumped her.

At first she was stunned.

Then it was like something inside her collapsed. Then she could hardly walk. She could hardly eat. The next few days passed in a dark blur, like she was no longer really there, her eyes stinging with tears, mumbling – *It* wasn't *real, none of it* was *real* – until her friends were knocking at her door.

Sezen, they said, *we're worried about you.*

They came to her room and they talked to her very softly like she was a very sick, very weak person. They said that she should really take the ferry across the Bosphorus – the easiest, simplest way to feel better – just to get her outside.

And then they took her hand, down to the water.

They were queuing for tickets. She could hardly feel the crowds.

Sezen felt like there was nothing else in the city, nothing else but her, as the engine growled for Asia, the boat full of workers going home, the kind of people from Anatolia that, if she'd fallen in love with one of them, there would have been an even greater cultural chasm between them than the man she'd now lost.

'I was imagining myself, like I was in a movie.'

'That this was my tragedy.'

'Like I was waving a handkerchief goodbye.'

The wind was in her hair as she looked back, towards Europe, at the great domes and towers and minarets, black against the sun, at this enormous city, that hid everything, where he had never been and might never come, her whole body tightening, with a building pain because she might never see him again, never hear of him again.

'I'd blocked him on Facebook.'

Sezen thought she couldn't cope with seeing him there, but now she sat scrolling through friends' photos, trying to see if he was tagged somewhere.

'One day I saw him tagged in a landscape. Just his name.'

'But it set my heart beating like I'd actually seen him.'

Things had already begun to change.

Her exams, they came and went.

Her graduation day, her happy parents, it came and went.

She was working now, at a law firm, doing the full year she needed to qualify, her inbox exploding and often her clients too, but wherever she was on her laptop, she left Skype open – she hadn't blocked him there – just in case.

Sezen kept glancing at it, she kept hoping for it.

But nothing ever came.

It was too hot in the city now.

The streets were filled with tourists, red in the face, happy, lost or getting scammed for knick-knacks, as she left for the summer house her parents had on the Aegean, still thinking of him, still writing in her diary, *I love him*, the same thoughts crowding in on her, weeks later, when she finally left and returned home.

'That whole summer. I was still in love.'

'I never got over him.'

Normally Sezen flew back to İstanbul from there, but for some reason, this time she took the bus. The summer was ending. The traffic meant the journey was taking hours. She leaned on the window, her music loud and mournful, eyes drifting over the countryside, so dry and yellow, everyone falling asleep around her, until she began to feel something building.

'This feeling that I would see him again.'

Her music making the sensation stronger.

'That night, I wrote it in my diary.'

I know today that I'll see Andi again.

And her mind began to clear, she started to be able to catch the beauty of the day and a few weeks later Skype made a sound.

He'd messaged her.

hey, it's andi

i'm back in vienna . . .

Her eyes began to swell.

i was sitting on my couch imagining how great it would be
if u were here

In that moment the office seemed to disappear; the case, the director addressing one of her colleagues. She began to tingle, slightly, as a whole storm of emotions gathered and one of them, her strongest, was pride.

yeah it would be nice i guess . . .

but we broke up

They kept chatting.

And she kept being cold.

shall we turn the video on

It was getting late in İstanbul when he wrote that. Night outside her bedroom window. The yowls of street cats. But the moment Sezen read that she sprang up, and rushed to put makeup on and fix her hair.

yeah give me a few minutes i'm doing something

There was his face. That was his voice.

That was his bedroom in Vienna.

I was thinking about Amsterdam, he said, almost shy.

How we were never fighting and how nice it was.

But now on video, she gave him a shrug.

Yeah it was nice but we broke up.

About a week later, a package arrived from Austria.

Sezen's heart started to pound the moment she saw the handwriting – it was his – and, as she ripped open the package, Mozart brand chocolates, postcards and a letter tumbled out; a letter saying that he loved her, saying that he'd made a terrible mistake and if she'd take him back he'd come to İstanbul, in fact he'd come almost right away.

Then she was crying again.

But not tears of pain.

It's ectopic, the doctor said, quietly.

I'm really sorry, he continued.

Before she really knew what it meant.

It had all seemed too easy. They had been living in Vienna for the past few years and when one day Sezen walked in and told Andi she wanted to move back to İstanbul to run her own firm, they had just made it happen.

What do you mean, it's ectopic?

They had got married, his vows had been in Turkish, her vows had been in English. Thanking him for giving her a life better than fiction. They had found a beautiful apartment, then within a few years her business was a success; the firm she had made from nowhere was in the legal five hundred. They acted like you only had to be ready, that you only had to decide, then the baby would come.

Then pregnancy tests piled up.

The boxes and the kits, until they made her shudder.

And now she was hearing this.

Sezen started to feel cold.

I can't see the baby, the doctor said.

He was pointing at the ultrasound.

I'm really sorry.

His face said it all.

But it's lodged in one of your tubes.

You have a calendar. You think.

This time will work for me, or then.

It doesn't work like that. You're not in control. You learn that lesson first.

This means we have to abort it, the doctor explained.

It's a methotrexate injection, it's quite heavy. And normally we have to do it around twice. I'm so sorry. Then he looked away.

There was nothing else to say.

The next few moments passed very quickly. They left the building. Sezen was crying, holding on to Andi in the taxi on the way back from the hospital, thinking, *I didn't sign up for this, why isn't there some technology that can just take my baby out and implant it in my womb?* Her head echoing with everything the doctor had warned her about. *There could be internal bleeding. The thing could just explode inside me and it could even kill me. Will it?*

All of the confidence of all those years, gone.

That night, those thoughts didn't stop.

They woke her up, they stopped her sleeping. They caught her off guard in the office, speaking to a client. They'd be crowding in on her. Then suddenly she would feel faint. Like she was dizzy. Like she could hardly think.

Each time, Andi rushed her to emergency care.

Her Austrian boy spoke such good Turkish now: with his export business he knew this country of factories almost better than she did.

But it wasn't the bleeding. It wasn't that. It was the stress.

It wouldn't let her go, or leave her alone.

The alarm went off on the day.

They left for the hospital.

They laid her on her back for the injection.

It was a burning sensation, she felt, entering her. Sezen could hear herself sobbing as it stung: crying harder than she ever thought she could. Then it was over. Except for the cramps, then exhaustion and then the migraine. And once those cleared she was back to the tests, back to the doctor, her heart sinking when they told her blood tests were still positive, that they were giving her the kind of scores she had so wanted, only weeks ago.

Because it was still alive.

It died after the second injection.

Slowly they went back to their routines.

They woke up every morning, early, when it was still cool, when they could still walk together without sweating. They would stroll down to the water, round the backs of villas, talking about everything, about work, about life, about what had just happened and what they so wanted to happen. There would only be them, the joggers and the fishermen on those mornings and sometimes the old man with the rabbit whose bite on a piece of paper would tell your fortune. Those were the moments they told each other everything.

We'll have a baby, she said.

We will. Just not this time. I can put this behind me.

Then for a few weeks, it really seemed like she could. They went out to their favourite rooftop bars, they met friends for dinner and they made each other laugh.

Andi buying her more small presents than usual.

He was always so attentive.

Then one morning she started to feel sick.

You're pregnant, the doctor said, grimacing.

But I thought I couldn't, she said, *just after.*

The doctor shook his head, telling her that she would be coming in for a weekly ultrasound.

We'll be keeping an eye on you.

There was something worried in the way he talked.

Sometimes your injection's after-effects can linger. They can deplete the body of what a baby needs.

It was a feeling of angst.

It's a mistake, she winced.

I'm pregnant, she kept muttering.

It was happening again. This thing she'd so wanted, but she so wished it wasn't happening now. She could feel those very slight changes in her body again. Her hormones were playing tricks again. Swooping in and tugging at her until her anxiety became overwhelming, until her mind was spinning, uncontrollably, the paranoia eating into her, *Something not right, it's not right.*

Can you hear the heartbeat?

The doctor passed her the headphones.

Then she did the same to Andi.

But you know when something's not right.

You lie in bed catastrophizing. You feel something terrible creeping in. You don't know what it is. You can't say what it is. Then it's suddenly there.

Sezen was at the ultrasound with her mother.

I can't hear the heartbeat, the doctor craned in, squinting.

That's when they told me I'd miscarried.

Why are you crying so much, she caught herself thinking. *It's not like you were really pregnant.* She saw herself, almost like she'd slipped out of her body, sobbing against Andi on their couch at home. *Why are you so sad?*

Then her mind would swing the other way. Her work would fade away and there it was again: the agony, whispering, *You'll never be a mother. Never.*

Andi was asleep, it was only her sitting at the table, the red and white of passing cars still rushing along on the nearby motorway. *I'm like a walking cemetery*, she wrote. *I've got two dead babies inside me.* Then she kept writing this dark story, like it was addressed to them, until she burnt it.

The operation to remove it came quickly.

They put her in the gown, they took her on the trolley, the cold of the anaesthetic went in and then, without a moment of darkness, it seemed she was back. She shook her head, groggy, confused, unable to remember little things, until she realized they had parked her in the maternity ward. There were cries of newborns. There were fathers and grandfathers with balloons. Their women holding and caressing their little ones that had journeyed so far. As it all, as everything, started to sting her and prod her and humiliate her, she felt rage.

This would never happen . . .

If miscarriages happened to men.

That night, when she came home, she lay in bed, holding on to Andi, crying, feeling his presence beginning to heal her, ever so slightly, as they watched Netflix and, bit by bit, he tried to make her laugh.

Then the summer came. They went to Çeşme, to her parents' house on the Aegean, where the bougainvillaea falls over the stone cottages, purple against the walls, whilst you wander your way down to the sea.

'I began to mourn.'

'I really mourned that baby.'

'I think it was a person.'

Sezen lay there at night, the cicadas singing, the sounds of someone else's happy summer, touching her belly, mourning what might have been.

The memories, she might have had. The love she might have felt.

'They did a genetic test afterwards.'

'It was a girl.'

That summer, they would be on the beach, the water every colour of blue, the families around them, all complete, until she only felt cold, until she only felt numb, like joy was something she could no longer feel.

'Then one evening, I was walking, I was alone.'

'And I heard a miaow.'

It was a cat, just outside her window, calling to her. Sezen, like a moment in a dream, began to follow her, to where she lived under a bush.

And then she saw the kittens.

'And first she was so scared, she only came out for little bits of food. And then I was watching her. Mum, I called her . . . and I was so moved by how she was taking care of her babies. I started coming every day, to feed them. Until I was mothering them too . . . until I was learning about motherhood.'

She gave them names. Like Cotton and Brave.

She was talking to them, a little. Telling them how beautiful they were.

Until she began to heal.

That winter, they were walking in the forest in Poland, near Zakopane, where their friend was getting married.

If we can't get pregnant, he said.

Our lives . . . they are still beautiful.

They are still full.

We can consider adoption.

The birds were singing. She felt calm. A calm that stayed with her as they went back to İstanbul. But still they kept trying.

The pregnancy tests mounting up again.

The same routine.

Worrying it could happen again. Another ectopic. Another miscarriage. Or not at all.

'You're in a very vulnerable place after you miscarry. You blame yourself. And these emotions around motherhood and pregnancy . . . They aren't emotions I'd ever really experienced before. Especially this yearning for a child. It doesn't make sense if you haven't reached it. But once it's there, it takes over, this longing . . .'

'And it becomes the very centre of your being.'

Sezen realized she was pregnant in the mall.

It was next to the office and in the toilets there, there it was, positive.

Then it began again. The doctors. The scans.

Those nights she lay there shaking with anxiety.

The worry it was only hurting the baby, only making it worse.

This is the most important person in my life, she'd lie there thinking. *And I've never met them. I don't know who they are. And again, I might never meet them.*

The dawn was blue and the hospital lights bright when she finally saw him. Her little boy. That moment she held him, covered in blood and tears, she had a flash of the amazing pressure, at that moment, to feel. And then they passed him to her husband. When she saw Andi holding him, they called him Lucas, and she felt it instantly: there was nothing more beautiful in the world.

A week later they were walking by the Bosphorus; the white wooden mansions, like filigree, on the water.

This will be our thing . . . won't it? she said.

We'll walk with him . . . like we walk with each other?

At that moment, Lucas began to scream.

But they looked at each other and started to laugh.

4 AVDIIVKA

Olya breathed. Zipped up her winter coat, and stepped out. The door clicked behind her – like it always did – like nothing had happened. *Yes*, she was going to leave him. Outside, it was December. Already. It had taken her months to get here. But now she was doing it. Fast. Olya held on to her baby; he felt so warm; and for a moment she hovered in the gloom. The smell of fried potatoes and boiled cabbage filled the stairwell; that smell that was always there. That's when she left the Builder.

'I have no fond memories of that apartment.'

It could have been anywhere in Ukraine; anywhere that used to be Soviet. It just so happened it was in Vinnytsia; that it was *her* small town in Ukraine.

'It wasn't even his apartment. It was his parents'.'

Olya tried not to think about it. Why she'd been pregnant there; how she'd given birth there; when she'd heard baby's first words there. Because she couldn't stay there. *No*, she had to go. But it wasn't the fights that made her go. And it wasn't the Builder's mother, even though, truth be told, she was terrible too. *No*, it wasn't even those nights, when the Builder said, *Take the baby; make him shut up; I need to sleep alone.* It was the messages: there were other girls now.

'That's when I picked up my boy.'

She told them she was going out. She was going to stay at her mother's. On the other side of town; in a block, almost exactly the same.

It was her mother's birthday when she arrived.

They were all there, her brothers and sisters; there was that noise they made when they were all together. Happy. You could hear the little one laugh. And there it was: that same old, big Ukrainian

birthday table – the same one that came round every year; her fried schnitzel, crab-stick salad and mashed potato, with that same old roast chicken, soupy gravy and chips. She missed it. And after they passed around the baby, she told her.

Mummy, I'm not going home.

You know love changes first to contempt.

She began to despise him on the sofa.

You know only much later does it turn cold, indifferent.

'The protests started around when I got pregnant.'

The light, the chants, coming out of the TV.

She sat there watching her country change, feeling her body change.

The Builder didn't seem to care.

She went to work thinking about it.

There was a morning and an evening rush at that bakery; and like everywhere there was an afternoon quiet. There was a smell when the day started that was so strong; the sweetness of fresh bread that always faded too fast. And then her mind would wander until suddenly a thing would happen to remind her.

Something was happening.

'One day, they all burst in . . .'

'All the protesters, who were heading to Kyiv . . . I'd just been paid and without thinking I bought a ton of food and gave it to them.'

Aren't you coming with us?

No, she couldn't go, she was pregnant, she was having a baby.

That's what she'd say. Sometimes they'd text her.

you should have come!!

She felt strange and jealous. Olya locked up the shop.

Evenings came round.

Olya sat at home: watching. Night after night on the TV.

The protests. The speeches.

They got bigger. The reporters were live. The anchors talked faster and faster. There was breaking news. There were sudden alerts. Before too long they were running feeds round the clock; from that big square in the big city, where everything happened; that is, apart from anything that happened to Olya.

'I couldn't take my eyes off Maidan.'

The Builder was usually out. He had friends. He did his thing.

But Olya kept watching. They were marching now; the people were marching. They were putting up tents. They flew the blue flag, with the gold stars; the one they never used to fly before. *No*, she couldn't stop watching. It was on Facebook, it was on TV, it was all around her. Right there at the till.

'I tried to read everything.'

She began posting, she kept scrolling, sharing.

Everyone was doing it. You couldn't escape it. It got behind her eyes.

She lay there at night clutching her phone.

'I was huge, I was heavily pregnant.'

'But I wanted to read everything and to watch everything that was happening. I just couldn't stop. I was obsessed, about what was happening, to us as a country . . . because of the baby. I kept worrying what future he'd have. I kept wanting my country to be free, to be wealthy, to be better . . .'

'Just for him.'

Maidan was still there in the morning. She woke up thinking about it; the sounds of the Builder's mother clattering around through the door. She went to sleep worrying about it. It wouldn't let her go. It became tied up with him inside her.

The baby. Her baby.

Then it all seemed to succeed: the jubilation on the TV, the people in the palace, the cheers in the street. Their own revolution. Then it all went wrong.

'My baby was eighteen months when it started.'

The shooting.

'Then they started enlisting.'

Men started leaving for the front. That's all anyone would talk about, even in Vinnytsia. That's all anyone seemed to post about. Olya sat on the sofa; she kept watching TV and she even started to think that's what the Builder would do – *enlist* – because he was strong, he was young, he could do everything on site. *Yes*, her husband would fight for them. He would fight for their future. He would fight for their baby.

One evening, she dared ask him.

'It crushed me what he said.'

'That if the recruiters even knocked on our door . . .'

'I should say I didn't know where he was.'

That was when she started to despise him. On the sofa watching the news come in. Knowing he was the kind of man they ridiculed.

'That was the last straw for me.'

His face was ugly now, that of a coward.

'That's when I knew it was over.'

It was crowded at her mother's home.

Her little sister was still only seven. A family of ten; and she was back cooking for them: mashed potatoes, *kasha*, stringy chicken. The same old stuff. And it was weird being back there, with the baby. But things couldn't be the same.

'I had to start working because my husband didn't give me enough money to raise the child. And I couldn't rely on my mother and my stepfather as they had other children to take care of . . . I had to earn it all myself.'

There was nothing for it.

She got a job selling vegetables. Olya would sit there and think, *How has it come to this? Why has it screwed up like this?* How she had always had work like this. Work that meant nothing: the pizza place, the bartending, the bakery.

The bleeps of the till. The rhythms of the day.

The smallness of their lives.

The mornings were the worst.

She would wake up and baby Dima would still be sleeping. She'd kiss him and leave for the store. *Don't worry, I'll look after him.* That was what Mummy said. *Don't worry*, it was just like having an extra kiddie.

'Around then I started to see him less and less.'

She sat at the till. She swiped, she sorted, she counted. She found it hard to feel.

'But the war kept me busy.'

Inside her mind. She followed the battles on her phone.

She listened on the radio. Donetsk. Luhansk.

Maps pointed to where mattered now.

'I couldn't pull away.'

The frontlines were moving.

'I got used to . . . leaving the baby.'

Olya took more shifts.

'I had to, you see, otherwise there was no money.'

'And when there's no money there's no future.'

Olya got used to not being with Dima.

And when she got back late from the store he was already asleep. That's when she would sit for hours in front of the TV and let the war envelop her. She watched the reports. She watched the lives. She started to feel she was needed there.

And that was when she saw the advert.

Volunteer.

Volunteer for Ukraine.

Women and men wanted.

They were marching. They were ordered.

There were women who looked just like her.

Heading into war. Heading into history.

Her eyes swelled.

'Then I remembered.'

It stirred something inside her. Something from childhood, a fuzzy memory of bright days; when she used to see the little boys and girls in uniform, marching in and out of the military academy. And how she wanted to be one too.

'I couldn't tear myself away.'

The advert never stopped playing.

It swallowed her. It was like it blotted out all sound around her. Her mother would be talking and she couldn't hear her. And then she'd be back in the room. That was it. That's when she realized she had to help.

'It's strange,' said Olya.

'When I saw this advert I felt like a horse.'

'Being led by a horse-whisperer.'

Olya was waiting at the recruitment office.

Are you sure about this?

They looked at her funny at the enlistment centre. They, yes, and they were men, mostly; they sat, more often than not with furled-up flags of Ukraine behind them; with incredulity, or was it mockery, she wasn't quite sure, pinched in their smiles.

Twenty-four years old . . . a mother.

And you want to serve your country?

Yes, I am, she said. *I'm ready.*

We are at war, they said, that smirk, still there.

Are you aware of what is happening in the Anti-Terror Operation?

She nodded. *Yes, officer.*

The letter arrived. Her heart beat at the postmark.

A positive assessment has been reached with light to recruitment.

Mummy didn't try and stop her.

If you have to go . . . go.

She held her baby; and she let her go.

'I felt I was needed there.'

'I felt that I must be there.'

Friends asked how she could leave the baby.

I'm not a very emotional person, she told them.

'I had to be there.'

It didn't happen at first. They took a bus to Vasylkiv but there were no spaces and they sent them back home. And then nothing happened. Olya went back to the vegetables, and the early mornings, and counting change as quickly as she could, and boiling cutlets in the evening. And then they called.

Citizen, we have a vacancy.

It was the recruiters on the line. She held the phone close, as if she might lose them.

It's at Starichyi, near Lviv, and we need an army chef. Understood?

Of course I can be a chef, she thought. *I could be a great chef for the army.*

I've been cooking for ten people.

I'm fit to cook for thirty soldiers.

She left as soon as she could.

When they first arrived, they signed their contracts. Fatigues to the left; boots to the right; the base thrust them into these. Those uniforms, which stank of dried sweat, and those army boots, which came on sore and never stopped hurting. *Congratulations,* they told them, the recruits, in that special army language she would get so used to.

Basic training now begins.

The base was huge.

What they called a polygon.

A whole area of military operations. With little buses that took them from point to point. And slowly Olya noticed it was in the middle of a swamp.

One of those swamps in western Ukraine; where everything is green, a strong, bright green; where the mist clings for a while after dawn; where if you blink it can feel a little out of time; like a woolly mammoth, like a German tank, could appear between the reeds. Their feet squelched through it to the sounds of orders as their boots turned black and oozed.

They scrubbed them constantly.

The mud got everywhere: in their clothes, matted hair, soles, into places she couldn't understand how it had got there. And here they were strict: they ran through everything quickly. *Understood?* They introduced ammunition, mines and grenades; then the shooting range; then they were running and jumping over the obstacle course, until they were out of breath, but they kept on going.

'I'll never forget it.'

They dug a trench and told them: duck and cover.

'We fell into it, face down, we had to cover ourselves . . . and we had to stay there when the tank passed over us.'

In that moment she felt something.

'I can't explain it.'

Something she'd been searching for.

'It was a very emotional moment. Full of adrenaline and fear and pleasure . . . lots of it. I mean that very moment, when the tank is passing over you . . . and the soil is falling down on you . . . that one.'

She wanted to cry or to laugh or to gasp. She wasn't quite sure.

She felt a rush; she felt like she'd always wanted to feel.

'And then they told us to jump out.'

'They wanted us to throw grenades . . . but because we were girls we weren't given anything to throw. So we just watched.'

It thrilled her; even to watch.

After two weeks they yanked them away.

As that was enough for military chefs.

Things became a little different then. The days a little longer. At night she told herself, *I won't go back*. And sometimes on the other side of that she would miss her baby; she would miss him so much she could almost see him.

'Every morning we woke up at 6 a.m.'

She never thought she'd turn back.

It sank into a routine: they slept on creaking double bunks; they showered in cold water; and they kept themselves to their ground floor.

The boys, they slept upstairs.

They stayed away from them.

They were shadows in the hallway.

'You know how the men in the army are.'

'Some of them were, like, starving for girls . . . they hadn't seen any girls in a long time. And they were looking at the girls all the time and making jokes or laughing at us. The others, the older ones, would start talking to us and say, *What are you doing here . . . Wanna find a husband here?*'

'Because of that we stayed mostly away.'

Sometimes, a priest came from the village, to bless them. He would tell them stories and sprinkle holy water on them, in that wide-eyed manner all priests seem to have. And they would light a candle in the church, for them, and pray for peace. For their children, for every mother and, sometimes, for Ukraine.

And the months wore on.

You learn war is about waiting.

You learn generals wait for their campaigns, soldiers wait for their orders. You learn the moment can seem never to come. You learn armies are always waiting: in the barracks, in the ministry; even when war finally comes there are stretches of waiting, again.

The logistics. The rotations. The offensive.

You will have to wait.

Spring began to come. The trees, the light, the sheen on the swamp: it all began to change. Little flowers began to show in the dirt. There were four of them who became friends in that base; four girls from Vinnytsia. They taught them how to cook in a

PAK-200 that looked more like a tank than a mobile kitchen. There was Marina, and they talked all the time. They were so similar, they even had the same bouncy shoulder cut. And then there was Masha, but they talked a little less; they weren't quite the same. And Raisa, but she was older, she already had kids. And, the girls, they would all cook, with heads plugged in; listening to their own music on their mobile phones, so not to disturb each other.

'But it was hard.'

'There was always shouting in the kitchen.'

It seemed the moment would never come.

Every now and then they would come for recruits.

'We called them the Buyers.'

'Those were the men who picked you for the front.'

There would be a ruckus; the Buyers would talk; men would jostle and push to serve on the fronts in the east. And a lot of them refused to take girls. They were four girls from Vinnytsia and at first there was talk of 59th Brigade, but then the orders were rewritten – no girls – and they got sent to 72nd Brigade.

That was when they asked them.

'Unlike the boys who were never asked whether they wanted to go to the war zone or not . . . the girls did get asked. So only if you wanted to . . . you went. Back when I first saw the advert on TV about hiring volunteers, I talked to my mother . . . and I was always clear to her that I would be sent to the Zone . . . sooner or later. So when I got asked, I had no hesitation . . .'

'I said yes.'

The Zone.

It was no different at first. The same sky, the same fields, as all of Ukraine. Then they saw the first soldiers, the first tanks, the first derelict homes, abandoned petrol stations, checkpoints, gaping blast holes.

When you entered, no matter who you were, they made you sign a form with your description in case the bombs made your body unidentifiable.

Short. Blonde. Blue eyes.

They kept on finding bodies they couldn't identify.

Bus arrival. Trucks, sandbags, shouts. They escorted her quickly through the position, through this world of camouflage, to the kitchen; and told her to get to work. The first night in Avdiivka, she cooked for the commanding officers, they told her their station was only one kilometre away from the front line. That was when she began to hear it; distant but there.

'We only heard the sounds.'

'But we knew that's where the shooting was.'

'That was where the platoons were.'

'But still, when you're not directly in it . . . when you're not directly on the line of fire. You still don't feel it yet. When you're further away . . . it still feels the way civilians in Ukraine feel. That the war's not here. It's somewhere there . . . far away. Even a kilometre away. You still feel it's not here.'

'You can still sleep peacefully.'

It wasn't long after they arrived in Avdiivka they split up the four girls from Vinnytsia. Masha, Marina and Raisa went their own ways into the war. Olya, they kept there, cooking for the commanding officers. Her days smelt like canned meat. Every day the same stuff: cereals, macaroni, peas, barley, buckwheat, rice. Supplies never varied. Meals repeating themselves; again and again.

The quickest breakfast was Fleet Macaroni, that old Soviet thing: spam and macaroni – that sizzled and stank like cat food on the pan. And then there was lunch. Two courses: those were the orders – rice and gravy; mash and peas; that kind of thing. And as for the dinner, the officers got the good stuff: steak or cutlet, or even scrambled eggs.

They didn't keep her there long.

They started to send her to the front.

It was only there that she felt something she hadn't felt before: in her stomach, and in her shoulders, at first. She began to feel scared. In that cold way it would come up on you; it would begin like this.

Often they gave the cooks a supply order.

Our men are out there.

We have five positions between here and the line.

Drive there. Do what you can. Deliver them their supplies.

Wait for a lull in the fighting.

They had five positions, Company One, between the motorway and the factories. That's what they were fighting for, for the coke plant.

It had a particular sound, the Zone, especially at night. A silence. A silence when cities, when roads, have emptied.

'Once you're in the Zone . . .'

'It kind of cuts off your emotions to a certain extent.'

And then, there was its noise. The rumbles. The explosions far away.

'And that was sometimes scary . . . especially in the evenings, to hear that, because you couldn't see anything. But you could feel those immense forces at play. Somewhere out there but not too far. And you could feel the immense damage it can do to you. How it can . . . just rip through you.'

It was strange. The silence and the noise.

Maybe how the end of the world would sound.

It wasn't like it was with the officers.

'That's where the soldiers were, in those abandoned houses.'

'Our boys would spend the night in those houses, just off the front . . . and then during the day they would rotate with another company returning from their shifts and head right out to our troop's positions. And that's where the actual war happened. With shelling and everything. But once in a while a stray bullet or even a stray shell could fly over us or nearby and we could hear it.'

That was what she heard on delivery.

The car on those empty roads.

Dusk. October. The sounds of the birds disturbed.

'One late evening we supplied the furthest front-line position.'

'And the guys met us, as they were so hungry. It was so dark already, they beamed a torch around to see who we were.'

Are you the last position in the area? she asked.

Yes, a voice came back.

'So then I threw open the boot and said, *Take whatever you can!*'

They ravaged the vehicle. They took everything down to the last potato. That was when she first saw him. Blue eyes, a thick side parting, slung with his rocket-propelled grenade launcher, in the 72nd Brigade. Strong, trim, smiling; in the dim lights of the jeep. One of the boys who jumped in to take whatever he could. And

for a moment or two in the dark, they spoke, without knowing each other's names.

A few weeks after, they asked: would she head to that final position?

Base herself there. Be the position cook.

'I was always open for new places, new people.'

'So I thought, why not.'

There were twenty of them right at the front line. Hutched like refugees in that ruined house. Soldiers, RPG operators, volunteers and hardened gunners from the Battle of Donetsk. In that wrecked kitchen, this was where she cooked.

That was when she saw him again.

He looked at her. He smiled at her.

The kind of smile and the kind of look a man only does when he looks at you for the first time and he sees something he wants.

But he wasn't that kind of man.

Would you like me to give you a hand?

He stepped into the kitchen. And then he began to clean. Lyosha, that was his name. He came back again and again. And this time he offered to make her coffee and began to play with the platoon's dog that kept her company as he hung around for scraps.

'He was so sweet to that little doggie.'

You quickly learn this is one of the most telling things about men at war. Because everybody in war knows the cruelty or the kindness they will show to animals is the cruelty and kindness they will show to man.

What's your number?

He added her. He started to send her chats.

She started to ask him about where he was from.

He told her about Kyiv. And what it had been like in Maidan. She told him about Dima. She told him about what had gone wrong. He told her how deeply brave she was. Outside they heard the war.

Will you sit next to me?

Would you watch a film with me?

'What happened was so unexpected. We were watching a movie and then we just faced each other and then it happened . . . our first kiss.'

And then it happened, much faster and deeper than it had ever happened before. There were eyes all around them. They felt awkward and embarrassed as they began. The gunners all about them laughing and making jokes. Everything between them felt significant, there in that ruined house. There was no courtship. There was no conversation.

There was just them and the war.

'We celebrated New Year's together.'

The sounds of fireworks, the strikes of the big clock in the big city were on their phones as the vodka went round, and they cheersed. That was when they posted their first photo together. It was late. The party had reached that point where anything might happen. And as it began to die, the boys sang the Cossack songs; the ones that were always about death. Almost like they were rehearsing.

Online there was a comment from Lyosha's mother.

who's this girl

They were lying together in that little room when he turned to her and said it. *We need to talk.* And her heart fluttered with curiosity not fear. *We really need to talk. I like you,* he said. *I like you a lot.*

'And I said, *I like you too.*'

And after that things changed.

Little things, shading how they talked to each other, or in the way they worried about each other. They began to be more serious. They were together.

'When he left our position, to fight, we could only exchange a few text messages with each other. Nobody could ever predict how long a battle would last. Was it a regular day of duty? Or would it last the night?'

She would never know.

How she would hope it was just a regular day.

'Sometimes, when it was all quiet, Lyosha could call me for a few minutes. We were always talking. So, I never said goodbye to him when he went to fight. Only sometimes, the shelling was so intense our boys would have to shut off their mobile phones and only use radio communications.'

That's when her mind was all him.

You can't explain it when you fall in love.

You only want to hold them. You only want to see them.

Because when you know – you know.

'It happened so much faster than it does in peacetime.'

'So I don't remember the exact moment of falling in love. There's only a moment when you look at a person and you realize, I love him.'

His face. His smell.

That was when they transferred her again.

They were always looking for basements, in the Zone.

They were scrabbling about in tumbledown houses, between broken-up roads and overgrown fields. You learn nature always eats what we leave.

They were filthy, the soldiers she would feed.

At 6 a.m. she would wake up knowing she had to cook.

All day only one thought: *Do I have enough? Enough rice? Enough barley?* There were thirty men, sometimes seventy; and they all needed to be fed. And another day would pass. The same pop song in the background. Something by Okean Elzy.

'Once you've cooked breakfast . . .'

'Once you've washed your utensils, it's time for lunch, it's time to start cooking again. And there were only the tiniest breaks. I only had time to drink coffee, talk to my mum on the phone, or maybe my baby. But he didn't speak yet . . . all he said to me was – *Ma* – and – *bye bye*. So I just watched some videos that Mum sent me, or looked at her pictures, and then it was time for dinner. But the truth is, I thought of my kid only sometimes, less about my mother. And once I was with Lyosha, I thought more about him, as I was worried.'

They were separated.

He was at another position.

Sometimes she would see beautiful trails of smoke in the evening.

Sometimes she would fall asleep worrying he'd been hit.

The shelling started very early that morning.

And then it kept going. That crazy, spitting – woosh. And then the thuds. One after the other. Thumping sometimes closer.

Sometimes further away. Rattling everything right down to the pins in the camp-bed.

It was the dogs, naturally, who felt it first. They would begin to whine and squeal, they would panic, something glassy would happen to their eyes and they would yelp and bark, and try to burrow. Minutes before the boys had heard anything. That's when they'd know to run. To get to the basement and hide. Somehow, the dogs always knew when it was going to be close.

Everything shook.

There were no dogs that morning.

And that was when she woke up. Another thud. Another morning outside Avdiivka.

Was it close? Then she heard it again.

Yes, it was over there.

That was the industrial zone, for sure.

She'd been through this so many times now: the drill. The sudden rush when – *yes,* it really was too close. The shouts of the duty officer. Those moments grabbing whatever they could on the way to shelter.

But this morning, there was nothing. There was no drill.

She could see the room around her.

The bricked-up window. The cracks of light. The empty bed.

'There was another soldier in my room but he was away for his shift when I woke up . . . I looked around and I could see nobody was fleeing. Everybody was calm and then . . . for some reason I fell back asleep.'

It was very sudden.

It hit with a loud kaboom.

Her ears were ringing. There was dust and bricks everywhere. The wall had caved in. Olya was coughing. Then she began to gasp. Her mouth was clogged with it. They'd been hit. The window was blown open.

And then she realized she was on the floor.

'As I tried to pick myself up, I saw what had happened. I'd been thrown off the bed and I saw that the other bed had also been thrown by the explosion . . . it was standing right there, upright, blocking the door.'

She couldn't get out. She knew she was stuck.

And that was when she began to scream.

She screamed for the soldiers. To get her out. To help her. To hear her.

But they were not thuds any more. They were blasts. They were angry and close.

'I heard the boom of another artillery round. And then I heard this sound, this swooshing sound, of a shell incoming straight and somewhere deep inside me . . . I suddenly realized it was coming for me.'

It was less than a moment.

Maybe she was still screaming.

But in that space her mind suddenly filled.

She was suddenly back at the training in Starichyi, the officers shouting to duck and cover, to get to your lowest point, to fall on your back. And that's what she did. Olya threw herself back and tried to cover her face. But she still saw it.

It was right there.

'I could see it coming, the shell . . . there through the blown-off wall where the window used to be, the very moment the shell hit the ground and burrowed in. I was seeing it all as if in slow motion. The shell was burrowing – deeper, deeper, deeper into that soil. And I'm falling, falling, but I haven't fallen completely.'

It was twenty centimetres away.

It was one second.

And in that one second she hung there, there were faces.

'Lyosha. My son. My mother.'

There were voices: the voices of officers telling the recruits in Vinnytsia how gashed and maimed the bodies were when they found them five or ten metres from a blast. There were thoughts. Or the fragments of thoughts.

'I thought that's it. It's lights out.'

And in that space, she turned on herself.

'Lyosha is going to be mad at me when he finds out.'

'Because I'm not waking up again . . . *I'm not waking up.*'

And then it arrived. The explosion. Fierce and full.

And for an instant darkness. Then nothing.

Then nothing at all.

—

She came to and she screamed.

But it was in her mouth: dust, clay, mud – whatever had come from the blast. And it was in her eyes: she was covered and she could hardly move.

The dust was choking her.

Again she tried to scream.

Are you alive?

A soldier came in. He was shaking.

The battle was on his face.

It was a trooper they called Socrates.

Are you alive? he screamed at her.

Yes, Olya shouted.

Then he yelled back. *Crawl to me.*

The ground shook. Then that swoosh again.

'I couldn't see a thing . . . But somehow I managed to crawl to the bed blocking the door . . . grab the guy's shoulders and neck and he carried me out of that house to where the soldiers were taking shelter. I felt an ache in my leg but I thought I just hit it pretty hard, or some fragment got inside.'

She was breathing. Her heart was beating.

Olya felt a rush through her: she was still alive.

'And then I lost consciousness.'

She was awake.

She was lying on her back in some yard.

The men were around her. Standing over her. Someone was bending down to strap something round her leg to stop the bleeding.

'I look at my leg and I see . . . there's my knee. I saw one foot and I thought it's going to be OK. But I couldn't see my leg and I was scared to look.'

They strapped her up. Then she felt them lift her.

'All the guys carried me and I went . . . *Where am I?*'

We need to get to cover, they said. *The enemy is still shelling.*

What's happening? she said. *Why are you carrying me?*

But they wouldn't answer.

It's going to be all right, they said. And they looked away.

They tried to soothe her.

Don't worry.

She began to shout.

What's up with my leg? I can't feel my leg!

But the soldiers said nothing. She became frantic.

Is the ambulance coming?

But their jaws were firm.

There's still shelling. That's why it's taking a while.

She began to drift: the colours, the trees, the soldiers – it became a haze. The booms, the shouts, the radio: it seemed far away. She could feel they were taking her somewhere. *Yes,* they were carrying her back into that yard. Then there started to be moments where she was gone. There was the stretcher. They were trying to strap her in. Something was going wrong. It wasn't working. Like they couldn't get her legs in right. But it seemed far away. Like it wasn't happening to her.

Then they lifted her into the van.

We're going to make it, Olya.

That was Valya. She remembered the name of the nurse.

Valya, it was a pretty name.

She knelt next to Olya in the back of the van. That clunky old Soviet kind, that stank of petrol and they called the Loaf, when they used to laugh about it. The light was coming in. But she couldn't see the windows. They hurtled between potholes. They skidded. The Loaf rattled and shook. She could still hear them. They were still shelling.

'It felt like a numbing pain in my leg.'

And then she began to feel something.

'It was so rough, the road, from the damage . . . I felt like I was being thrown around on the stretcher . . . and then I began to feel like my hip was moving, like my leg was getting away from me, so I screamed . . . *Valya, hold my leg.*'

Catch it! It hurts.

And the nurse ripped open the bandages and grabbed on to her leg. That was when she first began to see. That mess of blood and skin and bones.

'And then I felt calmer.'

'Because that movement had scared me, that I was going to lose it.'

The road shook.

Much, much later, they told Olya that two shells had landed near them.

They had landed so close it should have been over. But neither of them went off. Olya knew none of this on the floor of the Loaf: the nurse holding her, the potholes rocking her as she fell in and out of consciousness. She felt her eyes dropping, her head falling; and then she was there again.

Commotion. Shouting.

They were taking her out of the van.

It's a girl!

That's what they yelled when they reached the hospital in Avdiivka.

There were a lot of people at first when they first got her through the door. But they seemed to flee. They were shouting. The lights were brighter now.

She was on the operating table.

Who are you? they shouted.

What's your name?

Olya began to yell her name.

Blood type? Say it now!

Someone was taking pictures.

The knee's intact.

There was a nurse now. She was trying to wipe her face.

She's covered in dust.

And there was the dripper. The needle. They began to count.

And then nothing.

She woke up slowly.

She came to behind her eyes and then she opened them.

Her mouth was dry. She wanted to say something. But she couldn't.

'The first thing was I couldn't speak.'

It was fear. Sudden and sharp.

'Because I knew I used to be able to speak.'

She tried but she still couldn't and that was when she saw a nurse.

'I tried to communicate with her by whatever gestures I could.'

They yanked the oxygen out of her mouth.

Olya turned to the nurse.

Can you move my left foot?

The question hung for an instant. Then somewhere, half a memory, she saw something. She was back on the stretcher. They were loading her into the Loaf. And there was her left foot; twisted sharply to the right. Then she was back in the ward.

'I was hot and feverish and I turn to the nurse and go, *Can you move my left foot, I'm hot and it's hurting me . . . the way it's lodged.*'

The nurse looked at Olya and came closer.

What leg? she said and she ripped off the blanket.

It wasn't a scream that came out. It was a sob.

An animal choking sob.

And as it began to shake and convulse her the nurse snapped again.

Stop it! Don't cry . . . Don't get agitated. *You've got this monitor attached to your heart and you want to add tachycardia to all the problems you've got?*

Olya tried to suck it in, to stop it flooding out.

Until they brought her a phone.

She phoned Lyosha.

I'm coming . . . I'm coming, he said.

And then she phoned her mother.

Mummy, I'm OK, I'm OK, she said.

It was her voice. In the middle of her day. She was puzzled.

Why didn't you call me on Mother's Day? What's going on? What's this strange number you're calling me from?

She gulped and swallowed and said, *I'm in hospital, Mummy.*

But I'm OK, I'm OK . . . it's just one small piece of leg that's missing. Lyosha told me it's OK. He's on his way to me. Not to worry.

She cried a little bit.

And she fell in and out of sleep in tears until Lyosha came.

He stood there, her own soldier, like there were no emotions going through his mind. Upright and strong, like he was saluting her, like it was only a graze. It's going to be all right, he said. It's going to be all right. She was crying now. But she wasn't sure why. Relief. Pain. Love. Shock. They were all there.

And then Lyosha began to cry too.

You survived. It's a real miracle.

His eyes were red as he held her. Then he said it.

And you should know I will never leave you.

And in that moment she felt it: everything that love can be.

She felt safe. She felt needed. She felt like she was finally home.

5 BUDAPEST

Ibrahim liked to keep a strict routine.

He'd wake up at 9 a.m. The Spanish light, bright, coming through the window in Marbella. He'd start, the same way he always did, with a protein shake. Then he'd throw on his shorts and go for a jog. Ibrahim would run, until he was breathing heavily – he had to run, to keep his body, to keep his stamina like this – and already they'd be there, already he could see them, the girls on the beach. His eyes would wander – he'd be thinking about it already, he was always thinking about it – and then he would hit the gym, bench-pressing until he was dripping in sweat. He'd go harder. You had to keep at it. There wasn't much morning left. Then he would eat quickly – salad, chicken, very few carbs – check the cameras and wait for the buzz at the door. It was a beautiful flat.

'I'm very good at it.'

'When the girl comes, I try to talk to them. I touch them . . . you know? I make my mind believe, this girl, it's like I picked her up.'

The first few minutes are very important. He'd take her to the sofa. She'd sit down. Usually she'd put her bag somewhere. Then he'd always offer her a drink. Ibrahim had done this deft manoeuvre so many times he felt himself expert at it. He knew how to talk to them. He'd try to turn them on.

'There are ways you can touch them.'

Sometimes they'd be moody. This was a job, after all.

'But I know how to deal with all of them.'

They go over the plan, he'd hit the camera, then they'd fuck. The blowjob. The cumshot. There'd be things you'd have to shoot. Fuck, stop, cool off, start again. The whole thing took about two hours to get about fifteen minutes. Sometimes he threw the camera to the side whilst they fucked – so it would be there on the bed – often he'd

go at her also filming with his phone in one hand. This kind of raw footage was increasingly popular.

His heart was beating afterwards.

'I always do it very intense.'

Ibrahim would get up, click save, download and then send the video to the team to edit it and post it on the site. Sometimes, she'd already be half-gone – professionals, booked through the agency, a lot of them didn't hang around – but sometimes, he'd know if she'd liked him, they'd fuck again with the camera off, then they'd sleep a little, go out afterwards for a drink by the beach and sometimes try and pick up another girl. It happened pretty often. Because everybody knew there were two kinds of people who did it in porn. Those who do it for money and those who were addicted to sex. By now he knew who he was.

'I prefer it actually . . . fucking on camera.'

'You can do it without a condom. The girls are tested. But in private life you have to wear one. The girls in porn they are very nasty. You work, they work. But in private . . . You know, when you meet a girl they want to pretend they are not that slutty. On cam you can just be you. She can just be her.'

It had only been a few years. But now he tensed up if he didn't fuck every day. He started to feel crazy, like he was in some kind of withdrawal. That's why he tried to shoot all week. Not to stop unless he really had to.

'I get hard even if the girl looks like shit.'

Sometimes he'd think about Europe. And all those different girls. Russians. Now those were hard to read. Some of them loved sex and, some of them, well, they didn't. You never knew what you were getting. Spanish girls? They were not really that horny. Maybe a little bit. And they were dramatic. Like French girls. The kind that got jealous if Ibrahim shot with another girl. Or if there were two girls in the scene they'd get moody. But the French: they were horny. Central Europe was more disappointing.

'Hungarian girls?'

'Not really; you can tell they do it just for work.'

Czech girls, now they were a bit hornier. But not by much.

'It's the same, mostly just doing it for money.'

Italians, come to think of it, could be pretty good though.

'But British girls . . . now they are very nasty. They like hard sex, like . . . *spit on me*. And I love it because it touches me . . . as I don't like to do rough sex if the girl doesn't like it. I'm really into British girls.'

After work he'd check his numbers. Lately his anal scenes had been going through the roof. Ibrahim wasn't sure how many women he'd fucked since he got into porn. Maybe eight hundred. Maybe a thousand.

'It takes a lot of energy. You have to only have energy for this. I was only thinking about this. Just sex . . . and I'm still like that actually. And sometimes, I ask myself . . . I really need another hobby, you know, not just sex. But it's difficult because I've trained my mind just to be happy with this. I can't.'

These thoughts would linger late into the afternoon. Nagging him. After he'd napped and before he'd hydrated again. There'd be a grogginess in his mind as the sun went down. But at night it would focus again.

'The world is fake.'

That's what Ibrahim would often think. It would be dark outside. The sounds of the evening would be coming in: cicadas, car music, sometimes the squeal from a group of teens horsing about on the promenade. He'd get dressed, always Versace, Gucci or Dolce and Gabbana, then he'd pick out one of his watches, a gold Rolex or Patek Philippe, and then he'd go to the clubs.

It hadn't always been this easy.

He knew being brushed off.

'You see, when I first got all this . . .'

'I'd see the girls again and they loved it. And that's when I realized – the world is fake. It's all about what you have, not who you are.'

'I've changed my life.'

'To a luxury: friends, places, houses.'

'You understand?'

The hits were coming through. He had over a million followers on Instagram, more than 700,000 followers on Twitter, enough subscribers to make €900,000 that year – the messages, the requests, they never seemed to stop. Ibrahim could do whatever he wanted – two girls, three girls, four girls. When there were lockdowns in

Spain he flew to Brazil. When there were Covid problems there he'd fly back to Spain. And now he had the Lamborghini.

'I'm always training to focus my mind.'

But it could slip away from him. It would hit at odd moments. He'd be thinking. Always about girls. How the ones with a tiny bit of hair on their hands were the horniest. How there were some that genuinely did like anal and some that didn't. Ibrahim would be driving or he'd be in the shower after sex and suddenly he'd catch himself and for a moment it would feel strange and incredible again like at the beginning – *How did this even happen?*

'I don't really think about Syria any more.'

It wasn't easy to have sex in Aleppo.

At least it wasn't for Ibrahim when he was seventeen. He'd wander around the ancient city and he'd see them – beautiful women – and then he'd try. He'd be invited to parties and then they'd be there – they walked, they talked differently from other women – and he'd try. He would always try.

'I was loving girls.'

He'd always been like this. Ever since he was twelve, when girls spoke to him, he got excited, something came over him, something tingly.

'I was loving girls too much but in my country I couldn't have girls. Because in my country there's religion and there's the culture.'

'They want you to marry them.'

It didn't stop him. Not in the slightest. Ibrahim would try and pick them up. He knew how to smile. He knew the right eyes. But nothing. Nothing ever happened – a few numbers, a kiss, drinks, once, twice, he'd take them to one of the clubs they had in Aleppo – but of course, nothing could ever happen.

That was just how it was.

'I was frustrated.'

'I was getting more frustrated.'

And they were like that at home.

They were religious, both of his parents: they really believed in it all, in a God, in everything. Just normal, middle-class Sunni people, with his dad working in the car-parts business. It wasn't how he

wanted to live. Prayers five times a day. Continually asking above for stuff. Then the mosque on Friday. It had started when he was fifteen. He'd started reading about religion – about Catholicism, Islam, priests – and he'd found they all claimed they were right and the others wrong and it just didn't make sense.

'And after, you know . . .'

'Reading and reading, I got a lot of headaches. And I stopped, and I said I've become atheist. I don't want to believe in it. And then, you know, it took me two years to train my mind to not believe it.'

That wasn't it though.

That wasn't the thing that set it off.

That was the rich friends. Guys like Abdallah. They were all from Furkan, the right part of town. They were all really rich, with their own cars and swimming pools. They lived in these tall, beautiful homes with maids, and it was them that made him realize that the way he was living, Ibrahim, it wasn't the best, and neither was anything else about him. His dad wasn't in textiles. He was normal. Nothing, really. He'd be with them – they'd walk so lightly, the city would open up expectantly – and then he'd go home to that very simple house and it just wouldn't be the same.

'I have obsessive thoughts. When I want something I want it very intensely. When there's something in my mind it doesn't go away. It stays a long time. It's very hard. So I want to do it. And then: I do it or I die.'

That's when it go into his head. Ibrahim was watching films in the evening, and he's be watching the actors, the big ones, like Nicolas Cage, and that's when it started to ply in his head: *That's who I was to be – a star, a performer, a famous person. Someone like them.* He had to do it. He had to act now. *That's how a normal person becomes very rich.*

'I started acting in Aleppo.'

It was amateur, but it was still fun.

There would be plays at Aleppo University theatre, he was still at school but they let him come. He was so nervous at first – that time he played a tramp, a lover boy or a movie director – but he'd be up there, he'd be somebody else and everybody would be looking at him. It felt right. He'd go home and watch the series from Cairo, the singers from Dubai, he'd even watch Tom Cruise and Angelia Jolie, and he'd think – *yes* – I can be them.

'I told myself . . . if I believe, I will be. And I was sure that I will be an actor. Because, you know . . . I believe it.'

Then something happened.

Noise was how it began. Terrible noises. The crowds marching, men, hundreds of them, chanting – *the people want the fall of the regime*: that crackle, that started at night, of gunfire, somewhere over the city, then the bombs. That boom, shattering glass, car alarms, then shouts and wailing. Sometimes far, sometimes very close by.

Germany. Everybody was talking about it.

His brother was already in the army.

'Then I got my call-up papers.'

At the front they were being slaughtered.

'I'd have to go to the army.'

It wasn't a difficult decision.

'So I left, but not . . . by water or anything.'

Ibrahim didn't have any time. He found the smuggler. He kissed his parents goodbye and then he left. Only months after the start of the war.

'It was expensive. I paid $4,000 just to get into Greece. That was with the car. I just drove straight to Greece with a fake passport, with my fingerprints and everything. It was a Greek one. And then to Athens.'

It was all so quick.

Like a dream. Like it hardly happened.

He woke up in that cramped flat. Now he was in Athens, he was with family again, he was staying with them all day, at this restaurant they owned – it already felt like too much time he'd been spending with them – and at night he walked around the city. That temple, the Acropolis, glowed on a hill, like something in a Middle Eastern city, like photos of the Dome of the Rock. And in the narrow streets below, that only got busier the later it got, his eyes followed the girls. They were beautiful – that thick black hair – he wanted them so badly. Everything about them. But nothing.

'Still no action.'

He felt it in the restaurant. He felt it in the street. Ibrahim wasn't comfortable. It was like a panic creeping over him. The first time he went to the airport, with his second fake passport, they threw him out. They were women, in uniforms, and they spoke to him very badly. *Go out*, they yelled. *Out!*

'I feel really bad as I ask: *Why I cannot fly and other people can?*'

'I will fly.'

Then it happened again and again.

This wasn't a good situation. He kept telling himself, *Maybe it will come one day, maybe it will come. Women. Money. Sex.*

'I was still hoping.'

'Maybe I will get to Germany and I have some action.'

But it wasn't here. It wasn't in Athens.

'I'd be dreaming, I'll get to Germany, then England.'

'Then eventually, America, where they make films.'

Ibrahim would wake up and he would feel it immediately. He didn't feel good. He felt small. The longer he stayed with them, with the restaurant – cleaning plates, the sounds of waiters – he started to feel scared. There started to be questions.

They started to flood in on him.

'I was afraid, it's a new country to me.'

'I don't know what I'm going to do. I want to travel but maybe I'm not going to have enough money to be very rich.'

I'm going to go to Germany, he kept telling himself. *Then England*. On the way to the airport, for the fourth time. *I'm going to go to London and there I'm going to fuck*. The woman took his passport. She nodded. Then waved him through.

Cabin crew prepare for take off.

'I was so excited I hardly slept.'

He could hardly keep still. It was happening, at last.

'It was like my life was beginning.'

The hours passed. The seatbelt sign came on. Then the plane rattled slightly and it dipped through clouds, blinking, into Stuttgart. He was finally here. Sounds. Announcements in German and Greek he did not understand.

Ibrahim pulled his bag from the locker. Moved into the slow, funnelling aisle. Then it happened. Like a sudden twist where the monsters appear in his nightmares. *Polizei*. There were policemen at the door of the plane. Policemen waiting for him.

'They must have realized.'

'*Come with us!*'

'I was so scared I went limp.'

They were taking him somewhere. Somewhere bad. Through the tunnels of the airport. *I'm going to be sent back.* His mind raced as they barked at him and pulled him into a side room. *I'm going to be sent to prison.*

Ibrahim was in what looked like a cell.

Strip! – they shouted. And he was standing naked. They made him squat, cough and they patted him. He was sweating. He was so scared it felt like a fever. The light was bright. *Dress!* – they threw it back at him. And then the lady came. *How old are you?* She was Syrian, her hair free, middle-aged. *Are you here to claim asylum?*

The men seemed calmer.

'They took my basic asylum claim and they took my fingerprints.'

That was when he knew it was over. The moment his thumb was over the scanner he knew England was over for a long time. *They'll never let me in now.* He was stuck in Germany. The lady, she looked tired, explained he was going to a *Kinderheim* – a children's home – and he'd be there until they had further notice for him.

'They took me to the house.'

'And that's where I slept.'

Ibrahim woke up in Germany. The other kids, they were about his age, seventeen, they spoke no English. And he knew no German. At least they let him out and he wandered – no internet on his phone, not knowing where he was, or what was going to happen – in these strange, silent, empty streets full of trees, that were like nothing he'd ever seen before. He stopped at a bench.

'I just sat like I was in prison.'

'You know nothing. It's like you're starting again.'

Two days later they came for him. *You have family in Cologne?* He nodded. *You have been registered at a Kinderheim in that city. Do you understand?* It took a moment for the translator to help him understand. *You're free to go.*

'I rushed to the station.'

To get a ticket to Cologne. The people, they looked different, they smelt different, the girls were different, right to their shape. Ibrahim stepped into the pleasurable crowd and let it wash over him.

'I will be safe, I will be an actor. I will make my dreams come true. And I will be someone special. I will be different.'

This is what he kept thinking as the train went faster – forests, castles, small, misty towns – sped past him and he smiled.

'I've always been thinking this.'

He fucked Stefanie in Cologne.

It started on Facebook. She threw him a like on his gym shot: a six-pack in the mirror. Then he added her.

why dont we meet???

It was in the street he first saw her.

'I could see how nice her body was.'

He wanted her, he wanted her so badly, and then they wandered, trying to talk – him with his shitty broken German, her trying to talk very slowly – into the park. She said she liked cats, he liked them too, and for a while they talked about that. Until they kissed.

That same day she let him have it. Finally, for the first time. 'You're my favourite,' she'd shriek. 'You're very good at sex. You know how to do it. You know how to do it intense.'

He fucked her every day.

'She loved it so much.'

You make me scream, she said. Then they'd fall asleep. They'd start again. And then sometimes they'd talk. Ibrahim would tell her about Furkan, about Syria, about how he was going to be an actor and then they'd fuck again.

'I'd go round to her house.'

There were a lot of Arab men in Cologne, hanging about on the main square, working in crap jobs, waiting for something to happen, but she only wanted him. He'd be in her room – her girl's room, with photos all over the wall – and they'd fuck, for what seemed like hours, as the cat sometimes watched.

They did everything. She wanted everything.

'She taught me German.'

She taught him how to pronounce things correctly – '*miene Liebe*,' she'd say, '*ich liebe dich*' – as she looked at him, so pale and beautiful, when her eyes wanted him. One night, when they'd played Xbox afterwards – he was always Mario and she was always Princess

Peach – she told him her dad had raped her when she was small. And that's why her mum was on her own.

They'd fuck for hours.

'Then she moved to a different school.'

They'd fucked so much it was like they were together. Then something changed. She'd gone to a new school and she'd stopped texting him. She'd stopped calling him. He came round that last night.

I'm sorry, she said.

She was crying.

But I don't love you any more.

The cat was hiding.

For a moment he tried to ask why.

I don't know, she said.

And then it was over. She was gone but Ibrahim didn't stop thinking about sex.

'It's like I was addicted.'

'I got it and I just wanted more.'

Time had gone by so fast but also, he thought, so slowly at the same time.

Ibrahim had been two years in Cologne. The migration Ausländerbüro had put him in school – *you are a child refugee*, they said – they had him in classes, in a normal, everyday school, where they'd look at him because he couldn't speak German, where they had everything, but they still made fun of him, laughing at his Arab accent. It made him feel so awful, even now, he didn't even want to think about.

'Always I have this anxiety about losing control.'

But not in sex.

'I loved it so much.'

'I'm in charge. I'm the boss.'

'I had so much fantasy in my mind . . .'

You keep going. You get there. Then it's all gone.

You can feel a little sad afterwards. Everybody knows that. You can feel a little sad even when you're in love. But it wasn't like that. What would come over him. It was big, it was heavy, it was some kind of emptiness: so misty and vague at first he didn't know what it was. Ibrahim would fuck. Harder than ever. He'd fuck like this when he was with Stefanie. And the fucks he got after her. But it would always come back.

'I wasn't happy so much. It's like I always felt something was missing. It took me a long time to figure it out.'

During classes and nights out and German lessons, it was in the back of his mind. It was inside him, always there. Cloudy. Heavy. He couldn't really hear it properly. Like somebody was shouting from far away. And then it became clear. He would be on the morning bus to school, the streets would be passing, Cologne would be out the window, and then it was almost like he would see himself.

'Many things were missing.'

He could see it very keenly now.

'My goals. My life. My future.'

What he wanted. The reason he'd left Aleppo so happily. All of it was missing in the *Heim* where he lived here. It was missing in the clothes he wore. It was missing in the places he went. In the places he ate. It was missing with the girls. He'd see them on the bus, outside the cinema, his eyes would follow them, their skirts in summer, their shapes that made him ache, outlines in pullovers in winter. Hardly any of them wanted him. They looked at him – they looked right through him – so many of the ones he wanted, because he had nothing, because he was not on their level. Just a refugee.

That's when they started telling him no.

No, you can't apply for acting school.

'They told me my language was not good enough. That you need to study all this. But acting has nothing to do with studies. It's all about you.'

No, you can't graduate.

You've failed the tests. You need to repeat.

He could hardly argue with them.

They had a system here, this people, they had rules, they liked setting them down and they liked to follow them. That's when he started to feel it again. That creeping panic. He had to become an actor. He was stuck repeating the school year – they kept failing him – until he was older than the other kids, who looked at him funny.

'I will make it, I said, I will.'

You feel awful if you need to be seen.

You feel awful if you're not looked at.

Another summer. Another winter. The carnival – it filled the streets – was a great day to pick up women, drunk and flirty and ready to talk to anyone in a funny hat, it came and went. They did let him pass in the end. His days were his. Really his. But there was nothing to fill them. *I should have got to England,* he kept repeating to himself. *I've got to get there, or to America. There's something wrong with Germany.*

'It was like everything was closed.'

I want to be an actor, he said, over and over.

But it wasn't working. The schools they'd all said no. The system had come up blocked. *I can go round the system,* he kept on telling himself. But that wasn't working either. Twitter. Facebook. Email. Every day Ibrahim was messaging – *i want to be an actor* – and nothing. *i'll work for free. i just want experience.* He'd messaged all of them – producers, companies, theatres – and there was nothing.

Almost nothing.

Do you have the right to work in Germany? Ibrahim would tell them he was Syrian. The replies would stop. *We'll contact you later,* some said. After that he'd be waiting: until he realized that also meant no.

'What else could I do?'

'I worked in restaurants.'

It was almost no money.

In Cologne, he could hardly pick up a girl.

'I was thinking: *When's it coming, the money?*

'When's it coming, the success?'

He'd hardly get a glance.

Ibrahim wasn't even a waiter. He was a dishwasher again. Running hot water and soap over his hands for ten hours a day, until they were slightly numb – the plates, they never stopped coming – and he'd be thinking. Those same obsessive thoughts would be crowding in. *Maybe it doesn't really matter who I am. Who I end up being. Maybe it's not an actor.*

Maybe just someone different.

Nothing. No emails. No DMs.

Nobody was responding to him.

Ibrahim would watch porn in the evening when he was working

at the Turkish restaurant, after he'd spent the day scrubbing dishes – two, three, four girls, this kind of fantasy. He'd be masturbating, when the thought first wormed in. *I don't want to have a regular job*, he'd be thinking. *I don't like this. I don't want to be like everyone else. I've never wanted this. Not since I was little. I want to be an actor.* And then he'd see the men fucking.

Not just the girls.

'It came slowly.'

'I like sex. I have a lot of fantasies, sex with women.'

It didn't happen so often. But when he picked up girls in Cologne, he liked it. He liked it so much. Nothing made him feel so good.

'I wasn't thinking of money when it started.'

'I was only thinking of fame and leisure.'

Those guys, fucking. The ones on his phone.

They have that. They had all the fame and leisure they want. All they do is fuck and fly around the world to pools and studios and they don't wash oily kebab dishes.

'I always knew I'm better than this.'

Ibrahim would be masturbating again, watching porn late at night: searching – *arab, syrian, arab guy* – and now it wasn't letting him go.

It was obsessing him.

'I like it. I like this fantasy.'

He could fuck like that. Like he fucked Stefanie.

'And I said to myself: there are not so many people doing porn in the Arab world. If I do porn, I'm sure I can be successful.'

I've got to get out of here, he told himself – the owner screaming to wash faster in the kitchen – and after a few days he walked out. But the only job he found was in the refugee *Heim*, first on security and then translating.

In the morning, he'd be there, a witness to their battered faces, the eyes of people who had seen men explode in front of them. Mothers, pleading, to get their benefits quickly. The videos they'd show him. The stories he'd hear of what had happened to Aleppo.

At night, he'd watch porn.

He'd be masturbating. But he couldn't stop thinking about it now. Him. Doing this. Again and again. The obsessive loop. This was the hack. The way in. He'd storm it. He'd make a name. And then he'd transition: music, real movies, it was all possible. And it was all there on the internet.

'I could see so many ways in.'

You find things on the internet and then they find you.

You pull out your phone and then you're in it. You're mainlining porn. You start to see it everywhere. It's in every phone. It's in every pocket. It's something anyone can do. It's a way to be famous. It's a way to be you.

It was then he started messaging.

That was all he could do.

Porn accounts. Companies. This was going to work. It had to work. On Instagram, on Twitter, on their websites. He sent hundreds and hundreds of messages.

'There was nothing back.'

Then he applied with a German name.

'I was almost thinking it's impossible.'

Then two companies, out of all those hundreds, pinged him – saying they'd be interested. And when he told them he was Syrian, that actually he was a refugee, they were still interested. Just as much.

Then the first email arrived.

It was the fee, date and location.

'I couldn't think about anything else.'

Ibrahim was nervous when he arrived in Prague. The city was old, it was full of tourists and trams and there was something off about it, like something weird had happened there. There was the address, it was a private porn location, and when he turned up, it was like a movie. There were cameras everywhere and a team and a set and all kinds of protocols. He showed his passport, the Syrian one, like you have to before all porn shoots to prove it's you, and they nodded. That's where he got ready. His mind racing.

'Will I be good? Or will I fall?'

'Because it's my only chance.'

And then there were the girls.

Czech girls. They were cool and professional, to him; they had no interest in him, because why should they, as they got ready.

'And it was very clear to me. It's all about who you are. The girls always react about who you are. People always treat you like who

you are. If you are strong, they treat you like you're strong. If you're weak, they treat you like you're weak.'

They got naked and so did he.

The lights were brighter than he'd expected.

He'd taken Viagra but now it was giving him a headache.

'It was a little bit stressful and I was feeling stressed. I was feeling excited. I can do it. I want them to see me: *This guy, he can fuck.*'

Two hours. That's the usual slot.

It felt strange, fucking under the camera. *Stop*, they made them do it again. *Doggy*, the director shouting positions. *Cumshot.*

'It felt like I didn't enjoy it so much.'

Then it was done. Just like that.

Like he'd just finished work. He stepped out, it was cold in Prague in the winter, and that night he went out. His heart was racing. A friend, Big Josh from Iraq, had come with him from Germany; they went to a party, they drank, they had something about them, a hungry glow, and they picked up.

'And I was fucking, a second time, more excited.'

They paid him €500.

He went back to Germany pumped, like he'd crossed the border, like he'd lost his virginity all over again, so strong was that sense it was all beginning.

They were going to get back in touch. And for weeks he'd be checking and checking. Then it never came, the email he'd been expecting, the next scene. It was just a weekend, it wasn't the start of anything with these guys.

'And then I got another email.'

But the same thing happened in Brussels. They invited him, he shot – he was better, he thought, he fucked better – and then it was over. Another €500. And nothing. They didn't contact him. Like they didn't like him.

'I was worried about many things.'

'There were many worries around me but I just ignored them.'

Or at least he tried to. Because they never stopped whispering.

What if you do this, you make a fool of yourself, then you close all your doors?

What if it's not so easy?

It was following him, calling after him.

That feeling of being a fool.

'I began to see how difficult it is for a guy to get into porn. They choose the guys they work with all the time. They don't want to change the guys.'

'I'd thought it'd be easy.'

Three months. No offers. No emails. No calls.

The girls from Prague and Brussels were busy.

'The people I shot with were all on new scenes.'

All day he'd be at the *Heim*.

Translating: benefits, traumas, migration appeals.

The day would pass. Their stories washed over him.

Then he'd be up late, watching more porn, going at it, thinking: *What can I do, where can I make it?* He was clicking through streamers. He was clicking through sites. *You don't really need the companies, do you?* It was all becoming clear. *I'll make a video with the money I've saved. I'll post it myself.*

I'll quit the Heim. *I'll get out of here.*

I'll do it all myself.

This time he screamed as he fucked.

Bring me my slave! She was brown, Spanish, the girl he'd hired to film in Barcelona. It had taken for ever to find her and fix this up. The stress had been really getting to him. *Bring me the wine!* He had her for two hours. *Do you want some wine? Yes*, she said, over and over, pretending to speak Arabic as he barked orders at her. It was almost ridiculous, her saying that, he thought. *Now give me your ass!* But she did look kind of Arab – a look of a lot of Spanish girls, actually – and he had her for two hours to make this fantasy work. He'd read so many stories about this. He'd watched so many videos. It had to work.

'It's like: *a long time ago . . .'*

'The story was I'm an Arab king.'

That night Ibrahim was watching himself.

It was good, he thought. He looked good. It made him hard. And it must have worked because the ratings, the reviews, the numbers, were all up. *It's a syrian guy doing porn,* people were writing, *100 percent real arab bull.*

Then something started to happen. They didn't stop. The ratings. They got higher and higher. The clip was going viral. And then the messages came in death threats. Then that cold feeling. What he was feeling was fear.

disgusting arab. we will kill you.

Messages from his family.

you can't do this. think of your family, what you are doing is disgusting.

i'm ordering you to stop it now.

They were phoning him, friends from the *Heim*, saying people were looking for him – saying everybody knew it was him – that there were men in Cologne who said they were coming for him. That they were after him.

'And then I realize . . . *I'm fucked.*'

He was back in Cologne.

For all the ratings, the video hadn't made a cent.

Friends saying, *Keep away from here.* His family weren't speaking to him. His father incandescent with rage. Syrians, in Germany, men who felt he'd humiliated them making his video, looking for him, wanting to humiliate him too.

'Or even kill me. That's what they said.'

He'd felt like a star fucking her in Barcelona.

Now he could hear it again, those doubts roaring at him.

You're a fool. You're nothing. You're done.

'I'm fucked. I've got no money. Everybody knows me.'

'This porn fucked me up.'

That voice in his head. It was panic now.

Ibrahim skipped town. His cousin, who lived in a small city not too far away, took him in. And those were the worst days. The rage online against him. The texts. The DMs. He sat there thinking again and again: *I'm an idiot.*

'I can't work at the *Heim*.'

'I can't even do porn because nobody wants to hire me.'

'What am I going to do?'

And then, like a dog following him over his shoulder, he began to hear something worse. Another voice. *It's over. There's no way out.* It came automatically. Again and again. The same thoughts that lingered there until he pushed them away.

'I thought about killing myself.'

It was there in his head. It was there for days.

'Then I said, *OK, let's give it one more chance.*'

'*Maybe my life will change.*'

He slipped back into town. Avoiding the Arabs and the *Heim*.

Now Cologne was greyer than ever. There were videos of him fucking online, ticking up likes on porn sites, but it had almost killed him. It was like he'd gone through another door and been punched in the face. He was still eating the cheapest food, walking for an hour because he couldn't afford an uber, avoiding the police document checks, the whole time messaging, messaging – *Here are my videos, I'm ready to work, I want to make Arab porn* – then trying not to panic about money. Those same obsessive thoughts coming after him, *I've got nothing – almost nothing – left in my account. I can't afford that. I can't go on like this. Just keep messaging. Don't stop. Don't even think about what will happen if you stop. You choose to live.*

The same message.

i want to shoot with you.

i'm doing real arab porn.

And most of the time nobody answered. It was as if there was nobody there on the other side of the internet. Like this was all just a joke being played on him.

And then one day there it was.

ok let's meet

That was the reply from Ryan.

She was a name in porn, a mature – in her forties, American.

come to hamburg I'm touring ;)

'And I don't have any money. I have nothing. Zero.'

But nothing was going to stop him getting to Hamburg.

They fucked the moment he got there. It was so much better with older women than with the very young ones who said they didn't know what they were doing – and then he told her about his dreams. About everything.

'She liked me. I had nothing.'

'She just liked me. I don't know how.'

It was like they were together, in a porn-world kind of way, after that. And the more they talked, the more he realized she was like him. A very honest person. He was very honest with her and she was very honest with him.

'I just want to make it.'

'We can do this,' she said. 'We can do that.'

And then she lent him €10,000.

'I'll pay you back when I get famous.'

A few weeks later Ibrahim arrived in Budapest.

It was drizzling, the autumn was already becoming winter and the taxi slipped past the ornate city on the river towards the flat. The one he'd rented, the one he was going to furnish, to shoot his scenes. Ibrahim let himself in, the place was bigger than he expected, his mind already planning it. *There.* That's where he'd put the sofas. There needed to be some better chairs. And he'd have to rent a new bed too.

'Budapest, it's like the capital of Euro porn.'

'You can still do everything so cheaply here.'

Ibrahim picked the girl. That's the look he wanted. That's who he wanted to fuck. Then she turned up: they fucked, he filmed and they uploaded.

'And nothing. It didn't become successful at all.'

Pale winter light streamed in through the window. Ibrahim was slumped on the sofa, alone, clutching his phone. Nothing. That feeling of being followed, of being haunted by failure, it was getting stronger. He kept refreshing the sites, but his numbers – they weren't moving, they'd stop ticking up, now it even felt like they were still.

It had started the first hour he noticed the likes were flatlining. That panic, those voices, he could hear them again very close by. They were hissing inside him now – *It's over, you're nothing, you're never going to make it, you couldn't even make good on this. You get all that money? And what do you do? You spunked it up the wall.*

Things were going wrong with Ryan.

'What am I going to do?'

He'd be on the streets. Lisping questions and doubts inside him. He'd see the trams and the girls, also the world, passing him by.

'How am I gonna save my ass?'

The noise of traffic, the glint of the night.

He'd be back in the apartment, the whole thing, the sofa, the bed, the whole porn set he'd tried to make himself, mocking him –

like a monument to his folly. *Fuck Budapest*. There was nothing to understand here. He'd be online – more porn, only porn – trying to understand that. Only the internet mattered. *You win that – you win everything*.

Fuck meeting people here.

'I'm gonna make a website, I decided.'

'I'll do it in Arabic, I'll Tweet it out . . . and maybe.'

It was awkward at first.

Hi, this is where I live, I'm shooting in Budapest . . .

He'd hold the phone, trying to be natural, streaming. Still nothing. The hissing would be so loud now, it'd be with him in the gym, it would be there when he woke up, his mind racing, when he was watching more porn, trying to join the dots – *I need content, that's what I need, content*.

'I flew back to Barcelona.'

The money was almost gone.

'There was a festival, I'm wandering around the festival, Tweeting, and I'm saying to people . . . *You want to see more? Subscribe*.'

The whole porn world was there.

The studs and the bulls, the PAWGs and the matures.

'It was then I started to feel scared.'

It was like cold hands grasping on to him.

'If nobody subscribes, I've got no money, I can't go on.'

That feeling didn't go away – that fear – when Ibrahim flew back to Budapest, when he got his first few subscribers, when he was back in the flat, or even when the first few payments trickled in.

'I was making a tiny bit of money.'

'But not enough to survive.'

It was ending with Ryan but he asked for more money.

Of course she said no, that €10,000 was all he was getting. He had to pay the rent in Budapest. He started to feel clammy, it was physical, that fear. Like someone was about to get him. He started to feel stress, it was painful, like something burrowing into him. Like it was just outside the door.

He couldn't hide from those questions now. It was like they were screeching at him. *You're going to have to be normal. You are just like everyone else. You belong in the kebab house*. Then he would pull himself together. He'd train his mind not to hear them.

To only focus on porn.

'I've only got €500 left. And at the end of the month the rent's going to be out. That's it. I don't have any money any more. I don't have a home. I don't have anything. Nobody is going to give me any work. And my girlfriend isn't going to lend me any more because I already burnt it all for furniture.'

You know what it's like to feel stuck.

You know those mornings. You can hardly get up.

You've hardly eaten. You open your eyes and it all comes flooding back. The logic of desperation takes over. You're this close to being broken. You can feel the cracks spreading.

You'll do anything.

'So I tell myself.'

'I've only got €500 but let's try one last time. So I contact one girl and one guy – a husband and wife team. And I tell them to come to my flat. And I tell myself I'll just film with my phone – even though it was actually broken, with a cracked screen, and just barely working.'

It was almost time.

Ibrahim's heart was pounding when they turned up, like it did the first few times he knew he was about to have sex with Stefanie in Cologne. She was nice – and he looked pretty good too. *I want to do a cuckold scene*, he told them. *That's what sends Arabs wild: they are all stuck-at-homes – mum, cousin, step-sisters, that's all they have to fantasize about and all they search.* And they laughed and said that was something they liked doing.

'I began filming them.'

'And I'm shouting at them in Arabic. *Come here! Go there.*'

'*Look at me . . . I'm fucking your wife.*'

'I'm calling him names and something comes over me.'

You might have fucked like this once or twice.

Like it mattered. Like something depended on it.

He was screaming as he went faster and faster.

'And I did it intense. I did it with my heart. Because it was my last €500. And I knew as I was going that this was good, that this scene had everything. It was like I was fucking for real. Not fake or something.'

He fucked with everything that had happened to him. He fucked with Syria. He fucked with failure. He fucked with a sad freedom and he fucked – *Why can't I be an actor, even this kind of actor* – he fucked with rage. Ibrahim came. He was covered in sweat. Like it doesn't happen very often. And then they went at it again. Even harder. And then the two hours were up. Ibrahim was buzzed. Like he was drunk. So that was it. He'd paid her €300 and him €150. He was down to his last €50. But that night he hardly cared.

'I uploaded, I showered and then I slept.'

Ibrahim was tired when he woke up. He grabbed his phone, like he always did, the moment he woke, and then he saw the notifications, red and green, still coming in, like the thing was exploding.

'What's this? I'm thinking . . .'

There were subscribers, hundreds of subscribers.

'All of them in just one morning.'

And the numbers were shooting up. A cold feeling raced through him like water: that was it – he'd hit the magic number. That was just enough subscribers to get by. And then he saw the views.

Edging a million on Twitter.

'The whole, whole Arab world had watched it.'

There were DMs from producers, fans, even stars. Ibrahim wanted to laugh. He wanted to shout. He felt something shimmering through him, from his head, something electric and cold. What he felt was joy.

'And I think: *So what are we gonna shoot next?*'

6 SABETTA

It was in quarantine he finally had time to think.

Alexey stared at the map. They looked like blood vessels, he thought, the pipelines coming in from Russia. And he was right at the edge of it.

Almost at the top of Yamal.

He was still waking up late. There was no point getting up early. That strange northern light, the kind he had only ever seen here, on mornings in Yamal, seemed to linger. There was not yet snow. Alexey was running down the clock till they let him out. They couldn't afford Covid at the gas site.

Leaks. Subsoil. Positioning.

They had enough problems as it was.

One more week, he thought, *one more week*.

Until then his life was frozen, in that tiny room.

Alexey had time to make tea. He had time to play with his phone. He had time to keep looking at the blueprints. But his mind kept drifting to big things. Like what this whole system looked like when you finally zoomed out.

Or what threw him into it.

You probably have them too.

Family parties your year revolves around. You've also noticed how they start to change. It happened to Alexey when he was at university. His sister got married. Suddenly, it was two families that got together. Her husband Kirill brought his whole family. They all lived in Samara on the Volga.

'So – *why not?*'

Alexey would turn up at the restaurants the lot of them had

booked and, now, at the heart of it, clicking his fingers and sending waiters back to the kitchen was someone he had trouble getting used to. Big Vladimir.

This guy was always, now, the head of the party.

Big Vladimir, of course, was Kirill's dad. His sister's huge father in-law.

It was a familiar type. You see it in soldiers sometimes.

'He's one of those guys used to ordering people around in very difficult conditions. He just can't change his behaviour. Even on holiday.'

But Big Vladimir wasn't in the army.

He was an engineer, or at least he *was* an engineer. He'd made it good in the north. Now he was a boss. His whole life on rotation, running his construction company in the Arctic. Building oil and gas sites, which whatever you were doing in this country, Alexey thought, never felt far away.

But he wasn't thinking about that.

The day it happened was his sister's birthday.

Alexey had been out of sorts. *Yes*, he could see that now.

Big Vladimir was circling.

Hey come here, put some sexy music on.

The waiters rushed to it.

We need more shashlik . . . That's right!

He was coming closer.

Alexey! You'll join me for a smoke . . . right?

He didn't smoke, as it happened, but he followed him. You couldn't say no to a man like that. You feel strangely beholden to them.

So what are you going to do, then?

It happened on the staircase. Alexey could see it now: Big Vladimir was taking a drag, holding himself in that way men who are used to bossing around other men hold themselves. He looked straight at him.

You've graduated . . . What next?

Alexey hesitated.

He couldn't tell Big Vladimir that he was listless. That he's lost motivation. That he felt like a tossed tin can bobbing on the river. He couldn't tell Big Vladimir that he didn't like the things he used to. That those last months at university had felt pointless. That he'd woken up and gone to bed thinking: *All I want is something new.*

'That I felt like there was deep shit inside me.'

Alexey didn't say any of that.

That's not the kind of thing you say at a family party.

That's not how you hold yourself when big men invite you to smoke.

I don't know what I'm going to do.

Alexey mumbled half-heartedly about some places he might apply. Big Vladimir kept smoking, then came a little closer, like he wanted something.

You speak English well, don't you?

Alexey nodded.

You know, Big Vladimir grinned, *I've got a new tender phase, with some foreign companies, up in the north. It's a new liquified natural gas installation. State of the art. If you've got some balls . . . why don't you come and join me?*

Then he went back inside.

You know that parties are like life. You're suddenly here, for a moment you can't imagine it being any different, and then they slowly die. Big Vladimir had been drinking. They'd all been drinking. And Alexey knew that if he never mentioned those balls again Big Vladimir would never even remember.

He woke up thinking about them.

Maybe, I can do this, he thought. *Maybe, I'm not a loser. Maybe, I can just go to the north.* Before he knew it, he phoned Big Vladimir.

I've got . . . some balls. I want to do it.

I knew you did, Big Vladimir said, chuckling.

Then it all happened very fast. They took him into the office, in the middle of Samara, sat him down and he signed papers. They took him into the computer room, ran him through the software, and told him to learn.

I've got no clue about any of this, he kept thinking.

But that wasn't the way he wanted to think.

I've got to make this work.

Two weeks later he flew to the north. Alexey didn't remember leaving Samara. That moment didn't matter to him. He didn't remember the flight out of Moscow. But he would never forget the approach to Novy Urengoy. The gas capital of Russia. This was nothing like the country he knew. Alexey pressed his face close to the window. What he saw was horrible and strange. This land was perfectly flat. Punctured by thousands of silvery lakes. Little trees that looked bent and sickly. Like a world that didn't want people.

'It was already snowing.'

The airport emptied fast. There was nobody waiting for him.

This couldn't be right.

'I called the office, expecting someone. *No, this is not how it works*, they said. *Get a taxi. Here's the address. You'll spend the night there before the chopper takes you to site.*'

He had a sudden cold feeling. So this is the way it is up here.

Night lamps made the ice glint orange as he waved for a taxi. Burly Chechens in leather jackets seemed to be driving everyone. Each cab with the feel it might be moonlighting for the mafia. Worn seats reeking of diesel and smoke.

'I wasn't expecting Chechens here.'

'But it only took a few hours to realize they ran half the town.'

Novy Urengoy passed in the dark.

Neon lights. Weather-beaten concrete. Snowdrifts. A few old wooden houses. A brash new church preening like some kind of iced gingerbread house. The kind that criminals liked to build all over Russia once they'd made it.

'The taxi left me at what felt like some random building.'

That block could have been anywhere up to Vladivostok. Its stairwell stank of trash and fried potatoes. Here was the address. And the moment he knocked, it clicked.

'The door opened and I'll never forget it.'

'I'm arriving in the north . . . just imagine it like this. You open the door and it's like the shittiest place, kinda like where some poor people who don't care about comfort, or cleanliness, or anything might live. It was a complete shit hole.'

'It's just a complete mess.'

Beefy men stared back at him.

Hello, I'm Alexey, I'm new . . .

I'm twenty-three years old.

They eyed him like fresh blood.

Their faces haggard from years in the snow.

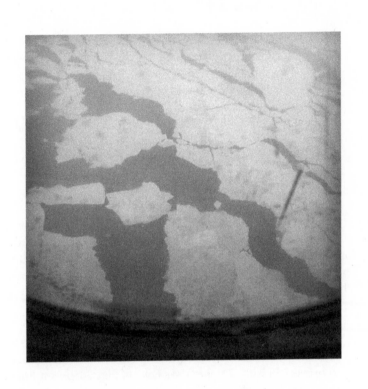

These were the guys he'd be working with on site.

'They were having some emotional conversation over vodka.'

No sooner was his bag on the ground than a shot glass was passed in his direction. Then came the pour. The toast to new company. And they carried on as before. One guy was bragging about how he'd used to be a model as a young man. Another was warning about the site. A third was chortling. It wasn't clear what about.

Who are you? Once they established that they kept going.

Like he'd always been there. And they went on with the vodka talk.

'I had enough emotional intelligence not to go deep with them.'

The bottle kept turning.

Then the manager told him to arm wrestle. If he was a real man, that is.

'And that's how my first night ended up, wrestling on the floor.'

'That was my first taste.'

But only when Alexey saw the bed did it really hit him.

'This is where I was gonna sleep.'

'This shitty bed, cracked in half, the pillow completely yellow.'

Stained from the forty people a month coming through this flat for a few days on the way out to the site. The room was filthy. Filthier the closer he looked. The way these men live without women. The flat so overheated he sweated and the pipes burnt to the touch. The sheets were foul. The pillow was bare.

'And I found there was no linen.'

Next door they were still wrestling.

'I knew not even to ask the guys. I tried phoning the woman I was to check in with. But there was none of this. Forget any linen. Because they didn't change anything here.'

Alexey took a towel out of his bag and put it on the pillow.

'I would have expected the company would care about me. That somebody would meet me. No . . . *this is the north. Just take care of yourself. No, nobody is going to give a shit about you.* And it hit me very hard because it was very different than if, you know, if I'd got a job at a posh and luxurious Moscow office and been taken to the coffee station.'

But it was a kind of excitement he felt falling asleep.

'*Welcome*, I kept thinking . . . *this is the north.*'

The next day, when he woke up in that space, his eyes catching new bits of grime on the wall, the company told him that weather conditions were too severe to fly. That the helicopters simply couldn't take off.

'You can get stuck in that flat for weeks.'

That corner of the airport was crammed when he finally made it. Crowded together, at the airport were the men for Sabetta. That was the name of the site he'd been hearing since Samara: that's where he was heading. His site, still three hours to the north. Shoved between huge bags and the mishmash of multi-coloured uniforms Alexey could smell booze on men's breath. Then he started to wait.

'There was no way to find out what was happening.'

'When this thing was going, if at all.'

The longer he stood there the less he knew.

Until they were ushered through security.

'We were waiting in a bus for, I don't know . . .'

'Maybe two or three hours.'

'It was a small bus. There were twenty people inside it, which is as much as it can take. And there was not a single word at all. I mean, there was a complete silence inside the bus, complete silence, and I do mean it.'

These were severe people, here in the north.

Comically so. That's what was starting to dawn on him.

Then, finally, it moved. And there it was.

'I'd never even been in a helicopter before.'

Get in, they said. Then they began to load it with no ceremony. They sat on benches along the side, facing each other. But there were so many bags and boxes loaded in, that by the time they were done weighing them, you couldn't see the row opposite for the supplies.

He started to wonder if it could even take off.

This is your captain speaking . . .

The engine whirred. The chopper rose, beating its rotors.

Then it came down a little. It was too heavy.

Then it finally took off.

Quickly the buildings were gone.

The first thing you notice when you fly further north, apart from

the impossible noise, is how suddenly the land changes. There are trees in Novy Urengoy. Not many, but at least some. And then as you fly further and further north they simply disappear.

You look out and you realize something.

You've never seen a world without trees before. You've never seen an infinite number of small lakes, everywhere, everywhere.

You keep looking out the window. And then you realize something. You've lost all sense of scale. There are no trees. There are no buildings. There's nothing. You can no longer tell whether you're five metres or a full mile high.

This is how the north plays with your brain.

'It's a very strange feeling.'

'You can't say how big this lake is. Or how small.'

'You don't have any clue about that.'

It took three hours to reach Sabetta.

Old hands pointed it out first.

More a moon colony than any kind of town.

The helicopter powered down. He was finally here.

'The weirdest thing about what I saw were the colours.'

Alexey blinked at these toy town-like dormitories clad in orange and blue. They told him, as he was getting his stuff, that this rainbow was for your mental health. That when the winter came and it was all white – the snow, the ground, the sky – that they wanted you to see colours. That, and when the storms came, this was the only way to find the buildings.

'And then, by a huge sand bank, I could see the sea.'

It was not yet frozen. And on that day it seemed green.

'As soon as I could, I went down there.'

'The first thing I did, I put my finger in the water and tasted it. The Ob River runs out here . . . it didn't taste of salt. Nothing at all.'

A feeling began to tickle.

For the first time in a long time, he felt good.

The alarm went off at 6 a.m.

And with that sound, the smell of the other men would hit him. They were all sharing, not only the room, they were sharing the whole dormitory and one of only two bathrooms. Minutes later he'd been queuing, between sour faces, until finally he got into the shower room.

There was ice on the opposite wall.

It smelt of forty men, that toilet.

A smell, so strong, you can almost taste it.

This is how his days began in Sabetta.

'It's much more like prison than anything else. It's prison rules, people have here. You've got to adapt. You've got to speak to them like that.'

'And you've got to keep your head down, too.'

The queuing went on. They would be in line at the canteen. Maybe for an hour or more. Waiting to get fed. The voices were angry. Then suddenly, scuffles would begin: someone had cut the line, or grabbed a bit of food.

He'd seen fists pounding into faces.

He'd been startled to see fights over food.

'People are tired.'

'You could smell their breath wasn't . . . *fresh*.'

'You know what the truth is? It's got more in common with the Gulag. You know what that is? When you're on site it's a hierarchy, it's a system.'

'People get beaten when they step out of line.'

The engineers stuck with the engineers. They were a caste apart. Nobody touched them. The labourers stuck with the labourers. That's where the fights happened. And when the beatings would happen, Alexey would step back. He'd be reading, once, he remembered, it was Vladimir Nabokov, and would try not to look up at the shouts. The specialists never fought. They'd just look the other way.

Then it would be time to work. At the beginning, the whole company, even the office, the command room, was shoved into this creaking wooden building; its floor crooked and sinking, like it was about to collapse. It's like that all over the north. On anything built on the melting permafrost.

His mind would focus on the blueprints. Calculating over and over how compression and deformation would shape their foundations.

The wind moaning at the door.

'The wind is the nastiest thing. When you're in the city, it stops, it slows. But in the north, it just never stops, it blows and blows. It catches a mixture of sand and snow. It gets it in your teeth. And when you start to breathe . . . the wind, it just swipes off your breath. It chokes. You really can't even breathe.'

You had to cover your mouth to do it. You had to almost gulp the air and that sound, when you first heard it, sounded almost like you might be choking; as you measured foundations, as you oversaw cranes, as you tested soils, because you had to go outside.

That was the job.

'The weather started to change.'

They said it was coming, they said this was nothing. And he wasn't quite sure what they meant until it was finally here.

Suddenly and abruptly.

Alexey knew it had changed for good when he lost his boss. They had to drive across Sabetta to another office. It really was urgent. But the snow, it was falling so heavily, he wasn't sure, even now, how to describe it. It was white, everything was white, like being in a waterfall or sandstorm. And they could see nothing – *nothing* – but the shine of their headlamps. It was then the driver gave up. There were normally signs, there was a road here, somewhere. But it was all gone. They had no idea where they were or what they were driving over. It was dangerous.

'It's not a big site.'

'But we had no idea where we were. Or where we would go. That's when my boss went, *Let's just go by foot – I'm gonna risk it,* we've got to get there – then he opened the door, slammed it back and began walking, and by the time I'd thrown on my coat, I already couldn't see him. Just white, white . . .'

Alexey stood there.

His feet sinking into the drift.

The cold biting, the cold burning you.

And he couldn't see him. He couldn't see him at all. A few seconds passed: a feeling of panic. He couldn't see anything at all. Alexey tried to focus: *Was that the corner of a building? Or a shadow?* Now it was gone.

He stepped towards it.

'And somehow, I found my boss.'

'But when we got there, we couldn't even really open the door from the ice without help from inside.'

They had to pound at it.

'That night I began to see it better.'

'Why they painted the dormitories orange and blue.'

'Why they said it was for your mental health.'

He could feel it, the white, playing tricks on him.

There was no privacy in the north. You'd cross the so-called street running between the wooden hutches, or at least that's what they looked like, built by Soviet geologists back in the day, and sometimes he'd spot the old sign – *Glory to Labour!* – like the leftovers of another world, and then you were back at your dorm again. In this place both vast and tiny.

'It's like this in Sabetta.'

You're never alone.

You were surrounded in the office, in the car, in the dormitory and sometimes you'd think, just over the perimeter – where technically they were never allowed to cross – there was nothing, there was nobody, an uncrossable way, a surface like another planet.

You couldn't get away from the smell of feet, the sound of men. And the moment you felt you were alone, someone suddenly was watching you; trying to talk to you, just nodding at you or looking back just as vacant.

'You cannot be alone.'

'You can't be alone at all.'

'It's heavy, it's almost impossible.'

You want to call someone, in the dorm, but you're not alone. You can't bear them all hearing. You try and go to the car – the one company car – to call, but there's already someone there. You try to hover in the corridor, but you're jostled past, there are guys smoking, you just can't.

'You feel trapped.'

You start dreaming. You start seeing things.

You start feeling things when you wake up.

Knowing you'll already be last in the shower.

'You start to think of your friends, back on the mainland . . . and what are they doing? What are you missing, being here, with your colleagues, drilling and calculating, spending every hour shoved together? While they're creating things, visiting places, doing normal life.'

'I used to think about this.'

'But I know it's bullshit now.'

At night they'd sit around.

The men swapping stories, sometimes with an illegal flask of something, they were strictly supposed not to drink. Stories of ten-metre flares erupting against the aurora. Stories of earthquakes triggered by fracking. Of explosions like brief red suns that burnt whole deposits. Or huge forests on fire beneath the polar sun. The army called to contain them, like they'd made a warzone. But the stories they liked to tell were comic.

Especially those about Cargo 200.

'It happened my first time there.'

'There were these guys, labourers, bottom of the food chain, who kept coming to the office all the time begging to go home. Like, *Why can't we go to the helicopter? We need to go home, please, please.*'

It was then this happened.

They found the old engineer dead in his room. An important guy on site. Or more accurately, when the guys woke up, they found he wasn't moving, that he was cold, they began to shout out, but they already knew he was dead.

You didn't need the doctor to tell you that.

It was a heart attack, he said.

'I didn't know him, we had maybe five hundred people cycling out of our dorms at that time. In and out every month or two. But I'd heard of him. And that's when I first heard it: Cargo 200.'

That's the aircode for a dead body.

'And those two labourers, they were already back at the office. Saying, *Please, let us go home.* All right then. Somebody stood up and smiled. *There's an option. You can go home but with a dead body. You'll fly to Novy Urengoy, the medical car will come and all you have to do is give them the body.* They looked at each other and said: *OK, we'll go.*'

'They left the same day like VIPs by helicopter.'

'Just with a piece of Cargo 200 between them.'

The thought of them – *was there a smell?* – getting what they wanted made everyone burst out laughing until they were too tired to carry on and the lights went out and they were too tired to remember falling asleep.

Then came the alarms.

'You can't tell your days apart in the north.'

After a week you first started to feel it. The weight. It was supposed to be thirty on, thirty off. But it didn't always work out like that.

'The biggest, the longest time I spent up there was two months.'

It doesn't sound like much.

'But that was pretty hard.'

'It works you, it really does.'

You begin to feel heavy. You began to feel worn. In a way you never have before. It was always about day forty-five Alexey started to feel it. These bad things inside him. Alexey kept finding himself counting days. *Ten more left. Five more left. One.* The people around him, the ones who had come on the same chopper as him, you could see it in their eyes too. The fever was building. From being here too long.

The longer he was there, the more stories he'd hear.

And the longer they spoke the darker stories they told.

'You'd hear about the misfits.'

He'd hear about them, sitting in that room at night, the boys trying to unwind. Or were they sharing this, they weren't natural gossips, for another reason? There was the man they said – *disappointed* – in his relationship. The older ones knew him. He'd been heartbroken, they felt, but they weren't sure. At any rate, something had really broken him, because he walked into the tundra. He set out and he didn't turn back. Into that endlessness of moss and ice, lakes and nothing, nothing. Alexey imagined him looking back, at the beginning of the site, wanting to die. They found his body a few weeks later. Frozen.

'And when I was there, there was the girl who tried to jump.'

She said her mind had been scrambled and she couldn't go on.

She'd been there too long. He'd seen her in the office. For months he'd passed her by. He'd wondered if there was something in her eye, or was she just like the rest of them, tired. And the next thing he knew she tried to jump from the construction site. They caught her just in time. Maybe, just as she wanted.

Maybe, that was the only way she felt she could leave.

'I will tell you . . .'

'That misfits cannot work in the north.'

The people with problems back home, the people with issues, with things that weren't resolved before they left, they broke down first, they began to have problems, or before you knew it they were in fights. They'd be begging, by the end of it, begging to be let out. It was like this. Here they called that the mainland, like they were on an island, somewhere as remote as the Pacific, separated, far from Russia. *He's gone back to land*, they'd like to say. *I'm land-bound*, they'd say, *I'll see you in a month*.

Alexey didn't remember how he first left Sabetta. That moment wasn't important to him. He didn't remember the helicopter. The lakes, his eyes couldn't begin to read, repeating underneath. The flight to Moscow. The sound and the light and the options in the airport. Then the flight to Samara. He remembered his family telling him he looked tired.

That he really must rest.

The trees were what you noticed when you finally got home. All these green things, everywhere. Over the cars and between the houses. You looked at them, puzzled. You looked at them like you had never seen them before.

At these lifeforms that we live with.

But his head was still in Sabetta.

In the cables and the clumps of frozen soil.

It had been a long time, now, in the north.

Years had passed. Those workers had become his friends. They would meet at the dacha on the mainland, outside Samara, the boys from Sabetta, the big engineers from the company, Big Vladimir and him, and they would waste away those afternoons drinking beer, grilling meat and when it was done, shotting vodka. They'd toast the job, they'd toast the end and each other. There were birds in the countryside. There was colour. There was everything not in the north. But the stories kept on circling back there. Big Vladimir told them, again, about the time his car had stalled in the snow – when you're between these kinds of stations, out of signal, out of radio, that can mean death.

There are some God saves, there are some He won't.

That was one of his favourite sayings.

There were stories about fishing trips and bears.

And then Old Valery the specialist mentioned herders.

You see them in the north. The natives, at least that's what they called them. The Nenets tribes. Summer comes. You see them in the distance through binoculars. You squint and make out stick-like figures on the horizon. Then a mass of blurry herds. You know they migrate with the seasons. The rains come. Then the snow. You see them close now. Begging you for food or fuel in their skins. Hammering at the office door. You give them what they want and they leave. But often you can see something in the corner of their eyes.

Like they know what you're doing.

Like you're destroying something you don't understand.

Alexey had seen more and more of them.

Everyone in Sabetta knew why. The climate was getting warmer.

Everything they were doing was changing the seasons. They weren't as they used to be. It seemed just a little thing that it rained too early and then it rained too late. But these showers quietly brought death. Anything at the wrong time froze the land. And the grasses and the mosses vanished. Coated in a thick ice. The reindeer grew hungry. Then agitated. They brayed. Then they grew weak and one by one they started to die.

The geologists would see it.

You step deep into the tundra and there are carcasses every-where. You know some of them say the end of their world is here. The rains are doing it. That this warming is part of it. You think about it. Then your mind turns elsewhere.

The party was still going.

Old Valery told his story.

It was a flare, years ago . . .

And we had to fill up the site with sand to begin digging.

And this is what he said they found: strange wooden carvings, fetishes, shaped like small little gods. There was a sleigh with pieces of textiles on it, like it was carrying them. And there was a sense we had to step back. It was very weird.

You didn't need to tell us this was holy to them.

The shaman appeared before too long.

He said we couldn't use this place.

He said that we couldn't use it for the gas flare. But, you know how it is, the higher-ups, they made the decision. They ignored him. Finally they sent in the workers and the shaman . . . he cursed the construction site.

They had been drinking for hours.

It was late at night when these stories were told.

And the site was bought by a very powerful private company. And when it was eighty per cent done, it was nearing completion . . . the director of the company was incarcerated and the financing stopped and the contracts too.

The work was over.

Old Valery moved on.

I forgot about it. I forgot about all of this.

And then years later I find myself again, at this site.

They were trying to lay foundations. They were digging into and turning over the frozen soil but everything was collapsing. Nothing would hold. And then one of the engineers, one of the old guys, he remembered the shaman.

He said we have to bring a priest.

It didn't take long. He came.

They lined up. And in the interior of what they were trying to build he blessed them. Turning and flicking holy water into the corner of that space.

Then everything stopped.

And as it often is with these stories, somebody scoffed, another jeered but something about it logged in Alexey's mind, long after the gas was flowing.

And then he was back in the north.

At the beginning there was no airfield.

There was no liquified natural gas terminal. There was only the chopper. As they beat the air, he thought about these stories. Alexey thought about them on the days it took him to Sabetta. Sometimes you'd see the herders far below.

He'd spend hour after hour daydreaming.

The flights delayed. The chopper shaking.

'You feel like it's easier to get to the moon.'

At least that's what he thought at the beginning. The rotations had become his life now. One month in. One month off. He could feel himself changing.

'They say it's the winter that's the worst.'

Alexey wasn't sure about that. He was sure it wasn't the darkness. Those were the months the sun never came up in Sabetta, where it was dark by the time they made it to the office. His life by electric lights. There was only this brief twilight at dawn. Sometimes he'd see the polar foxes, white and rifling through the bins. There would be bands of red, like sunset, overhead. Then it was gone.

'Sometimes we'd get warnings of polar bears.'

The alert would go out through the site that they were here. They were hungry, they said, clearly, something was wrong. Something about climate change pushing them close.

But he didn't think too much about them.

'The worst, it's the summer. The worst, it's the sun.'

'When it just gets dark it's easier than being under the bloody sun, beating down on you, making you hot, making you bothered . . . all day. It's awful, when it never disappears. That's when it screws with your sleep.'

It feels like it's playing tricks on your mind.

Like it's telling you something you don't want to know.

It's only brief when the snow melts.

'It's not a time I look forward to.'

Nobody does in Sabetta. And you know that when it does, something is coming. You know it when you see it. And even when you do – even when you've seen it summer after summer – you can't even begin to imagine how horrible it is; how many mosquitoes there are in the north. You wake up and within one or two hours, they're unstoppable, they're everywhere. You see them rising, in an enormous swarm, like a spaceship, coming towards you under the pale sun. You can't bear it and you take your shovel and swat at them. You turn it up and its metal side is caked in dead bugs.

But it's made no difference at all.

So you keep going. Face inside your mask. Trying to focus on the installation. On building what you need in this impossible place. This place that doesn't want you. That wants to spit you out with the bugs and the salt water and the sandy clays that cover you everywhere and every day.

But you keep going.

It's hard to describe it, the white nights in Sabetta. A strange eerie blue. Brighter than it should have been. But not with a colour you'd ever seen in the day. It would fade for hours into a lingering pallor. Like the faintest light seen through a smeared glass.

You want only for it to go away.

And then it does.

The seasons turn, the air chills and the mosquitoes die.

And at the end of every summer, one of the old men will shake his head wearily, saying it went on for longer than ever before and with more of those pests. And then it gets colder, but every year the sea freezes later and later, until one day, those same old engineers warned, the whole world would be warm and it wouldn't freeze at all.

Alexey tried to focus on the job.

They were imposing their reality. That they were conquering this place with red and white chimneys and silvery hulls the size of apartment blocks.

'The liquefied natural gas terminal was appearing.'

'They call it LNG. It's a critical part of the system.'

'The same one that heats your home.'

By now all of Europe was in Sabetta.

There were Poles, there were Brits and there were even more French. Like colonials, they held themselves above the people who already knew here and tried to do things differently, until they were defeated by Russia and eventually followed the Russians sullenly.

'You know how French guys are, they prize themselves. And you always have the feeling working with them that they think they've come to some no-name island in the Pacific on navy ships and we're the natives.'

'Until things start to go wrong.'

Sabetta was changing.

That was the first change.

Then the icebreakers began arriving. That enormous cracking sound announcing the beginning of gas to Murmansk, even Rotterdam.

It was becoming almost a small town.

But you couldn't say it was becoming safer.

'Man is always the most dangerous element on any site.'

You learn this quickly.

Alexey learnt this when he got thrown back: his head struck hard by two steel beams. They left his ears ringing. Telling him, whatever had just happened, it might have killed him without the helmet.

You can't let your wits drop in construction.

You can be tired, you can be cold, you can be on a sixteen-hour day but always, *always you have to check* – and you have to run the protocol.

'Your life has led here.'

You find yourself in an enormous construction site that sucks the energy out of you and everyone around. You dig like your whole future depends on it. Because it does. You never have time to think about its ultimate purpose, about its place in the system or its consequences. Your mind is mapping every screw, every sediment and every steel beam on site. You know the forty thousand components.

'You're swallowed by it.'

'You have to focus.'

If you don't, it's dangerous.

'There are accidents.'

He'd never forget what happened to the Serb.

They'd been digging the foundations. They'd been clearing and piling out of these huge shafts twenty-four metres deep. And somehow, at the end of the shift, when they were so tired, so cold – *they couldn't go on* – they didn't notice that one of the workers had fallen down inside there.

'So they left him there.'

'And they looked, but nobody noticed.'

The night passed. Work began in darkness.

'And so the next shift came for the drilling. And they only noticed something was wrong when the drilling machine stopped. And they pulled it out of the ground and they noticed there were, ugh . . . some clothes on it. Wrapped around it. And immediately . . .'

'They knew.'

There were bits on the spiral drill.

'They knew they'd gone right through him. I just hope that he wasn't conscious when it happened. He was fully in the hole.'

'I hope he was frozen, at the bottom of the pit.'

'That he didn't feel it.'

'How he died.'

It only happened once or twice.

Alexey, normally, never got scared.

And only at the beginning. It was during the worst of the winter, that once, he did. They were preparing to leave by helicopter. But the wind was blowing, it was howling, filled with snow. It seemed too strong to fly, he thought, it seemed wrong to take off now. But he did not say no. Once again he put the earmuffs on. Then came the awful sound.

Stop worrying, he told himself.

'These guys were pilots in the war in Afghanistan.'

'They know what they're doing.'

'They've done this hundreds of times.'

His heart was pounding faster than it should have been.

Alexey turned but Sabetta was gone already. His mind began to race almost with panic. *Does the captain look anxious? He does, doesn't he? That sound, it's not normal, is it?* He could see nothing. *They had to crash-land, didn't they – his colleagues – not that long ago?* One of those nights, they'd told him about it – *the cracking sound* – and how the chopper had shook. And they'd had to power down into the tundra. By a miracle it flew again. They could have died on the icefield.

The chopper shook. Alexey breathed.

Is it making that sound now?

What if we have to land? We can't.

There's no way we'll survive a night in the –50°C outside.

There's no way of knowing where we are. Hundreds of miles from roads. No other way to reach us but helicopter.

What if the radios fail?

He was spiralling.

Then he began to notice something.

The flight had steadied. The wind had calmed.

It was like this in the north. The weather could change – *not just change, transform* – in minutes. And then he did too. The snow

began to clear and so did his mind. The tundra, the emptiness, the lakes opened enough beneath him and, for a moment, he could think.

'It's always like this.'

'The landscape, it's telling you . . .

'You're just a guest here.'

It was dark outside. A complete void.

Set against it something finally felt clear.

'You look into the tundra, from the helicopter, from the site and you finally realize . . . the only thing you can find there is yourself.'

He knew it now. And he slept a bit, till Novy Urengoy.

7 LIEPĀJA

That's a lot of money.

That's what Nora sits thinking, looking at this ad in the newspaper. There are cute little patterns around it: *Looking for girls willing to moderate chat rooms on friendship, fashion, marriage and dating. Get in touch!*

That number keeps staring back.

Really that much? Almost €15 an hour?

She reads it again and again to make sure there's no mistake. That really is a lot. That's more money than anyone she knows is making round here. Nobody gets paid that much in Liepāja, in Latvia, her small city by the sea.

Nora tears it out. Telling herself: *I'll email.*

Later she's at the computer alone.

Hi, my name's Nora and I'd love to moderate the chats.

Click send. There's a quick reply: *Hi Nora, how old are you?*

She types right away: *I'm fourteen years old!*

New mail: *So sorry! Get back in touch when you're sixteen!*

Nora sighs. That isn't what she wants.

Whatever, she shrugs.

You either grow up like this or you don't.

You're constantly worried about money. You're always counting. Always thinking how little you have. Can I do this? I can't do that. This every day. It can make you ache with a physical, hungry, kind of worry. Like it's eating you.

This is how it is for Nora.

Not having money is the taste of buckwheat. There are weeks when that's all they eat. Not having money is her mother on the phone: *We don't have much, could you please not eat our food.* Her brother's friend ate a sausage after school from an empty fridge.

Now she's calling his mom.

It's embarrassing, Nora keeps thinking.

It's embarrassing to not have any money.

But this is the same for everyone.

You grow up, it doesn't really matter where; and the world's always somewhere else. This big house, this small house; this town, this city. You've got to get out of here to really live it. You spend days staring at maps, seeing yourself in films, imagining how things could be different. What it really means to live. She isn't even in Riga, where everything happens – apart from anything to do with her. And she isn't even close to the Europe where it *really* happens. Then one day a letter arrives promising to change her life.

A real actual scholarship letter.

Look, look, she rushes to show her mum, but then, like a kid with the wrong Christmas present, she suddenly feels pissed because it's only a scholarship to the United World Colleges campus in Italy and not the one in Canada she really wanted. Then she reads the small print. *No.* That can't be true. They can't do this. She's showing it to her mum.

They're not going to pay for the plane ticket.

It's in Italy. That's so much from Latvia.

You know the feeling of being on top of the world. Now imagine yourself plummeting down a lift shaft from that very high spot. That's how Nora feels.

Another life: for a minute she holds it.

And then just like that it's gone.

No. Maybe not. Maybe there's a solution.

I could always ask Mum to borrow the money, she thinks. Then she feels awful. She feels guilty. She can't make herself a burden like that. *I can't do that to my brothers,* she thinks. She does the sums: anything she takes, it's an opportunity, or something even more crude, she's taking from them. Mum's a single mum. And she's just a teacher. The salary is not enough for four kids. *No, no, I can't ask her,* thinks Nora.

I'm going to make it myself.

Her mind is racing with how to make money. She wants to get there. She needs to get there. Jobs. Shops. It's the school holidays. There's still time. That's when she remembers the advert. *I'm sixteen*, she thinks.

They can't possibly say no.

'They answered right away.'

'And they were like, yeah, fine.'

We can even meet today if you want.

Evening light. Nora leaves.

The familiar half-Soviet streets of Liepāja.

The address and the apartment she comes to is in a rundown part of town, in one of those old communist, low-lying apartments blocks. Nora rings the bell. The door opens and she meets this girl. Her name is Anna, or at least she says her name is Anna. She's tiny, super, super skinny with long black hair.

'And she immediately shows me the flat.'

It's a rundown three-bedroom apartment. But there's nobody in this apartment. Nobody lives here. There isn't an office here. And it's not clear that anybody works here. Anna takes her room by room. There are three of them and they all have these big, bright curtains, these grey old PCs and these dingy sofas set with these bright pink pillows perched on top of them.

'And she doesn't explain anything really.'

Anna smiles, sits her down on one of those sofas, then turns to the computer. She's letting her know there are two programs you need to open and when someone types – *PVT* – that means they want to talk in private. And, by the way, you only get paid for the minutes they spend in private chat.

You can do whatever you want in private chat, says Anna.

She's looking at her now. *Is something wrong?*

You know I work here too.

Nora nods: *Sure, sure.* Anna moves to the door.

I'll go and make you a profile, she says.

Then she giggles, turning to leave.

That's strange, thinks Nora.

She can hear Anna's actually left the building. She's alone now.

It's already so gloomy in the apartment. It's later than she'd normally be out. *That's strange*, thinks Nora. They've somehow locked this PC so it's got no internet browser so you can't just search anything. They must not want us wasting time.

She logs in. *Ba-bing*. That's a message.

Ba-bing. There's another. Then another.

At first she doesn't understand.

'People were writing in the chat room – *tits, show tits* – and I didn't know what it meant. So then, I just asked them, *What does that mean?* Because there was no Google or Internet Explorer I couldn't just Google it. And someone typed: *it means boobs*. And I was like – *Oh my God, wait – this is not what I think this is*. And so I was like, *OK, I think I'm in . . . Like, you know . . . a sex chat. I think I know where I am now.*'

This isn't right. She feels cold at first. Then tingly. She starts to feel scared. She doesn't know these people: this Anna, this grotty apartment. She's shaking a bit.

What's happening?

Ba-bing. Ba-bing.

They keep messaging: *PVT. PVT.*

She's at the edge of panic.

She feels it coming up her spine.

No. No. She doesn't know what to do.

Decline. Decline.

'At first I refused, because I was . . . *scared.*'

Stress creeps over her like a rash. Stinging her.

I haven't been with a guy, she keeps thinking.

I've never done anything like this before. Nothing close.

What's going on?

tits. TITS

'I'm a very timid person. I was generally scared of guys. And now for the first time they want me to get naked for people I don't know online.'

PVT. PVT.

Decline. Decline.

There's the door, she thinks.

I can still leave.

Ba-bing.

Mavrick 123 must not be happy, she thinks, because he's sent her several requests but Nora keeps clicking decline.

Maverick 123: *what's wrong bb*

Maverick123: *why u keep rejecting me bb*

Hesitating. *What am I doing here? What am I even supposed to do?* Pausing. She looks around. Then she just replies. *It's my first day*, she types.

'What else can I even say?'

i don't really know what to do because I thought I'd be talking about marriage, friendship, fashion and dating

A pause.

Maverick123 is typing.

in that case, just show me your breasts then and that's fine

The room is still but her mind is racing.

Nora's heart is pounding. Her hands are shaking.

I can get up, she thinks. *No. I don't have to do this. I can get up and run and I can go home and I can sleep in my bed. Fuck.* Then another thought rushes in answering: *Or I can do this thing that I'm very, very, very scared of. I can get naked for the first time ever, in a second, for this person I've never met online. Then I can go to Italy and maybe have the life I've always dreamed of. Or it's all over and I just go home.*

It's all rushing in front of her eyes.

Liepāja or the scholarship.

Ba-bing. Ba-bing.

Maverick123 is typing.

Her body tenses.

Italy. The flight. Europe.

She's trembling. She's scared.

Thinking. *Maybe I have to.*

'I was like *OK. I can. Maybe . . . I can do it.*'

'But then the thing is . . . I'd never done it in my life to anyone.'

Nora's dressed normally, even smart, like you would for the office. It's a shirt, it's a plain jacket and trousers. It's taking ages to get the whole thing off. And when finally – *flick* – her bra unstraps, she hunches forward, animally in shame, not to show them. Then she pulls herself up. Screwing her eyes closed.

'I was actually way fatter back then.'

'So I was also not happy with the way I looked generally.'

Maverick123 sees this and enjoys this.

Maverick123: *oh don't worry, u r pretty, dont be shy*

'But I wasn't shy. I was just super nervous and scared.'

Maverick123: *it's OK, just show me your breasts, touch them*

'And so I did it. But I didn't open my eyes.'

'Because I thought if I don't see it, it's not happening.'

Then it's over. He's gone and he's tipped her 350 tokens.

Buzzing. That's her phone. It's Anna.

Oh My God! You made so much already!!!

Nora's heart is beating very fast. That's going to be a lot of money, that's what she keeps repeating. Telling herself – *over and over* – it's not that hard, it's not that terrifying, *I'm only showing breasts,* nothing more, *that's it.*

I can't cry, she keeps telling herself, *I can't cry.*

Ba-bing. Ba-bing.

They keep coming.

Accept. Accept.

LadiesMan69: *open cam, open cam*

They all speak like they do online. *HRU BB* – how are you baby.

i'll give you 15 tokens, pings LadiesMan69. *Shit. That's a lot of money.*

I can open a cam, she thinks. *Yes, I can do this.*

She flinches stunned.

'It's a close up of a penis.'

'And my first reaction was, because, like . . . I'd never seen one like that before. I mean I kinda knew what it looked like . . . but not like that. And my first reaction was – *Oh my God*, this looks really bad – and then he types. *Do you like it?* And I'm thinking: *Are you serious, guy? Can't you see it yourself?*'

LadiesMan69: *oh, what u like about it?*

LadiesMan69: *what would u want me to do with it???*

He's thousands of miles away. His profile says USA.

I've never been with a man, Nora keeps thinking. Sweat rounds her neck. *I don't know how to improvise. What the fuck should I say?*

So she just types the first thing that comes into her head.

i like it, she types. *i like the size*

Then he explodes.

It's so nasty to watch.

She wants to close her eyes.

It's horrible. It makes her shudder.

'It's so gross. The first ejaculation I've ever seen. So yeah, so that was when I realized that men actually like to show their penises.'

She keeps going. It's been hours now. You can hear the streets go quiet outside. That's how you know how late it was.

Nora sits there and they keep requesting – PVT, PVT. She's never really spoken to an American. She's hardly spoken to anyone Anglo. But that's all there is on here – *Ba-bing, Ba-bing* – it seems from the profiles.

They keep typing: *oh my god, you're pregnant*

i can't believe you're pregnant . . . it's so bad for the baby

It stabs every time that message. *Am I really that fat? That they think I'm pregnant?* It's awful. But no. She can't let herself cry. And it gets worse – *your fat, your ugly* – they hit her with DMs. But she really wants to cry because she doesn't understand what the hell they are talking about.

why r u asking me if I'm pregnant?

i'm not! I'm not pregnant!!!!

Multiple users are typing.

where's your strap on?

what's a strap on?

They call them the members. *Go away*, she thinks. *Just go away.* But that's the one thing that can't happen when someone requests – PVT. It's money. This is what they're paying for. It won't stop.

tits. TITS

yur parents must b proud of u

It doesn't stop until she logs off.

It's summer light. It's hard and sharp. It's 6 a.m.

She's crying, sitting there – sobbing, uncontrollably, painfully – like she can't hold on. She's only doing what she's been told: wait until the next girl comes. But for some reason she doesn't show up immediately, so Nora keeps sitting there, in this run-down apartment, where everything is old and needs to be thrown away apart from those horrible pink pillows, the only things giving the game away. It doesn't take long to get home. The streets are busy now. Cars passing. People talking. But she draws the blinds, wraps herself tightly in her bed and sobs thinking about what she's done, about the flight, about the money.

Italy. I have to get to Italy.

Afternoon sky. Summer birds.

Ping. Nora wakes up. Anna is texting: *are you coming back?* The money, the scholarship, the flight – it's all pounding in there – and between tears she replies: *yes i'm coming back!* And then she starts crying.

That evening she's back at the apartment.

And then it starts again.

HRU BB

PUSSY. Pussy

show me pussy bitch

No, I'm not doing that.

She's on the sofa on the pink pillows.

I'm only showing breasts.

It's not just that they don't talk nicely. It's that they say they're going to come and find her – come to her city – and rape her and kill her and stuff like that. They keep saying it but tonight it bounces off her. It seems strange. Stupid.

'I obviously knew they were never going to do it. Living in Liepāja, and being in the neighbourhood, and knowing that nobody speaks English . . . I was just trying to picture . . . how are they going to come and rape me? Like nobody knows me. They couldn't talk to anybody in my city in English.'

The light from the computer.

She's alone in the apartment.

'And I keep thinking: I know you're all grown-up men.'

'You're supposed to be like mature people not spending your free time on here telling me I'm fat or you're going to come and rape me and stuff like that.'

Ba-bing. Ba-bing.

r u lesbian?

what do you like to use your strapon on??

Where's this coming from? She doesn't understand.

Now they're in PVT.

your a fat bitch !

It keeps going. It won't stop.

Until her lip is trembling and she feels roughed up.

But she goes back the next night. And the night after that.

You can't keep secrets in a small wooden house. Her mother catches her. Then catches her again. Her eyes red. She can hear her crying. She knows something's gone wrong. Something's not right. She keeps asking: *Is everything all right? Why are you crying? What are you doing?* But Nora only says this.

I'm fine. I'm just moderating the chats.

Then she tries to find herself online.

She's got it now.

www.myfreecams.com.

That's what it is. That's what she's got herself into. How can this be who I am?

She finds her profile on the home computer. That's why Anna giggled at her as she turned away to make that for when she first arrived. Her heart sinks. There she is.

Click on MargoX.

It says she's pregnant and likes strap-ons.

That's what the men are clicking on. It's not even her photo – it's someone completely different, someone much, much slimmer. So that must be why they start typing – *oh my God, you're ugly* – the moment they get to the live view. At least it says she's from the country next door.

She can't stop crying.

It's tearing up her insides. Her mother catches her again.

Nothing. I'm just moderating the chats.

Nora goes back on the fourth day knowing she's MargoX, she's pregnant and she likes strap-ons. Knowing this is really www.myfreecams.com. Her phone buzzes. It's Anna pushing her: *Look how much money you've made!* It's clear now the idea she works there too is a total lie. She's not a camgirl. She's the camgirl.

She's back in what Anna calls *the studio*. And it starts again.

She can feel something snapping.

'It was like a psychological breaking point.'

Ba-bing. Ba-ing.

They're asking again.

panties down BB

show PUSSY

hot bitches are doing it all 4 free in public chat and everybody tips why can't you do that???

'And I was like, why would I do that?'

'Go away if you don't like it.'

She can't take it. And then she thinks of the money.

She's doing this. She's doing it for a reason.

She can't do this and then not get all the money.

'I mean, I had decided that I will take my panties off and maybe touch myself down there. The tips were so much bigger.'

Decline. Accept.

It's a new guy who takes her.

drop panties bb

And then she does it, she does what they want – what they all want – for the first time. She starts. Then it's all over. In that cold moment she feels something breaking. And then she does it. She does it again. She does whenever they ask for it.

The morning comes, the other girl comes, and she goes.

She unlocks the door and there's her mother.

She can't keep it from her, what's happening, any more.

'I told her that actually it's a different kind of chat. *You don't have to do it*, she said. We'll figure out a way, you know, how to get the money and so on. And I said: *Yeah, but I've already made so much money.*'

She raises her voice.

But what if they don't pay you?

What if someone sees you? Someone from Latvia?

What if someone plays it back against you in the future?

'She said I didn't have to do it. *I'll figure out a way.* But the thing is we all lacked money, and I thought, *Oh my God, if I could make the money . . .*'

'I could give some to my mum.'

The studio pays out every two weeks.

Nora does her night shift and then Anna comes in the morning to give her this envelope. That's how the girls working in that apartment always get paid. They all have their little nicknames on it. Nora's, in pen, says – *MargoX*.

'And I counted the money.'

It's a cold, beautiful, mounting rush.

'And I was like, *This is the best thing ever.*'

Nora can't wait. She runs away.

She bursts in to find her mum. She's still sleeping, she's still in bed and Nora is climbing over her, laying the money over her – *Mum, Mum, wake up.* And she's shaking her head, asking – *What, what?*

See I told you they'd pay me.

She never says anything after that.

'As I did share that money with her.'

'And I think it was a lot of help.'

She's alone now.

She keeps on counting the money.

'I had this feeling like everything is possible. The world is my oyster. It's like . . . like it was one of the best feelings of my life.'

It's all clear in her head now.

'Everything that everyone ever said to me, I was like I don't care. They can say whatever to me, that's so much money. I made in two weeks what my mom makes in a month. I could do it for ever. Yeah, the very first payment felt very liberating. And I don't know . . . I instantly got this sense of security. That I had never felt in the family.'

And she sleeps without crying.

They want her every day.

Summer is one big block of camming.

Mornings. Nights. Anna texts and Nora comes. Every evening – it's twilight, it gets dark late in Latvia in the summer – she's back in that apartment, in that block, surrounded by so many other crumbling blocks that look exactly the same. Every night at the computer she's always alone. The lights are off in the other two rooms with those clip-on cameras and she'd be in the third with this lens that makes the cam girl look thinner on that frayed sofa.

She logs on. Members enter the chat.

And it starts all over again.

hi BB. TITS

tits. SHOW Tits

Then the birds. Morning.

She logs off and she waits for the other girls. Anna keeps telling her: *Always wait for them to show up.* But sometimes they didn't for hours. Morning after morning she's sitting there exhausted. Realizing it's been eighteen hours.

Falling asleep on the sofa.

There are three other girls at first.

This older one, she looks mature, she only works in the afternoons, she doesn't talk to anyone and when she's done – she never waits like Anna says – she just locks the door and she leaves. Then there are these two other girls. They're younger. There is this shorter one with black hair and this taller one who is actually pretty. They smoke and they drink and they bring beer to the studio and it's like them gabbing all day. They're not there at night.

And every afternoon they're sitting there on their sofa. Making up stories about her. Trying to get a rise. Mocking the sounds she's making. Saying things like – *You must have stuffed the whole wardrobe up there.* That's stupid because it's not as if they just did nothing in PVT and still got all the money. *As if.*

Anna keeps hassling. She needs her in the day. She needs her to cover for them.

Oh my God, we don't have anyone this afternoon!

Can you come? We really need someone now!

She's almost nocturnal.

Then it starts again.

HRU BB

You do this for a certain amount of time you get regulars. You find the same guys hanging out in your room all night, they're jacking off, from eight until six. You start to know them – or at least they think they know you – with their questions and their requests and their fixations. Some nights were worse than others. The things they'd keep saying. They'd be too much. They'd make her break down on camera.

'I think there was a movement that did enjoy this.'

One night a regular told her in private chat that the members, they have this lounge, where there are no girls and they chat amongst themselves. And sometimes they decide, they're gonna all choose a room, with a girl in, come in all together and see if they can make her cry.

'At first I was definitely crying a lot.'

Then she grew numb.

Some of them want in and out, quickly. But a lot of them, they really do seem to want a relationship with their cam girl. A real one.

why are you doing this?

i'm saving to study, she replies.

Member is typing: *what u wanna study bb*

MargoX: *architecture*

And then they try and chat. About everything, about anything, and then sometimes she begins to see these are sad, lonely men. Some of the saddest, some of the loneliest. And then there are the members insisting they aren't like that. Members like Rich Guy. He'd be there every night saying, *I'm so rich, I'm so fit, I'm so tall, I'm blonde, I've just changed cars.* Of course, Rich Guy, he was American, unsurprisingly. Never shows his face.

'You know a lot of the members, they actually want to be your friend and they befriend you. But I found that disgusting.'

They kept on trying to talk, to really talk.

how r u? what u up 2 today?

what you thinkin about bb??

And they'd tell her stuff, insane stuff.

Like the American who was constantly wanging on about his wife. How he loved her so much, but how after the menopause, she's been different. How she doesn't want to have sex, but they're best friends, but he really loves her and he just wanted her to know how great she is but how the menopause screwed everything up. They opened up. Really, they opened up too much. And then come the weirdos.

That made her uncomfortable with their requests.

'There's this group of men who have small penises.'

They'd want her to open cam – then point and laugh. And the louder she'd forced herself to laugh the more aroused they got. The more they enjoyed it.

The more they wanted it.

She can't keep it all inside her.

Her friends are the first to know.

'And they actually wanted to do it as well.'

'They actually joined the studio. *Because they wanted to make the same money.* And I was selling it. And that was kinda cool because all of them . . . not that they had all had boyfriends, they had all had sex. So, for example, I was finding it hard to find my vagina.'

'*Does that make sense?*'

'And my friends were like helping me, with like, explaining where the clitoris is, because sometimes the members would be like . . . *that's your foot.* And I would be like . . . *I'm not sure where it is.*'

'So yeah . . . I would just ask my friends.'

'So that was a lot. That was very helpful. That they decided to join the studio because, *you know* . . . we had that summer together and we had, *you know* . . . kind of a secret thing and I had someone to talk to . . . about both the members and when they were asking me for things . . .'

'*Should I do it?*'

'*Should I not do this?*'

The summer shifts. *Accept. Accept. PVT.* The weather changes. Very slightly. It's getting cooler. You can feel it in the morning. It's almost September. Just one more payday.

It's the envelope: MargoX.

She has it. She has the money. It's a feeling like no other. It's a feeling like bliss. Nora buys her ticket and slowly she starts to say goodbye. To her friends, to Anna, to the two other girls. She even tells some of the members. The ones that she had been watching jerk off every night for months.

i wanna keep in touch . . . what email BB? + what ur number?

That's Rich Guy typing.

And she gives it because, maybe . . . maybe they are friends, friends, *friends* – he's asked so many questions.

And then she leaves for Italy.

The campus is beautiful, it's like a castle, on a rock over the Adriatic and there are students there from the whole world: Africa, America, everything. It's another life. It's a better world. It's so overwhelming, there are so many activities, so many classes and courses, she starts to forget very quickly what she did over the summer. But they're still messaging her; her regulars. These two French Canadians and these Australians.

how r u bb?

And she's writing, just making things up.

That it's good at university.

That architecture's fun.

He keeps on calling her, Rich Guy.

'And then one day he said I'm a waste of skin and he hopes I die in a horrible way as soon as possible. He was sick in the head, I think. But if you don't count the times when the weird American guy called . . . other than that . . .

'It felt like it never happened. Or it was a dream.'

8 LINHARES DA BEIRA

You drive deeper from Lisbon.

You look at the map. It shouldn't be far.

Then you see the castle. There on the outcrop. Still guarding the village. Its two tall towers have battlements a bit like teeth. You're here.

You see the vultures. They perch looking down on the gentle valley. Silent, on some days; unless you listen very closely. You notice the swallows. They dance and dart at dusk. They sing their song and then, before too long, they're gone.

The first time David saw this place was on the internet.

Hours and hours on a property website. Scrolling. Dreaming. Then he clicked. He tapped through and he thought: *This is what I've been looking for.*

Now he knew it like a map.

Like a historian. Like a shepherd.

There is a small chapel outside Linhares. They have them all over Europe; isolated chapels, their doors locked, out on the high points. Mouldy places that have been sacred for thousands of years. Somehow closer to the gods. They might have been Celtic temples or the site of some kind of sanctuary. At least that's what he thought.

Because there was still a ceremony.

It hadn't happened for two years now but David knew, with a certainty you can feel for very few things, it would happen again. As it did every August – for St Euphemia's Day. As she was the patron saint of the village and those around her. And in Linhares it still felt like the day around which all else revolved.

'It always begins the same way.'

The sky is blue, but fading – it's the end of the day.

The bells begin to toll. There's the sound of closing doors. People are making their way to the main square. Anticipation, noise. It is almost sunset when the icon appears. You look up: there is orange in the sky and a haze over distant hills. With a thud the doors of the church open and, lifted on the shoulders of men, the icon begins the journey it makes every year up to the high chapel. David watches at the back.

'I'm always a bit detached from what's happening.'

Wondering what it all means.

The air is cooler now. The first breeze of night.

Maybe a hundred years ago, he thinks, *Lisbon had this kind of thing.*

'These traditions are dead in the cities. Yes, they are pretty much dead. But they are still alive in our rural areas. And what it tells me is that on some level, out here . . .'

'We are still a Catholic people.'

The icon glints in the vanishing sun.

Soon its heat is gone, a perfect disk of red; about to disappear. He begins to follow, a few steps behind. Sometimes David helps the old men to carry it. They are out of breath. The thing weighs a tonne. It makes circuits in the village before turning to leave.

The priest walks ahead, blessing them.

You hear fragments of prayer you do not understand.

You hear snatches of conversation that if you were from here you'd be able to place instantly. Town. Country. This is when David turns and spots something he doesn't that often. Young people. Not that many of them. Maybe they were the children or grandchildren who'd long gone to the city. But they are there.

Those city voices filled him with a little hope.

'I have no illusions that these worlds are disappearing and a lot of this will die with this generation. But still it's not so abrupt.'

Finally you see the chapel.

'It's always the same.'

The icon approaches. The men cross themselves. The doors are open and with a final heave they lift it into that cool space, filled with the smell of stone. There is a purple light. Where the sun was, bands of fading red. Darkness falls. You can hear the insects sing. Candles are lit. The icon is surrounded by light. One by one the villagers take turns to pray.

Some will stay all night.

Making a vigil for her – whoever she was.

Young faces are gone. David hovers at the door.

He catches a sincerity in old eyes, and looks away.

'But I don't think all this will outlast the generation after me.'

Night. The village sleeps lightly.

Morning. The sound of bells. Bleats and the sound of hooves. The shepherds are coming. He watches them gather their herds – their dogs keep the order – and then one by one they present their sheep to the chapel. They take off their hats. They drop to their knees with the sign of the cross. And his eyes follow them solemnly around the chapel with their sheep. Everyone knows what happens next.

'And then they perform some tricks.'

The shepherd whistles, he takes a step back, and with another whistle he sends the sheep spinning round the church. They bleat. Their bells tinkle, faster and faster, until they blur and the dog barks; and a whistle again, they're off in the other direction. The tail touching the head of the herd in a perfect circle of trampling sound. David's heart beats faster and it makes him smile.

'It's fantastic, fantastic to watch.'

The faster, the better, till they have all had their turns and the wine comes out and the little tables are set out and the auction begins. You can barely tell one sheep from another. You can hardly spot a male. But they can read the herds perfectly: out of eighty, a hundred sheep – 'You didn't have that one last year.' They laugh. They mock. They tease the sheepdogs. They hug. Then the bidding begins. You think fleetingly about raising your hand.

I'll have her for twenty euros.

I'll have him for thirty euros.

And then the music starts.

It's an old man's band, in an old man's country, all drums and trumpets and flutes. Every village used to have one. But now there are too few of them: the band has to be rented in. And with a farting trombone the march back to the village begins. Out comes the icon. Her carriers heave, fights and feuds between them suspended for one day. The flutes trill. The drums rat-a-tat-tat like the circus. You pass cut stone walls. Little windows. You see deeply etched crosses to the right of the door. Markings centuries old. Maybe half of this is abandoned or empty. Either neatly locked away or with roofs fallen in.

David walks with them. Today he doesn't want to stare at the haunted-house windows filled with cobwebs. Or at the plants that have swallowed gates and the wooden doors and the rotten window frames waiting to fall. His eyes linger, though. There is still life in the village. But not much.

The village square has a big stage on it. The band blares out. Wonky tunes and wonky sounds that melt his heart. The young faces slip away. Like they're allergic to that kind of melody. The village is so dark you can see the stars. A Portuguese night. The old men gather round a table: there are only eight people left here and, at a push, half are over seventy. There is only one baby. And his.

They play a sort of waltz.

David watches, holding a plastic beaker filled with something strong somebody just came up and poured for him. He notices there are never more than two couples dancing over the wide cobbles. And it is on nights like this that David dances with his wife and thanks her for coming to live with him in the dying village. So far away from what she expected and from her own country.

It's on nights like this he feels content.

It was a few years ago now.

They had met climbing and quite by chance. David had gone to a spot outside Lisbon when his friend bailed. *Sorry, I can't make it.* That was the call. Which was a lot, he thought, as he was already there. Ropes and all.

No. He wasn't going to let that get in his way.

There was a group, some Europeans, he'd ask them.

Mind if I climb with you? asked David.

I just need someone to strap on to . . . I'm experienced, I won't fall.

There was a Portuguese guy with them: *Of course . . . of course.*

That's when he noticed the girl. There were quick introductions. From Germany. Also from Germany. From Denmark. *I'm from Slovakia,* she said.

What brings you to Portugal?

He'd noticed her.

That thing was happening.

Just a master's with Erasmus.

You know when you like someone.

You know even when you can't really explain why.

She was next to him. He tried not to look at her and focused on the rocks. They reached the top. He liked the way she smiled.

Then it was down again.

It was great climbing with you, said the Portuguese guy.

That's when David tried something.

There had to be some way to see Slovak Girl again.

You know when something is pushing you.

I can drive you to Lisbon, he said. *If any of you fancy a lift.*

The Germans clambered in. He glanced at her in the mirror.

I'd love to meet again, he said, as if to the Germans.

Maybe we can all go to a gym or a real peak.

You know when you're trying to sell something.

How about a more ambitious climb? We can even stay the night?

And they met up again. He was only half expecting it. But they did.

His heart skipped when he saw her: Slovak Girl had come too.

Do you want to climb with me?

She said yes.

Now they were chatting.

She studied English language and literature.

That was when he told her.

I just bought a farm, you know, deep in the countryside . . .

Nothing had mattered more to him.

But he was trying to pass it off so casually.

I'm planning to move.

Slovak Girl smiled: *If you need any help at some point . . .*

Let me know!

You know when someone's inviting you to get closer.

You notice the eye contact. The way they move.

You start texting them.

A little more than a friend might.

you want to come to the climbing gym??

You never know if that's going to be the text that goes unanswered.

yes! sounds great!!!

Echoes. Ropes. The sound of clips.

The indoor wall he always went to.

They came down sweaty to have a coffee and take a break. Slovak Girl was flicking through one of those magazines: glossy, jagged peaks.

That's the real deal, she said, finger pointing.

You might have had a moment similar: something almost silly, where you suddenly feel – *Is this it? Is this the one I want?* It was the way she said it.

About something he really loved.

David asked: *Do you want to go to Spain?*

And see some real mountains?

They went alone this time.

She told him about her mountains, about the Tatras, about how spring and the winter was there, about woodland and the villages, like the little one she was from, Zilina.

They climbed and then they went back to Lisbon.

You might have had this too: when it doesn't happen when it was supposed to happen, so when you meet the next time, it happens, faster, more sudden than you'd expected. You feel it carry you along.

It was in a garden, near where she lived.

That's where he kissed Lucia.

When you know, you know, and then it all goes very quickly.

David and Lucia got engaged. He met her parents in Slovakia. Next he was driving through the gentle valley to Linhares: to show her the farm.

'I was telling her . . .'

'We don't have to do this. As you know, I lost my job . . . These are my skills. I can do any number of things. We could go to Slovakia. We could do some mountain business. I could become a consultant. But before I met you I bought this abandoned farm in Linhares.'

The car climbed the hill to the village and the castle.

They stepped through its silence: the stone friar, carved over a door, seemed to watch them, like he did everyone, from the medieval inn.

They turned at the tiny stone house.

And there was the castle.

It's like a Christmas postcard, she said.

They went down the country lane: oak trees and blackberry bushes, where farm cats might follow you, onto the hillside. They passed between pines, under boulders and tumbling slabs. They were in a small glade.

And there it was. The house, at the foot of the hill, under Linhares.

David asked: *Do you think you could be happy?*

They stood by the ruined house and she spoke.

I love it here.

Her face was serious.

But I don't know anything about it.

She turned towards the walls.

What I see is an abandoned farm.

David pointed to the broken roof, he pointed to walls and the fields.

'It's about transformation, I said . . . You have to imagine yourself like an architect. That you're making a drawing and mentally you can already see it . . . You can already see the house. Even though it's not there yet.'

He asked her to imagine a home.

It's beyond my ability to imagine such things, said Lucia.

But I trust your judgement. So if you want to . . .

They walked on. He asked her to imagine children.

You can always hear so many birds at this time of year.

The wedding was in Cascais a few weeks later.

Water lapped the rocks. There was laughter by the sea.

The priest spoke in English the best he could. There were twenty-five Slovaks. They say vows carry a greater meaning if you say them in your own language: she said hers in Slovak, he said his in Portuguese.

And that night it did feel very Portuguese at the dinner: the fish course, then the meat course, the multiple, multiple desserts and the bride's cake. But then something changed with the dancing. The DJ began to drop what Lucia asked for: Slovakian folk.

The guests were on their feet now, the Portuguese weren't quite sure what was happening, but they were spinning. They exchanged

partners with the Slovaks, back and forth, back and forth, in pairs. Until it was unclear who was Slovak and who was Portuguese. Until they had all danced with him and they had all danced with her.

And they went to bed happy.

You want to go back.

You want to live a different way.

You don't listen to the nagging doubts.

That's it over. That you can't.

David didn't remember leaving Lisbon. That day itself meant nothing to him.

He remembered the first days with Lucia in Linhares.

He remembered his first days on the ruin with the builders.

'I wanted a chestnut roof . . . because that's a very noble wood.'

'I wanted special tiles, like in the old ways, not modern techniques.'

It is an excitement like few others: building your own home. It was still not fit to live in. They rented a small house in the village and every day he went down to the glade with the builders. Dry leaves crunched underfoot. Grasses and bushes had yellowed. He ran his fingers through parched dirt. It was October but things hadn't turned yet. In Linhares it was still hot. And, as far as he knew, there had been no real rain since June.

'They said it was climate change.'

You wake up one day and you see the news.

You hear something. It disturbs you for a second. Then you file it away. *What are the chances? It's just a tiny chance*, you think. You're busy almost immediately. You forget about it. But one day it will happen to you. Morning radio. Scrolling his phone.

That was how David first heard about the fires. They were spreading nearby. They were at the edges of the county. He was busy. The roof, the chestnut roof, had been up for five days. There was still so much to do. Sleep followed work then dawn.

He was alone that day. Lucia was in Slovakia.

And it was that night the fires reached the village. That smell. That crackling sound. It was suddenly close. The wind, it was blowing towards them.

It was a strong, fast wind. The kind that carried flames.

They all gathered at the edge of the village. He called Lucia.

It's burning, he said.

They stood there pointing at it.

The old bells tolled on the hour.

'It looked orange, on the black mountain . . .'

'And there was this orange, red patch . . . moving.'

They stood, bickering, about the monster at their door.

I don't think it will come our way.

Yes it will.

It will blow out.

The old men were arguing, as they all stood on the slope looking out of Linhares.

It shouldn't, no . . . it shouldn't pass that stream!

You've told yourself similar things.

'That night the fire did pass.'

'And the next morning it was already on our slopes . . . I woke up, the smell, the smoke, it was everywhere . . . It was already on my farm. There were two great boulders there . . . and behind you could see the fire.'

He only had to look out the window to see it.

'And the slope coming towards my farm . . . it was all on fire.'

They were at the edge of the village, looking out again. Close together, like they might have watched a siege. Shouting, guessing, at what next.

It's coming!

Where are the firemen?

A few were heading down to the trucks.

David joined them: they were on the right, on the farm's edge.

'And I told the firemen . . . I've got my farm down there. I've got some thousand litres of water stored there . . . if you can just get down there and do something about it . . . *it's my house.*'

Forget it. That's what they said. *We're trying to contain it here.*

David knew there was no point asking.

'And so I left them.'

They shouted after him.

Don't go down there . . . You're taking too many risks.

He could only shout back: '*It's fine*, I told them.'

'*I'll be fine.*'

The house was at the bottom of the hill. He walked towards it. Slowly, fire was eating the long grass: it rose up, swallowed whole plants and spat. It was warm on his face but he walked beside it: until he saw the house.

'I had some trees around it . . .

'And then I saw they were on fire.'

Flames like fingers holding the house.

'*It's hopeless*, I thought. *It's gone.*'

Burning trees lined his country lane.

'*It's hopeless*, I thought . . . *it's hopeless.*'

There was no way to get there.

And, if he wasn't fast, there'd be no way to get back.

'*The passage will cut* . . . I thought. *The passage will cut.*'

He couldn't stay to watch.

He turned and began to run back.

There were shrieks. The fire had reached the olive groves. Running with buckets, people called him to help. Trees were on fire. Groves were burning. He was there as olive trunks burst and popped with flames. The pails kept coming. He threw, he carried, he threw again. His face running with sweat. The fire stinging his eyes.

Smoke choked his lungs.

Until he heard calls.

It's receding!

That night he collapsed in his clothes on the blanket.

You pulse, you twitch when you have this much adrenaline. You can't sleep just like that. David tried. But it was behind his eyes. The flames. He kept seeing them. Imprints of light. Dancing there, burning there, in his brain. Flashbacks. He needed them to go away. He was tossing and turning when he heard: a rattling. It was the sound of rain. It grew louder and louder. Filling him with relief.

The next morning he could hardly move. Exhaustion. A kind he'd seldom felt. Finally he pulled himself up. There was no point rushing to the inevitable. As he showered the water turned black. The ashes had covered him: all over his hands and feet. Like a black tar running off him.

David walked slowly towards the house.

You would have walked at his pace too.

Where there had been green there was black; where there had been plants there was char; where there had been trees, these dark twisted things. The hillside, the farm, it was scrubbed with ash. He got closer, closer to the house.

You should never see this.

A skeleton of black beams.

David didn't cry.

The winds had gone. And in that moment he felt a tightness around his heart. He felt something in his throat looking at it. Things he didn't want to let himself feel.

OK . . . it's done. It's done.

There's nothing I can do about it.

Look forward. Look forward.

And he turned back.

The baby was baptised in Linhares, almost one year after the fires.

The prayers stopped. They stepped forward: up to the altar, so rich in gold. And they passed Maria Amelia to the visiting bishop; in his green cloak and mitre.

What do you seek for her? he asked.

Baptism, they answered.

They gathered at the font: candles, water, immersion.

The baby cried. And the service continued.

'I wanted us to say: *there will be life here.*'

Mr Francisco was at the back of the church.

The shepherd who had become his mentor.

You find yourself after a disaster in almost a manic state. Your mind races. Connections you had never seen before come fast and clear. You read quicker and you stay up longer looking for your answer.

Sheep. He needed sheep.

The hillside shouldn't have been abandoned. It should have been grazed. The hillside shouldn't have had a thick undergrowth of flammable plants. It should have been covered in herds. The way it used to be.

Sheep. He needed sheep.

He told his wife his plan. It was all going to be all right. The answer was shepherding. That way the village would also be safer.

Are you sure? she said.

How are you going to have time?

He could tell she didn't like this plan.

How can we ever travel to Slovakia if you've got sheep?

David began to promise.

It'll work out.

It'll be profitable. I'll make cheese.

They won't just be pets.

Until Lucia said: *I trust your judgement.*

She was working as a remote translator. It hardly mattered where she was. But she had made friends. There was life here, coming back. But it wasn't Portuguese. There was a Belgian who'd bought a ruin. There was a Dutch guy and a Brit from Gibraltar there in the village. And then just outside there was a German couple. Then a Czech couple. A Brazilian guy and an English girl. Then an Italian guy and a Brazilian girl. Not to mention the Brit married to a German. Or the French guy married to a Brazilian. And there was Lucia's friend Emily and her husband from England who were raising goats up the mountain.

Like Euro-settlers, they'd all been drawn to the ruins.

Retirees and dreamers. There was a new village within a village. A completely different sociology, plainly. But it knew nothing about sheep.

About the way it was supposed to be.

About the way it was going to have to be.

David began asking the old-timers.

If I wanted a herd . . . what would I have to do?

Where do I buy them? Can you tell? Who can teach me?

One by one they all pointed him to Mr Francisco. When he was a boy, and this was a story he had heard more than once, he used to spend time at night, looking at the sheep, watching them eat, studying them. Sleeping up there on the hills with them. When you had to keep the wolves away.

Mr Francisco was in dirty work clothes. Old trousers and an overcoat. He spoke very softly, almost in a whisper. And otherwise he was almost silent. But that only seemed to add to his authority.

He asked what David was doing, gave a sense he seemed to agree, and sold him his first two sheep. But that wasn't the end of it.

He kept coming back.

Fine, I'll come see your farm.

Mr Francisco came to inspect: the stables, the pastures. Good enough. He began to tell him very specific things about their hooves, things David had never thought of before. How they get infected and you have to clean them with a knife.

Mr Francisco taught him about all of this.

He was barely literate.

But what he knew, he knew inside out.

And it was Mr Francisco who taught him how to slaughter.

They're not pets.

'I thought, *It won't make sense to engage in this if I don't kill my own lambs. So if I want to do this . . . I must do the whole thing.*'

What was always done.

What it was all, ultimately, about.

He looked at his knives.

He had no idea how to do it.

'So I asked this man if he could teach me.'

Mr Francisco came to the pasture and gathered the lambs. Then took them to a rock where he did it. He never wanted them to be scared.

Mr Francisco crouched beside him.

Do it. Now lay the lamb down. Find the artery.

The first few times, David's hands hovered.

Mr Francisco grabbed the knife away. David watched him make the cut. The lamb was quivering on the floor: the blood spewing out of it. It takes ten minutes, normally, for it to go silent and still. Mr Francisco would sit there chatting about the weather or the herds with him. It's not only about killing an animal: it's about removing the skin and the heart and the lungs and the guts and all the other bits inside it. It's all still hot. The moment smells like blood. You might not be able to do it.

Mr Francisco came back.

But a second time David's hands dithered. The shepherd took the knife away from him and whispered: *Don't worry . . . I'll do it.*

And then the third time: it happened again.

David was starting to become ashamed.

'I thought, *I have to kill it myself.*'

He laid the lamb down, like Mr Francisco had shown him.

He found the artery. And then David cut.

The blood was hot.

'It felt . . . *it felt correct.*'

'It felt like . . . the right thing to do. The first time you make the cut. You need to have made this decision. This is an investment in will. It's really all about that. And you tell yourself that you will keep your feelings under control. That you will not be disgusted. You will not feel bad about it. You will not feel remorse about it. So you just have to do it at that point. And after that it just becomes a piece of meat.'

'And you start dismantling it.'

He learnt how to do it.

Once, twice, until it came almost by rote. Almost.

'Sometimes I wonder if I can help the animal . . .'

One memory: another man had come to kill a lamb. He'd cut it very brutally and hung it over a bucket where there were already the guts of another lamb. *Do you think it has a sense of what's going on?* asked David.

Of course it knows, came the reply.

Ever since then, he always covered their eyes.

He put his hands on them as they lay on the floor.

'Sometimes, I think . . . if I close their nostrils and their mouths, it will go quicker than there being these final breaths. I don't check my phone or my messages. I watch . . . I keep it company. While the animal's dying.'

You wait.

You notice the body is still.

The dogs don't come too close.

You tell yourself: there would be no herd without you.

And this is how we have lived together for so long.

It's hypnotic to watch them eat.

You sit there and it washes over you. The bleating, the tinkling bells, the scrubbing hooves, their little munching. You feel something.

You feel content.

'Once I was joking with a shepherd. And he was saying how we wasted our time like this . . . watching them eat. And then he turned and said . . .'

'But it was the best time we had.'

The seasons blow over Linhares and the Sierra da Estrela. Long ago, he'd heard, the shepherds had named it this way because of the bright star they followed up here to higher pasture. His little flock only went up and down the hillside. But still, sometimes, he'd imagine them and these ancient times.

The spring is green like the winter.

Plants begin to turn, from bare to green and pink.

Flowers cover the quince tree. That's the sign. Then the wildflowers show. The first are dots of white. And soon enough there's yellow and purple, covering the field. Days fill with sounds: swallows, magpies, cuckoos. The flutter of birds. The sheep have grown fat: the pastures are green and the grass is tall.

And the shearing comes in May.

The men come and do it for him. He sets out a little table covered with food and once they're down and the sheep are cool he toasts them.

This is the way it was always done.

Summer has sounds of night: insects that get louder and louder as it builds. Cicadas and crickets. Sounds that fill the darkness. The first hot days come. The pastures disappear. Greens turn to yellow and brown. The sheep become restless. They haven't got enough to eat. The shepherd, as he knows, must bring corn to them. The days get hotter: they wake earlier and earlier. Their bells drift into your sleep. They are eating from five until by nine, the cool air fades and they retreat to the shade. Lying under boulders and pines. The days are getting longer, drier and warmer. The sheep stay outside at night.

St Euphemia's Day comes and goes.

The sheep circle the chapel. And the days get shorter. There are gusts of cool air. Nights are cold again. Then the first rains come. Once, twice, and then the hillside begins to burst with grass and the shepherds' smile. The sheep can eat easily now. Acorns fall. Sheep butt and jump in a joyous craze. They are happy again. The pastures

turn green as the leaves turn yellow and red and float down until they crunch everywhere underfoot.

Late lambing turns. They bring them to the shed. Cries and bleats.

And now they're calmer, in the long grass, as they eat next to their young. You watch them nuzzle. You worry about predators now: about foxes and stray dogs in the night. You hurry the sheep a little to the stable. There, they huddle.

Winter is the sound of wind and rain, which rattle the window and whistle down the empty street. The trees are stripped. The birds almost gone. These are the damp days. The castle disappears in fog. And often David would take a little bottle of brandy to keep himself warm.

'I like to walk into the mists and just hear the bells of the sheep and not quite be able to see all of them. And just pet the dog.'

You watch the lambs grow and wait.

The slaughter starts for Christmas and often Mr Francisco and David would sit and talk afterwards. Watching the herds.

This pattern was fading. It was still there but it was breaking down. Summer seemed not to end. It would break only to come back. Winter, said Mr Francisco, they used to be knee-deep in the snow in the seventies. And now it never settled. What if the snow stopped completely? It would kill the streams. Their water would be cut.

And everything, on every farm, would have to change.

'It's a slow-moving thing.'

You accept reality for what it is.

'I think it's coming, the tipping point, where the climate breaks completely. But I think for the rest of my life we'll still have it, these seasons . . . under pressure, but still here. With ever more fires.'

'At least the sheep can help prevent them.'

They never rebuilt the ruined house. There were three babies now in the rental. They spoke in English, him and her, as children's TV blared out in Slovak now in the living room. He hardly watched the news. One day he went to an auction with Mr Francisco. Weighing. Assessing. He knew every sheep. The old man seemed to know his own better than him. He even knew who their mothers were and what they did at their age.

She was a feisty one, he'd say, kneeling to a lamb.

Her grandmother.

Francisco. An old man grabbed his arm with a grin. *Will this one last?* he asked, pointing at David.

The shepherd was silent for a minute, then shrugged.

Time will tell.

9 MADRID

He was a nice man but he wasn't for her. That was what she sat thinking at the hamburger place on Avenida de Europa. It was outside. That April. The suburbs of Madrid. A gap in the lockdowns. They had taken their masks off to eat.

His eyes were red.

I've got allergies, he said.

That's when Helena should have noticed.

It hadn't worked out. He had his own recycling business and everything but something just hadn't clicked. I'm too easily bored, she kept thinking. That was on Friday. He was still texting her on Monday.

my throat hurts and I've got a cough

it's been like this for three days

No, she thought. *No.*

are you feeling ok?

She was just cleaning up after lunch with her mother.

Recycling Man was being silly.

You fall sick very abruptly.

One minute you just notice: I'm not right.

Helena touched her throat. *Yes,* it was starting to hurt. She took herself to the mirror. *Yes,* she didn't quite look right. *You know what, maybe not.* Then it seemed to subside. *Perhaps,* she thought, *it is a spring cold. Yes, that must be it. Those still happened, after all.* An hour or two and she felt it in her nose: congested. *No, that is normal, too.*

Can I taste? Can I smell?

In the kitchen she picked up things to sniff.

This is fine, she thought, *this is going to be fine.*

It's not easy when you live alone. You always notice too late. It happened on Tuesday. And it began with chills. They rattled up inside her like rats climbing a pipe. There were more and more of them. *Yes*, now she was sure: *I'm not feeling good. Yes, it's like something's taking over.* She had to sit down. She was all cold: a strange cold. A kind that stung but also made her shake. *Oh no, these are the symptoms.*

And then she called the doctor.

Come in for an antigen test.

Helena sat waiting until they called her.

Bright lights. White tiles. The hospital.

SARS-2 Covid-19 – Positive.

'I couldn't believe it.'

No, this can't be true.

'I sat there reading the paper thinking . . . *this can't be true.* I sat there thinking, *I'm sick because I've got a cold . . . because it's April.*'

'I didn't want to believe it.'

You are now legally required to isolate, they said. She nodded. And that was it. There was nothing more they could do for her.

She took herself home.

'I wrote to this boy and told him to run and get tested.'

'And then I waited . . . I waited to get really sick.'

When she thought about what happened next, she thought about the fever. She thought about her hands: how she touched them. How wrong they felt: like cold meat. And when she thought about the fever she thought about one thing. *I'm swollen.* Everything was swollen. Her throat, her face, her mind. Aching. It had come in bursts, the fever: for hours, then it seeped away. It wasn't long: but she was floating there. Hurting.

In a place where minutes were hours.

'In my head I was thinking, *I don't know what to think. I have this virus . . . this weird virus inside me.* The worst feeling is you can't fill your lungs. It's horrible to feel them empty. Because when you need to fill them . . . You cough. You can't breathe.'

'You cough and you can't breathe.'

Her days scramble and fog.

There are knocks on the door.

That was Helena's father leaving her food. Those were his footsteps outside on the stairs. It wasn't like clockwork. She wasn't quite sure when it happened some days. It was morning, then it was evening. It was slowing: the time in between.

'I couldn't go to the bathroom.'

'I couldn't go to the kitchen for a glass of water.'

When you lie sick your eyes follow the light. It makes patterns: slats of white from the blinds. They climb up the wall and disappear. You try to focus. You doze off. And they're gone. You wake up at night: a growl from a passing car and headlamps race across the ceiling. One after the other you keep seeing them.

You've forgotten to close the blinds.

'They called me every day.'

Buzzing. Her phone. It's her father.

'Even my friend Pedro called me every day.'

But she couldn't talk for more than a few minutes.

She started to cough. Her empty lungs wouldn't let her.

And then she found out her mother was also sick.

Please, if you can't breathe, call the hospital, they said.

You never think it will happen to you.

You cross the road and you don't get hit. You park the car and you don't get fined. You get ill but you don't get really sick. You're always taking a risk.

'And then I couldn't breathe.'

It happened one evening. She tried. She tried again. But still her lungs couldn't fill. Even sitting up made her wheeze. They'd told her – *eight or ten days* – if you don't get better then, then it's going to get worse.

That was when Helena phoned the doctors.

I think I can't . . . I think I can't breathe.

Come in. Come in now, they said.

Helena sat there as they took her oxygen level.

She was right on the edge. She wasn't under yet.

'And all they could do was send me back home.'

Then nurses signed her forms and sighed.

'There was nothing else they could do for me.'

—

You wake up.

You can't think. You can hardly breathe.

You feel cold but you feel hot at the same time.

And you ache.

'I'm not well. All you can think is . . . I'm not good.'

When you're sick you almost forget what it feels like to be well. When you're well you never remember what it felt like to be sick. You want to forget it. You want to move on: to get up, to get out, to get back. You don't want to fixate on the night your mother was admitted to hospital. On the call your father said she had no oxygen in her blood. On the text saying she was on corticosteroids. You only want to remember her coming back.

'I kept thinking this is going on for ever.'

But she did get better. Helena sat up in bed. She spoke for a long time on the phone. It faded away. The quarantine stayed. After two weeks she began to feel bored. Helena lay there sunbathing on the rug in her living room thinking how small her life had become.

She missed the airport. She missed work.

She missed being a flight attendant. She missed who she used to be.

'How much fun it is. How much we laugh.'

She hadn't worked for months. Half the fleet was grounded.

Variants. Borders. Maybe it would never go up again.

I want this to stop. Helena lay thinking.

I need to come back to life. Everyone has to come back to life. None of us have been living since this thing began.

It had all seemed so mundane. So everyday. And now it had all been taken away. She missed her friends. She missed her mum. She missed getting up at 3 a.m.: crossing streets so empty – you could hear every car. She missed getting to the airport. She missed the faces at the gate – *hello, goodbye* – the first flight and the last kiss. Helena even missed the briefing room when they ran through the day: routes, *check*, weather conditions, *check*, special passengers, *check*.

They'd run through how many babies.

They'd run through how many wheelchairs.

They'd run through how many blind people.

And then of course the deported.

They made sure to tell them in the briefing room about that.

Sometimes police were with them and they were always right at the very back. There were faces she never forgot: the ones that burst into tears; or the ones that just sat there, wistfully looking out of the window as the plane took off. Faces like the black man deported from France; or faces like the Spanish man, police all around him, being flown out of the Canary Islands.

'I'm not even allowed to feed them.'

And on those mornings, the instructions would go on.

'Sometimes . . . they tell us there are bodies.'

There are more coffins than you'd think being flown around. You've almost certainly been on a flight with one. You'd know what it was if you saw it: a coffin-shaped suitcase that couldn't be anything else.

It's nothing special at the airport.

'I remember this was a flight from Catalonia, but it happens all the time. It was so hot and heavy and as we opened the doors to let them on, we saw the coffin on the tarmac.'

'Also coming home.'

It was months since she'd left Madrid.

It was months since she had left the blocks around Avenida de Europa. The lockdowns kept coming.

'There was still no vaccine.'

Her head was full of flying and her days were full of nothing. Helena lay on the rug sunbathing, thinking she'd not spoken to anyone in person but a doctor in five weeks. The words kept running through her head.

You are infected with Covid-19.

Please enter self-isolation.

Life wasn't supposed to be like this. In the airport she'd meet new people every day. An airport is a sea of faces: you only see more in a football stadium. And a stewardess: they see more faces than any footballer. Maybe, she thought, they see the most.

The Community of Madrid is under lockdown.

Please leave your home only for essential activities.

She didn't want to hear it any more. Helena lay on the floor sunbathing. Her cough was coming: it was tickling, it was scratching her, any second now she wouldn't be able to resist. But she didn't want to think about this.

Routine. Movement. Airlines. Every day she came in at 4 a.m. and it would be a whole new crew: you'd have to be in your fifties to have flown with everyone, it seemed.

Now everything had just stopped.

When the light faded, she sat on the couch.

She flicked through her self-help books and her motivational books. She turned on the TV: she needed some voices in the apartment and she tried to teach herself how to sew.

Outside the streets were dark.

Cabin crew commence boarding.

Little bits of things came back to her as she sat there sewing. It would be two flights a day, mostly, on her map of Europe: the map of budget airlines. It went north to Britain, even though it had left the EU; and it went south to Morocco and Tunisia, even though they'd never be in it; and it went east to Israel and Ukraine; even though she knew that was never going to happen. One flight out and one flight back; then all over again.

She could do it all by rote.

May I?

The man's face: exasperated, confused.

Helena takes his ticket.

16L. That's on your left, sir.

The man's face: *Thank you.* Hardly looking at her.

But they were different in every airport. The best were the Nordics. They were so quiet and orderly; they made natural lines. The only strange thing about them was how much they ate. They didn't drink much but when they flew they got hungry. And if it was an extra-short haul and there wasn't enough time to feed them all, they got angry. They wanted the tea and the sandwiches like a point of principle. The Spanish and the Italians: *Why is boarding so slow? Always so slow.* But the English, now that seemed to depend. They lurched violently between moods and a strange sort of exuberance.

'The English people always like to drink. But they get drunk when they think they are on holiday: it's like a switch flicks. And when that happens and they are flying to Tenerife or the Canaries they get loud . . . and then they drink. The flights run out of alcohol. At the end of it . . . there's nothing. No food, booze or anything. And they love crisps.'

Please put hand luggage in the overhead lockers.

No matter how many times they heard this, men never seemed to understand. It was the ones who hardly spoke English who were difficult. They kept trying to put bottles of vodka or huge food tupperware where they shouldn't.

I need to, they always yell.

Every airport, every country, they all had their own particular differences. But that wasn't what stood out to her any more.

'We're just clinging on to these small differences.'

Helena thought about Europe: what she'd seen of it.

'We're not really different in these ways any more.'

Italian. French. English. It only mattered so much.

'We're more similar than they have us believe.'

What really mattered were the types: the holidaymakers, the backpackers, the school groups, who each travelled in their own particular way. And the ones who were always bad were the businessmen.

'Those were the morning flights from Madrid to London.'

You could hardly tell who was British or who was Spanish. You could tell from the clothes: who was travelling for work and who wasn't.

'They're just always angry.'

Snapping at her – *I'm working, I'm working* – when she came to tell them to put the tray table up and the laptop down.

I'm working too, she said.

The same look. The same puff. The same table flicked up and MacBook stowed away. Their faces had no respect in them.

She missed them now. Even them.

There was too much evening. It went on too long. She played music: letting herself be carried away by it. Because she felt music healed. She talked to her family: because she felt family healed.

'It wasn't over. It wasn't ending.'

You are currently required to self-isolate.

You loop into yourself when you're locked in alone. The same thoughts keep bubbling up. Your mind becomes completely circular.

Take off. Trolley. Landing.

Helena was thinking about turbulence.

'If the passengers knew they'd never fly again.'

It did happen: when the plane suddenly shook. Not a little tremor. Those kinds of things happen all the time. But a big, nasty rattle: like for a second or two it was falling in mid-air. *Yes*, it really did. Helena had a colleague who'd been thrown up with the trolley once on a flight across Spain. Others, there were quite a few of them, she'd seen them with cuts and bruises on their hands and face, from where the turbulence got them in a flight.

'You can have the worst time of your life.'

You see fear when you fly.

Helena had seen faces full of it so many times: crumpled, shaking, streaming with tears. Men, calling her over: *How old is the pilot?* Or, *Is the pilot experienced?* Asking for more to drink. Women, clinging to her. All those people who screamed and grabbed on to her. They never knew when to be frightened.

'Sometimes, I suffer for them . . . when they have no idea to be scared. But mostly they suffer when there's no reason to be scared at all.'

Infectious fear. It would jump from person to person. Then there was no difference in the face of a German or an Israeli or a Ukrainian: they all started to look the same. The eyes twitching. Then there were the panic attacks. A man she'd seen grab the hatch door: *I have to get off this plane, I have to get off this plane.* Nothing could open it.

Go on, she said. *Try and open it then.*

She'd sit eating on the pull-out chairs next to the toilet, eating, thinking: *You think I'm here just serving coffee but really we're here to make sure we can get you all out in ninety seconds. That's how long they had been trained to evacuate for in an emergency.*

'It's a small risk. But it exists.'

'And I think, *If I explained it to them they'd never fly again.*'

Morning again.

Quarantine. Lockdown. It was all still in force.

Helena tried to keep exercising: following the videos they sent from the gym. But, at first, she could barely stretch without wheezing. *I used to text with my boyfriend*, she thought. *But now the messenger's so quiet.*

Only the doctor came back: you need to keep isolating.

That relationship. It ended by phone.

'We'd talked about it before but this was the final word.'

He was an architect, not a very successful one, getting by at his father's construction firm. They had the same opinions. They had the same jokes. They watched *The Simpsons* together and it felt right.

'Then I didn't answer my phone for a few hours at work.'

He began texting. He began calling frantically.

'He became suspicious for no reason.'

You know it's ending when someone says something they can never unsay. You know it's over when they say something about you – you can never unhear. Something paranoid.

That's what happened.

'Then he said he didn't want children.'

Then it all started unspooling. If that's what he said: *Is that what he really saw her as?* If it wasn't going towards children: *Where is it going? It is going nowhere, then.*

Now she was alone for this.

I don't need a man in my life.

Watching the news – without his commentary.

It felt like it was on repeat: 100,000 new cases in Spain, the battle for vaccines, a new variant in India. It was this huge global event and for once she was watching in her suburb of Madrid: but nothing was happening. Every day she woke up early. Each day like the other.

'I kept imagining I was somewhere else.'

It wasn't like that when she flew.

Cabin crew prepare for take off.

It happened once, an aborted flight.

Madrid–Birmingham. The last trip of the day. They rushed down the aisle: checking the oxygen masks, adding the baby straps, picking up filthy tissues and litter shoved in all the same old corners. They started to flood in: red, boiled, burnt.

The English after their holidays. Subdued.

What's that? she asked.

Is there something wrong with the door?

It had made a sound. A horrible sound.

Cabin crew prepare for take off.

They sat down. The engines whirred. Then it started.

Clack-clack-clack: like the door was opening.

Helena sat knowing what she knew: that airlines don't change the doors very often, they keep tinkering with them, a little bit in, a little bit out for decades. *No*, she trusted the pilot. She trusted the team.

Clack-clack-clack. It was getting louder.

They were off the ground. They were in the air.

Clack-clack-clack-clack-clack-clack-clack-clack.

And then the first passengers started to scream. They were climbing and their faces: she couldn't forget them. The couples kissing for the last time. The women screaming. The men arguing. The man hollering: *I want to sleep in my bed . . . I want to sleep in my bed.*

And it only got louder.

Clack-clack-clack: it was worse now they were cruising.

What am I supposed to do? Her mind was racing.

We'll be returning to Madrid, said the captain.

They sent the cabin crew to calm the passengers down.

'They were like children,' she said.

'But the truth is they are always like children.'

The man was still booming: *I want to sleep in my bed.*

There was a woman that grabbed her, wailing, she was going to die.

'But that wasn't the time I got scared.'

They landed. They changed plane. The rest of the day fades.

Flying is a risk, she often thought. It's only a small risk. A tiny risk. But everything about flying revolved around it. She knew it as she checked the airbags. She knew it as she gave the safety instructions. She knew it as she saw that strange picture of a slide popping out of a plane window. But then so is everything: it's all a complex system waiting to crash.

'The time I got scared was different.'

It was a flight to Vienna, Prague, or somewhere: one of those eastern countries. She couldn't remember. It was boarding. That was when she heard the noise – *wee, wee* – they all heard it, all the cabin crew. And then they heard it again – *wee, wee.* Is that it? Someone was pointing out the window. It was the wing. There was something wrong with it.

Helena saw the pilot: *I'm not flying with that sound*, she said. He smiled: *Don't worry, we'll never take off if there's a fault*. But she could see his face wasn't quite right.

Cabin crew prepare for boarding.

The same excuses every time: *I need to, I need to* – not put these bottles in the locker. *I need to, I need to* – keep my bag at my feet. If only they knew.

Do you think everything's OK? They caught a word by the toilets where the passengers couldn't hear. *No, I'm sure, I'm sure*. That din: feet, languages, bags – no matter the airport, it was always the same. And none of them could hear the noise – *wee, wee*.

Had they failed the test?

That's what people were saying.

Then she began to see it: the Madrid crash. Everybody knew the story. Everybody in the cabin crew. It had been delayed an hour before take off. It failed, it failed, then it passed its tests. The failed take off. The second attempt.

Cabin crew prepare for take off.

She could see it now as she sat down, strapped in and began to feel the velocity flowing through her: the sudden swerve, the red flames on impact, the plume of smoke, black like a forest fire, the bodies laid out in the sports hall. Helena began to concentrate: that judder, it was wheels up.

And they began to climb.

'I concentrated . . . I concentrated.'

Every bit of the safety instructions, she went through them. She mouthed them. She could hear them inside her.

'I couldn't . . . I just couldn't relax.'

Helena could see herself: not this flight, another flight, she remembered. Turbulence over Gran Canarias. And the woman was crying. Big choking sobs. *My friend*, she kept saying. *My friend*. Helena got closer: she stroked her, she held, sometimes she felt like a mother to them. My friend. The woman was still trying to tell her something.

My friend died in the Madrid crash.

Helena held her.

'And slowly, the panic attack stopped.'

They were still climbing.

We're not going to crash, she said.

We're not. We're not going to crash.

It's a tiny chance. It's a tiny chance.

'And then nothing happened.'

The tightness left her face. It left her colleagues: because every flight attendant knows turbulence, it could throw you against the ceiling: but never – or next to never – is that when the plane is going to crash. That's always take off or landing: that's what they tell you in training.

Tea, or coffee?

They make you drink water up there: there's a requirement. Because with two back-to-back flights it seeps out of you. You're dehydrated. Before you know it your head begins to pinch at some deep spot inside: then it begins to pound. You begin to get tired.

You don't quite hear them.

Tea, I said, tea.

Landing. Boarding. It happens so much faster than most people realize. They scurry. They check. They're smiling again. Their hair dry like straw. That faint feeling of too much time in the air all through them.

Please remain seated while the seat belt sign is on.

Taxiing. One stewardess faces forward. Another faces back.

Now the runway. Glinting lights along the tarmac.

Another memory. Another flight.

A man jumps up, he's yelling in English, but also in his language – *Help, help!*

Abort take off. Abort take off.

Helena ran. Then she found her. A woman convulsing. Her sunglasses have come off and her eyes: it pained her what she saw.

'She had a black eye. And I've never forgotten it. We paused the take off. Then we called the crew. They carried her . . . lifting her up and taking her away. She was still out of it . . . and we checked her bag to find her passport. And it was full of cash. Huge piles of cash. She was Russian, or Ukrainian, one of those eastern nations, and I can still see her.'

Helena's mind was racing.

Is she trying to escape? Is she on the run?

'One girl said she'd seen her taking pills.'

'Who was she? I'll never know. But that's who we are. Flight attendants only ever glimpse part of the story. We never know what it really is.'

Helena woke up from a doze.

She'd been sunbathing on the floor.

Slowly she began to get better. She couldn't get to the bathroom, she couldn't get to the kitchen without wheezing. But it began to pass. She started stretching. She lay for longer in the sun. She was alone for fifty-two days. The doctors came three times.

You're getting better, they said. *You're getting better.*

Slowly she started to leave the house. She saw her mother: she survived. And she started walking under the trees on Avenida de Europa again. But she would get out of breath and stop every few steps: gasping. She couldn't fill her lungs. Sometimes, she'd stop, gasping, and she'd see a plane above her. And suddenly she'd think how big her life used to be.

10 LE COL DE L'ÉCHELLE

It wasn't simple being a rescuer.

The calls would come in the middle of the night. They would come in the middle of dinner. They would come when he was tired. Simone was never quite ready. He'd been doing this for years, volunteering for the Piedmont rescue crew, but still, it was exhausting. It was heavy to race up to the hills. It was heavy to find lost hikers, injured cyclists or frightened mushroom-pickers who had lost their way.

But still, he'd never done a real rescue.

One up in the mountains.

One with avalanches, or falls.

Somehow the call never came when he was up there.

'I live in Turin and those are my calls.'

Still, it was hard to believe the mountains were full of death.

But they weren't streets, they weren't attractions.

The Alps were what they always were.

That was why he loved them.

It was in that excitement, he felt, on those bends up from Turin. Mountains rising over him, wrapped in thick woods; blackish, brown and green, like the hair on an enormous animal. That was what made his heart beat faster every time. His eyes on those peaks jagged like a children's drawings.

This had been his whole life. He'd built it all around this. Photography. Writing. Volunteering. Every few days he was here.

'I can't spend too long away from this air.'

He would park the car in Melezet, at the foot of the ravine. He'd strap his skis on and he'd go up. The snow sparkling like crystal behind him on a bright day. Simone liked to be alone up here. Like every parent, he needed his moments where he felt free. He'd leave the chalets and the pisteurs and once he'd got right up to the top, he'd be right underneath it – le Col de l'Échelle.

'This is one of the most dangerous passes we have.'

But one of the places he loved.

Its folds, its grey rock face, its glowing white peak.

One of those places you really felt it: how many centuries had passed through the Alps. Hannibal's elephants. Lost Napoleonic soldiers. Smugglers in between the wars. Like a fly in amber, that past was even in its name – Il Colle della Scala, or Le Col de l'Échelle. In both Italian or French: The Pass of the Ladder.

A tiny hint of old frostbitten lives. Once upon a time not even the shepherds could make it over unless they threw a ladder over the rocks. Even today this road is impassable to cars every winter. Both its two tunnels and those hairpin turns at 1,762m were buried in snow. Iced over. Closed.

'To climb up that mountain? And then to make it through the winter tunnels? Even a rat would struggle. It's just not possible.'

You still feel it, as you go further up. To that tiny chapel, half grotto, almost a hutch; Notre Dame du Bonne Rencontre, Our Lady of Good Encounter. You can feel it as you enter. Something hard and desperate. Because the fear of the mountain is in here: filled with candles, Madonnas, rosaries and offerings of flowers; the stooped walls lined with plaques of thanks from those who think the Virgin saved them, when they were lost, when they needed her, in the snow.

'This is a mountain that kills.'

It didn't feel like that though, most days. It felt like other people's Instagram stories. It felt like a park; not a world where anyone had to cross that peak. It was a world where most of what he did was pleasure. The click of the camera on a rare bird. The thrill when flakes started to swirl. His notebook in cold hands in the glades. It's a world Simone never wanted to change.

But that winter something did.

He started to see clothes – fleeces, hoodies, whole puffers, tossed into the snow – hanging from branches, on the side of the path. Human tracks going in circles. Or a pair of shoes, or just one Nike, flipped up there on the path. The one that went up, up there, to Le Col de l'Échelle. Simone didn't think anything at first.

Anything apart from that it was strange.

Then he started to see them. Straggling the kerbs of mountain roads, squinting into cheap smartphones, trying to find the path. Then he'd see them again. He'd be on his skis, halfway up the slope, then they'd walk past, in trainers, in hoodies, in the thinnest kinds of fleece – African men.

They're refugees, or something like that, they told him at the bar. *They're asylum seekers, so they can't work in Italy until they're approved.*

So they're trying to go to France.

The mountain rescuers were talking when it hit him: what was on TV was suddenly here. But what the hell are they doing up here?

Police at every station and border to catch them. They're not allowed to travel freely in Europe. So they're trying to cross the mountains.

But Le Col de l'Échelle? he said. *It's impassable.*

'You see the phone trick them when they see it on a screen. They hit Walking on Google Maps and this path to France looks flat and easy.'

Some of the rescuers had even heard it was an app.

Someone was selling it in the camps: a path to France.

And what about those clothes?

Simone already knew it but he still asked.

'If you don't know the mountain, if you don't know that as soon as you start walking in deep mountains, you get hot, you start sweating. But they don't know that as soon as you stop in five minutes you're freezing. It's hypothermia.'

The mountain rescuers drank in silence. It was one of those restaurants in Melezet that smelt of pine. The kind of place that felt like a refuge.

That night Simone drove back to Turin.

He was twitching to go back. There was going to be work this winter. He kept twitching as the weeks passed, he began to see more and more of them on his days in Melezet. There they were: African men, from their teens to their fifties, some of them in baseball caps, most of them in the cheapest jumpers. None with real scarves. Trudging up the slopes. The snow school, the orange ski tans and the bright Patagonia wear all over the Olympic snowboard piste didn't notice them. But he did. The rescuers all did. But still no call.

'It was not long after they found Mamadou.'

'They found him just over in France right at the beginning.'

His legs frozen up to his knees; walking in tears.

This man was from Mali.

He was crying, when they found him, because he had tried to cross Le Col de l'Échelle on the wrong night. They were two friends. They had climbed and clambered until they were wading through snow, but somewhere before the chapel they had slipped into a deep hole. It was snowing, it was night, and they crouched, hugging their knees in the snow, trying, trying everything not to fall asleep, until light, trying to hold on.

This is what happened.

The morning came. They were still alive. Then with the little strength they had, they pulled themselves out. But Mamadou's friend could not continue. He collapsed. *Mamadou*, he said, giving him his mother's phone number.

Call her and tell her I died here. But you go on.

There was golden light that morning. It was a woman on a dog-sled that spotted him, disoriented in tears. Alone. Like a ghost from the past or maybe the future. Three days later they amputated his frostbitten feet.

'It was after that,' said Simone, 'the alarm really went out in the valleys.'

There were more and more of them now.

Whole groups, dozens of them, marching upwards.

But still, Simone received no calls.

'I realized they're too frightened.'

A tension gripped him, like nails digging in. Then a feeling. The feeling of being useless. There was an emergency. There were dozens of them up there – hundreds, even – clambering over the pass. But they weren't calling. It made his mouth curl just to think about it. It made his stomach turn – watching them, in his car, on his way up and on his way down – knowing that they weren't calling. That to them he was just like the police.

'Then one day we did finally get a call.'

An unknown caller. It was broken Italian.

My friends, my friends . . . problem.

It was unmistakable. That was an African man.

'We don't know who called us.'

'Or how they reached us, but we ran.'

Whoever had called them, he wasn't up there. Then he hung up. The alarm went out. They were shouting, the rescuers.

Where is he?

Get the snowmobiles!

Two minutes and they were ready: a medical student, a ski-lift operator, a guy from one of the hotels and Simone. Rushing. His heart pounding.

It was his first mountain rescue.

This wasn't a lost mushroom-picker.

'This time I was up here.'

'With the real rescue heroes.'

Quickly they passed the political border.

It looked like a tombstone, the stone post. Swallowed by the snow. On one side: F for France. On their side: I for Italy. The natural border loomed over them. Like a monstrous wall, round an enormous castle.

They passed the first signs – *Danger d'Avalanches!*

Then the second – *Danger de Mort!*

After three kilometres they came to a stop.

Cramped onto snowmobiles. Belching exhaust.

'We saw the piles of clothes going up.'

Simone's blood froze. This only meant one thing.

The hypothermia had hit. They had been sweating. They'd thrown off their clothes and now halfway further up they'd be freezing. There was only snow, rocks and human tracks ahead. Towards those zigzagging bends. The medical student saw it first. Simone's heart sank when he saw what shouldn't be there.

'There was a rough path, a beaten path we had never seen before, that showed us that hundreds of Africans had been trying it. So we followed it.'

You know this if you know the mountains.

You know the human paths follow the animal paths. The paths are ancient. You might never see them but they have a logic to them.

You must always follow them.

'The Africans had not followed the path.'

'They'd avoided every hairpin bend and climbed the steep ledges to reach the road further. Because they didn't have a clue that in the

mountains it's easier and less tiring to go the long way instead of the short way. That's what saves you.'

The ski-lift operator hit the ignition. They ploughed on.

The snowmobiles gurgled and groaned. Snow sprayed as they bounced off rocks and drifts. That day the light was strange. It was noon when the rescuers went up, but this was the north face of the mountain; so in this kind of winter the sunlight was gone from there. Simone and the rescuers stopped, switched off the roaring engine, and listened.

But there was only silence.

The silence you only get in the mountains; without currents and without birds. Like the background noise was gone.

He could hear himself breathing.

'We were in deep shade. This is a strange light, the one you get in the deep mountain shade, because you see the sun all around but where you are it's all in the deep shade. It's strange because it makes everything look a bit blue. The light, the snow . . . it all seems blue. Almost, like you are underwater.'

Nothing. They kept going.

Higher. It was the medical student.

Quickly. Let's go.

The path rose above the slopes; above the forests; until the piste was far and tiny beneath them. The snowmobiles drove four kilometres, but there was nobody; only clothes on the path up the wooded slopes. Then they jumped off the snowmobile, Simone and the three rescuers, and put on skis.

Can you hear that?

Nothing. It was all in their head.

Can you see that?

Nothing still. The sun began to dip as they trekked.

They kept going for two kilometres on foot.

'Then we saw them.'

At the mouth of the tunnel of Le Col de l'Échelle.

'They were shivering in a really cold and shady place. And one of them, I could see he seemed really in a bad way.'

They waved.

They waved back.

Simone yelled: *We're not police.*

Come down, please. Come down.

The men huddled together.

'They seemed tired and scared.'

Simone could see their faces now.

And that was when he really saw it.

'You can always see fear in the eyes. You can see it by how a man looks around. How your eyes look around changes when you are scared. You start to receive danger from everything you see. That is fear.'

There were eight of them, in their twenties.

And they said they were all from Guinea.

Pitiful, in sodden trainers and snow-wet jeans.

'By the way they were walking I could tell they had frostbite.'

'They seemed like they might be falling down at every step. They weren't putting their feet properly on the snow.'

That day it was –6°C. The light was half gone.

France, they said. *We want France.*

The rescuers shouted back.

We can't take you to France.

It was after they said they could only take them down, something rippled through the group. *No.* They would not go back.

'They talked, in their language, what to do, whether to continue. Two were very, very determined to carry on. Very, very determined. We tried to tell them we were not police. We were there to help them. But the two that were determined yelled – *No, no, leave us*.'

We will carry on.

They became frantic, the rescuers. They tried gestures, they tried French, they talked louder – they tried everything to stop them.

'We told them it was dangerous. That it was soon going to be dark. That there were avalanches. We told them we ourselves would not go here at this time of day. But they didn't listen to us.'

They got up. The wind was whining.

The rescuers were yelling – *Stop, stop, we are telling you now the French police are waiting for you on the other side – and they will take you back to Italy. You have hypothermia. You could die.*

Do you understand? You can die.

They stared back impassively.

It's impossible even for us in our gear.

You can't make it. Not even a fox can make it. Please.

Those tunnels are packed with snow.

But it was pointless.

The sun had begun to fall. One of the men waved a certificate he said he had received when he arrived in Sicily exactly fifteen days earlier.

'He had a calm face, this man. He didn't seem to know this banned him from entering France. Or maybe, on some level, he did. Because, his eyes, they looked . . . defeated.'

The rescuers held back.

'Now they were debating very calmly among themselves. But the two more determined ones said – *We are going to try and make it to France.*'

'*Whether you follow us or not.*'

They got up first and then the rest, for a moment they hesitated, and then they followed. Leaving the rescuers behind. Simone radio-ed back.

They are continuing.

It was cold, like all shocks, that rushed through his body.

'We watched them stagger on all the way until they reached the tunnel. It was one of those moments you don't know what to say. So we didn't say anything. We just watched.'

He could hardly blink.

They'd never seen anything like this. They couldn't compute something like this. Never – not one of them could remember – had an SOS been called on the mountain to be turned away. They went down in silence. The horror silent and growing.

That scene in their minds.

Those shapes turning away.

They couldn't look back. It felt wrong.

Down in the resort, which always feels like any other, like it belonged to serviced chalets and ski instructors, they said goodbye. They shook hands. *See you around, thanks.* The medical student, the ski-lift operator and the guy from one of the hotels drifted off. Simone had to get home.

It was then that he realized he was shaking. His hands trembled as he turned the key to his car. It was something he hardly thought of, the border. Invisible to him. The world to them. It was almost

like there were two categories of human beings, he thought. Those that could and those that couldn't.

The road snaked. The mountains began to disappear.

The first turnoff was coming. He felt almost sick.

'I felt like something was broken.'

They were still up there.

'We don't know how many of them have died. We don't know what has happened. There is no way of knowing how many got lost. We have no way of knowing how many were caught up there but were too frightened of the police or of being deported to call us for help. We have no way of knowing how many turned back and how many struggled on alone.'

All winter they had found the clothes.

'Only in spring will we count their bodies.'

Motorway lamps glowed overhead as he drove. He thought of his children. He thought how it was never going to end. This emergency. He just knew it. They would keep coming. And they would keep trying to stop them.

TORINO – 50km. Simone was driving faster now.

But he could still see them. The faces.

The light. The underwater light.

Like they were drowning.

11 BRIANÇON

Brico wasn't sure what had come over him.

He was tired but he was also restless. He was nervous but he was also calm. There had been too much waiting. It would be any day now. Any day his life would change. But he couldn't keep sitting there, slumped in the gloom, his worried face lit with the phone. Brico wasn't that kind of guy.

That night he went for a walk.

'It's not like Europe, the streets in Africa.'

The dogs were barking on the streets of Abobo. That was his part of Abidjan. The part where the poor people lived. They were thick with mud, the streets of Abobo. They stank of sewage and weeks old trash. Brico caught the eyes of hungry cats squatting on the side of the road. They were yelling in the streets of Abobo; selling – *banana, plantain, banana, plantain*. They were crouching over baskets, shouting – *please, please*.

He was not those people.

The people who just make do.

But that night, they were quiet, when he came back. Brico opened his gate. His two cars were there. The boy who cleaned for him was there. And that was when he saw his wife, Blandi. There was pain in her face. *It's happening*, she said.

It's happening. The baby, it's coming.

That's when I knew.

He was rushing now. He was throwing open the cupboards. Rifling through drawers. He had to find it: his holy water and his holy string. That was what he tied round her. That was what he made her drink. She was shaking. She was hurting. But they had told him, in church, that this would keep Blandi safe.

All she had to do was drink it, with the string on her skin.

They got in the car and, his heart beating, he drove.

Abobo was quiet that night. The hospital was quiet that night. But that night he knew something already. He knew who this baby was. Because they had told him, in church, the name – Kris. The baby would be called Kris.

'That was what Mother Mary wanted.'

They left all his toys, the night they ran away.

They left the doll in the pink dress and they left the rest: the clothes, the sofas, the tables, the little knick-knacks and the fabrics and the lamps and the ornaments. The rest, they left it all behind.

'I left it all – all, all, all.'

Everything that made him Brico.

'It's so hard because . . . I was living like a man should live.'

The BMW E46 – he sold it.

The Peugeot 306 Sport – he sold it.

For 2.2 million in purple and green notes.

All of them West African CFA francs.

Those were shoved in his pocket. Shoved in his pocket as they boarded the bus. The bus out. The bus out of Ivory Coast. The bus from Abidjan to Ouagadougou. The bus to Burkina Faso. Not sure where he was going.

'I was ready to run anywhere.'

Morning was still night. Abobo was sleeping. But the bus was packed, like all African buses, even a bus this early in the morning.

'I had to get out so early so nobody saw me.'

It had all happened so quickly. He was holding Kris. Blandi held Noa. He was two now. She was five and she had beads in the braids of her hair.

'I had to get out as fast as I could.'

Dawn. Rose sky. Abidjan was gone.

Hours later, the sky turned bronze. Hours went and the bus was shaking. Hours passed and the road was bad. There were no more forests now. There was dust and red earth. The trees here: they seemed stubby, blown and bent.

And the sun beat over the lines at the border.

'When you arrive in a poor country you can see it.'

You can almost smell it: sweat, sewage, gasoline.

Where are we going? the little one asked.

We are going travelling, my son.

Away. Out of the country.

Hours more, over the border and the bus stopped – Ouagadougou.

'I asked myself how is this even a town.'

How poor they were here. How their buildings were scuffed. How their station was small. How they hardly spoke French.

'They are illiterates there. The people who live in Burkina Faso.'

Ouagadougou station stank. Brico held Kris. Blandi held Noa. They went into the ticket hall, they walked past the chairs, past the squatting farmers, past the toilets, and there they found a little place to eat rice.

Brico fingered what they served and tried to eat.

'But I couldn't even finish it. It just didn't agree with me.'

The electricity kept cutting on and off.

'That's just exhausting.'

The place was busted. Everything was broken, like it had been, he thought, the day it opened. He needed to get out of Ouagadougou. The next bus was at dawn, the one to the country next along, Niger, the one he needed to get.

Night came quickly, just like it did in his country, and he spread a cloth on the floor and lay there. Holding his family, like so many others in the station, so many others who were in between. But that night, he hardly slept. The buses, the bugs, the voices in the dark. They were all around him.

On the floor, listening to the dogs, it all came back.

Why he was running away.

Abidjan city, Abobo bus station.

Back when Brico was a Général.

The bus stations in Abidjan, they are all the same. Permits, tickets. Drivers have to pay the gangs. The bus stations in Abidjan, they all have their gangs. The drivers, they know who they have to pay.

Winzins. Madoubes. Kassoum Coulibaly.

'They're not tribes, they're just gangs.'

The bus gangs of Abidjan.

The station rackets: there are three hundred, they say, in Abidjan. Strong gangs run whole stations. Weaker gangs, they have to divvy things up. Monday, Tuesday, each day is divvied up to a different gang.

'This is what happens.'

Weaker gangs, you can knock them out.

'And when you win, the station belongs to you.'

Boys on the street, they want to be in.

They wanted to be Winzin. A Winzin like him.

'Because I was high up, a boss . . . a Général.'

And Générals had to win battles.

Like the battle for the buses at Treichville.

'That was war.'

It had not happened quickly.

The Winzin had been circling the buses at Treichville for weeks. There were already seven gangs there and they'd divvied it up.

'But who was going to give us his day?'

'We would come and take it: the weakest's day.'

The news came by text.

The Winzin had made a decision. Thursday: that was the day. The day with the weakest gang. The Daltons: that was what they called themselves. Everyone knew they were weak. That was the day they would go for.

The battle started the way they always start.

Treichville, 3 a.m. The buses were still parked, blacked out, sleeping. The Winzin were already in position. Their hearts were beating. Shadows fluttered as the first drivers were slipping in. Then the first Daltons – *Hey you.*

'We came, we took the terrain, and took them by surprise.'

There were fifty on his side. Fifty Winzins.

Then the Daltons saw them.

How can you come here, they screamed, *this is ours.*

We went to them, *No – we are here now.*

That morning the Daltons didn't have their blades. Because there are rules to the bus battles and one of the first rules is: you can't show the first blade. Only when he shows it, can you take out your blade.'

The Daltons at Treichville called for help.

'They were under attack.'

Help was coming. Now blades were coming.

But the Winzins didn't have their own.

'Now, we had to run. We had to run because the Daltons were bringing blades. And we know there are machetes everywhere in the markets.'

'So, we go get our blades.'

There was sun and blue sky when they came back.

'8 a.m. That was when we fought. Knives, machetes, everything.'

The bus drivers screamed. The passengers screamed.

It was happening again.

'We were stabbing each other.'

This time, the Daltons lost. This time, nobody died.

'You know, people often die. We suffered some casualties but that day we had victory . . . *it was ours.*'

Treichville on Thursday was Winzin.

That night the Daltons came to beg the Big Man. They were humble, the way beaten men always are. *We have to talk*, the Daltons said. *We have to work out who is going to give up his day at Treichville.*

So we can all work in peace.

Those were the bad days.

But there were calm days too in Abobo.

Calm days when he went to Abobo station. Calm days where he collected the permits, where he collected the coins, where he signed the papers. Calm days where the drivers all paid their protection money. Calm days for a Général.

Crowds. The smell of engines. Dust.

'Most of the people who do transport are Muslims.'

He wouldn't smoke with them. He was a Christian.

'When I said Jesus Christ is my God, they wouldn't want to hear it. With them, the thing is, when you wanna roll with them . . . they want you to be a Muslim. You see, everyone but me was using the amulets we Africans call *grigris.*'

Never, never – would he use those amulets.

Sometimes, whispering, he could hear them.

You dirty Christian.

But they were quiet, when he still had the Big Man onside. Those were the good days in Abobo. Those were the good days when he was a Général. When he was Winzin and when he got Winzin pay. But things went wrong for Brico.

The way things had gone right.

It was his cousin. His cousin had married the Big Man Winzin. And this man had called him in, when it all began, and said – *Come with me, come, and we are going to work together.* This is how Brico became his Général.

'I was already, y'know, an . . . *intellectual.* Because in this field, they aren't intellectuals. They don't even know how to speak French. They don't know nothing. But when you know how to read and write you have better chances to grow . . . and that's how I did it actually.'

This is how Brico got the Winzin pay. The money they shared from all the stations. The winnings for all they do. This is why people from Abobo to Treichville in the Winzin called Brico, *Mon Général.*

Those were the good days. The good days when his cousin was married to the Big Man. She had children with the Winzin king. She lived in his house. The Big Man, he could almost say, he was family.

It happened suddenly.

His family threw her out.

'They sent her away because she wasn't Muslim.'

They sent her back to Abobo.

They sent her back to the stench and the wild dogs.

'And when she went, I started to feel threatened.'

Winzins would come to him and say – *You dirty Christian.*

'He didn't divorce her. They chased her out.'

'His parents didn't want to see her. So she left with the children.'

Winzins would come up to him and laugh.

The threats began, bit by bit, at the station. But then they didn't stop. The Winzins, they would spit on the floor and say – *We sent your cousin away. We're going to get a new wife now for our chief, who's going to give us the right children. Not Christian children. We want Muslims.*

Every night he went home.

Every night he knew it was going wrong.

'When she was married to him, I had support. But now she was no longer married to him . . . I had no support. They started calling me. They kept threatening me. The Big Man's parents, they kept threatening me.'

Then the Winzin pay stopped. That was it.

Treichville. Abobo. The battles. It meant nothing to the boss.

'I tried to see him, I tried to see the Big Man. Because he had children with my cousin. I told him, the money it's not coming, I can't see my money any more. He said . . . he would sort things out.'

But the money never came.

'And I knew, it wasn't going to work out.'

But for a Général it never ends quite like that.

You make friends. You make enemies.

You win battles. You lose wars.

His phone kept ringing. Winzins kept calling him, when he was at home, when he was playing with the children, in the middle of the night.

A voice he didn't know.

We're watching you. You dirty Christian.

One day we are going to come and get you.

Private Number.

We are going to come and show you.

One day you won't go home.

They kept phoning, it would be midnight and he knew it was them. Until he cracked.

'One say I said, *That's it.* One day, I say, *It's enough.* Because, you know, sometimes . . . they attack people at night.'

He felt it. He felt the fear in the dead of night.

He knew it only too well. How they come with the machetes. How they come with knives. How they come covered in amulets. How they come and they kill. But it was only with the wedding he finally knew.

The Big Man was getting married.

The Winzins kept calling. This was what they said.

Don't come to the wedding.

The wedding was not just the Big Man's wedding. The wedding was the Winzins' wedding. Every Winzin would be there, like they too were getting married. He wanted to be there. He needed to be there.

But they kept calling.

You think you can pull a trick on us?

He knew that voice.

You think you can because your cousin was married to the boss?

He knew it from the battles.

Forget it. Now you're not one of us. Today, we chased her away.

Come to the wedding and we'll kill you.

They kept calling.

There was a voice speaking slowly.

Brico, we're going to come . . . and kill you, Brico.

They were coming.

The Winzins were coming. He felt it in his stomach. He felt it in his bed. He was so frightened now, he shook and he cried like a little boy. He was so frightened now, he thought he could hear them coming. Just outside the door. But his wife knew everything. He hid nothing from Blandi. He didn't have to tell her much. She knew.

'I ran, I took my family, and I ran.'

That morning they left as early as they could. That morning, which was still black with night. He, holding Kris. Blandi, holding Noa.

'They had toys. They left them.'

'We left everything.'

Engines. Dogs. Flies.

They woke up on the floor.

The bus was leaving Ouagadougou.

The bus that was taking them to Niger.

'We knew here . . . we would be safe.'

Niamey was the name of the city. And here they were not alone. There was an aunt here, an aunt of Blandi's. This auntie was married to a little mister. What the little mister did he never found out. Something small. Something very small. Buying, selling. Something on the street.

'We knew we were safe here.'

Safe in the little house, with two little rooms, where she lived with the little mister and his sister. Safe, where they slept on the floor.

'I just couldn't stay in Niger.'

It was hot, it was dark in the little house. There was no electricity. The little mister was too little even for that. Too little for his own phone.

'I knew I wasn't going to be able to work.'

A week, three, a month, they slept on the floor.

And the streets he wandered were not like Abidjan.

'Niger is real poverty, there's nothing to eat. Even in the streets you see it. From the moment I arrived I hardly saw a real building in Niger. Nothing, not one building I saw had more than one floor.'

Everything was worse than Abidjan.

Even the dogs were thinner than back home: he could see their ribs rising and falling as they lay sleeping and breathing heavily on the street.

'I had to get out of Niger.'

Panic was eating him. He had to get out for Kris. He had to get out for Noa. He had to get out for Blandi. *No*, he couldn't accept this. He couldn't let himself become nothing.

Nothing, like the little mister.

'People can't feed themselves here.'

Libya. He had to get to Libya.

There were friends in Libya. *Come to Libya*, they said.

Come to Libya, they said, *we're making it work*.

They spoke on Facebook.

He called one on the phone.

Libya. It began to stick in his mind.

'*Libya* . . . I had to get there. Back then they were doing nothing to stop the people-smuggling. Africans were crossing into Europe. There had been a war there and there was nobody in charge. That meant if you took the risk . . . you could get there.'

It began to sink in when he was falling asleep.

Europe. Blandi, Noa, Kris and Brico in Europe. He tried to sleep but his heart raced thinking of it. Inside he could see it. Them, living in Europe.

That was when he started looking.

Looking for a guy.

They were in the markets, the smugglers.

Hey you, where are you from? They would come up to you, from behind the stalls, and follow you. *Hey you, where are you going?*

'*Europe*, they promised you. *Europe, it's not so hard.*'

These were the guys who arranged it with the Arabs. This is what Brico began to understand. The Africans controlled the route from Benin into the desert. That belonged to them. But once you got to the border, the ones who ran it were the Arabs.

'Everyone pushes this in Niger. It's like a market there.'

'The guys there are pushing for clients.'

There were a lot of them. But he chose one.

'I heard word he was good.'

He made the route sound simple.

Desert. Boat. Europe.

That night he told Blandi. That morning they kissed her aunt, and they kissed the little mister and his sister goodbye. Blandi's aunt was crying and holding her tight. *We will pray for you*, they said. *We will pray.*

'That was when we left.'

They left before dawn. They left in darkness. There were few lights in this city. The smugglers had come in a Toyota, a 4×4 pick-up truck. And in the back was where they stuffed them. Twenty-five of them.

'There were too many of us . . . and all the way I held wooden pickets, like a fence, in front of my son, so he wouldn't fall off the back of the truck.'

This is what the smugglers did. They wrapped their heads in rags.

'You know, like the jihadis do.'

They had to be hidden.

When the pickup stopped, the smugglers waited.

The police were hunting them.

'They don't want us to cross the desert.'

The pickup kept turning and turning. This lane, that route. *Now we wait.* Until they reached the checkpoints at the edge of the desert.

The smugglers, they knew how they worked.

'They knew the windows when the police weren't there.'

That was when they entered.

This is what he saw from the back of that Toyota.

There were mountains in the desert. Mountains unlike almost anything. There was sand in the desert. Hanging in the air. Falling through the sky. Sand filling your eyes. Filling your throat. Haze unlike anything.

'You see bodies in the desert.'

You see them, and you see pickups, half sunk into dunes.

You see men, who have turned into white bones.

'You see death everywhere.'

There were too many of them in the pickup. More than it could take. Huddling, holding on. Ivorians, Guineans, Gambians, Congolese.

'It's all mixed together . . . whole peoples are on the move.'

The sand was everywhere. In his eyes, in his mouth, in his hair. Making his children cry. The Toyota threw it everywhere. Over them, over the children. Over the ones who talked, and the ones who kept silent.

'Everybody knew why he was crossing.'

He held Kris. Blandi held Noa.

'We hardly talked.'

The desert is huge. And drivers say it obeys no rules.

'There was not enough water.'

The cans they had given them: it was not enough. They were asking for water. There was a Guinean Christian who was begging him for water.

'The water I had, I couldn't give it to him, because of the children.'

The Guinean Christian made faces, and played a little with Kris. He liked seeing the little boy. On the first day –*water, water*' – the Guinean Christian asked again and again. On the second day, he went very quiet.

My friend, said Kris, pointing.

The Toyota was bouncing off rocks.

Buffeted by winds. That was when the Guinean just fell. Out came his tongue. There it was, hanging out of his mouth. His eyes, they seemed to close, as if they knew what was happening. Kris screamed – *Papa, what's happening, Papa!*

What's happened to my friend?

The Nigerians died next. There were two of them. Two of them, who kept passing a bottle between them. It smelt like alcohol. But what it was, he wasn't sure. They said it was a product that stopped the thirst.

'I don't know who sold them that.'

The heat. It beat into his head.

The cold. It dug into his skin.

When the Toyota stopped, he held Kris tightest.

The night was black, huge, like an enormous mouth.

The children, they saw things in the desert.

'The babies, they would tug me – *Papa, can't you see it* – but I don't know what they were seeing. They would say – *Papa hide, Papa hide*.'

'But I didn't know what they were seeing.'

There were only shapes, he half made out.

'When you grow up, you can't see anything any more. But the children they see everything. Often, they were crying, but we didn't know why.'

The last night they were in the desert, it was late as the truck bounced and the wind moaned full of sand. Brico couldn't sleep. It was so dark the only thing he could see was Kris's face, right in front of him.

He was so thirsty his tiny breathing was shallow.

'I was seeing my children suffer. So I cried.'

It was a week. They drove night and day. He was lucky.

'Some people, it takes them a month.'

Out, the smugglers shouted.

This is Libya. Get out. They saw the men. They were wearing head rags like men do in the desert. And they shouted – *Ta'ala* – Come here.

They were Arabs. And behind them on the desert road was a dumpster. *Ta'ala* – said the Arabs: Come here.

And they climbed into the trash.

'Yes, under the waste. Real trash. With the children.'

Eskot – shouted the Arabs, Silence, as they covered them. The stench. The rotting things pressing against their faces. The children shivering.

Kris clinging to him. Noa clinging to Blandi.

'You know if you refuse them? You die. And it's better to lie under the trash than to die. Isn't it? Because if the police find you, my friend . . . because if the police find you it's terrible.'

Everybody knew they raped the women.

Everybody knew they hit.

The stench and the flies filled his mouth, the weight, the rot, the points of sharp things, crushing him and his children, and he thought: *I am in the hands of God.*

He was there for hours: he did not know how long he was there.

Hands pulled off the trash. They were at a half-finished house.

Sabratha, the Arabs said, *You are in Sabratha.* They pointed at cars, small, little cars. *Get in the trunk. Four. Five. As many as can fit!*

'That was how they took us.'

Then they drove.

'The whole family for two or three hours in the trunk.'

The thing about being in the trunk of a car is how noisy it is. How hot and dark and cramped it is. You never realize until you get into one.

They were almost at the water.

'Almost at the boats, the boats to Europe.'

The were almost at the water when they said – *Now we walk.*

Eskot – the Arabs said, Silence, the police are hunting blacks.

'Then we walked, we walked for twelve miles.'

Boots, shoes – everything came off for silence.

'It cuts your feet when you walk in the desert.'

The Arabs, they had them in single file.

Blandi carried Noa. He carried Kris.

'I was in pain but he . . . he had no problems.'

They were so close to the water. They were so close.

It all happened so quickly. There was noise. There were men there. And they came out of the darkness. And then there were screams. Their faces froze in the white lights of torches. *Papa, Papa* – Kris was shaking, as he hushed him.

It was over. They were soldiers, Libyan soldiers.

Brico was shaking, as he whispered – *We'll make it out, my love.*

The soldiers were laughing, the soldiers who took them to the camp.

The camp with so many others. The guards laughed at them as they took them behind the wire. *No Europe for you*, the guards laughed, in English so they understood. *Europe . . . finish – now you go home!*

That was the night it happened.

'The Arabs . . . they like to take your wife in front of you.'

They come and they point and they take. He had a beard and a Kalashnikov, the man who took her. And when he took her he froze.

Ta'ala – he said, Come here, and in his shadow he froze.

You move, and they put a bullet in your skull.

That was when he felt it: what it feels like to be nothing.

'When he stood there . . . I thought about my children, I thought about their lives, I thought if he shoots at me, what will happen to them?'

Ta'ala – he yelled, Come here, and then he took her.

'It felt like I had no power . . . it's hard to explain.'

When Blandi came back she didn't cry.

'What good would it do?'

When Blandi came back they didn't speak.

'What can you say? What can you tell her?'

That was the night in the camp in Sabratha.

This was the day.

'You know what they do?'

'There they hunt for men. There men rape women. They like beautiful women. That's how it happens for the women in Libya. There, you're not allowed to have a wife. I ask myself if these men are even Muslims?'

'Do these men even believe in God?'

There are slavers in Libya. Everyone knows what happens when they come.

'Everyone knows one black in the market – is $400.'

It all happened so quickly, that day when it happened to him. They came with guns. They came in fatigues. The day they strode into the camp at Sabratha. *Ta'ala* – they shouted. *Ta'ala* – Come here.

'They separated the men from the women.'

They were screaming. The women were screaming.

Ta'ala – they fired in the air.

Blandi was screaming. So was Noa.

'That was when I lost my wife.'

It all happened so quickly. He was screaming.

Blandi, Blandi.

He was screaming and he began to sob.

My wife. My girl.

My wife. My wife.

He was holding on to Kris.

The slavers were taking the men, when an Arab guard – he saw Kris – and before he really knew what had happened, pushed him into a dark room.

They heard the screams. They heard the cars leave.

They were gone. The slavers had gone.

Noa! He was screaming now. They'd gone.

They had no phones. Nothing. Neither did he.

That was he started to howl like a dog.

Blandi, Blandi!

'That was when my son went to me.'

Papa, be calm, Papa . . . Papa, be calm.

His eyes were red. His eyes were hot with tears.

Papa, we'll make it out.

Bluish light.

Then the prayers, the megaphones, went off at dawn.

That dawn, like all dawns, the guards went back to sleeping.

'I had only been there a week. But it was just enough to spot this.'

'The only moment you can escape.'

Brico ran to the barbed wire and grabbed it and climbed as it punctured his hands and he told Kris over and over, *Don't let go, don't let go.*

He started to run. He kept running until he was lost.

That was when three soldiers saw them.

'*Ta'ala*' – they said, Come here.

'But one of the soldiers, he was a black. He was a Senegalese but he was like a Libyan. The only way he wasn't was where he was born.'

The Libyan Senegalese saw Kris.

'He told them I was a builder not a migrant.'

The Libyan Senegalese told him to get in the patrol car.

Otherwise you'll be captured.

They drove him back to the camp. But once they got there, once the other soldiers had wandered off somewhere, the Libyan Senegalese took pity on him. He gave Brico some money in their currency, seventy dinars, and, his eyes falling on Kris, told him, quietly in French, how to escape – and where cars left for Tripoli at the edge of town.

'Then he helped me run away.'

'Fifty dinars.'

That's what they wanted to get him out – out of Sabratha.

Get in – the smuggler opened the trunk.

The boy was quiet. The boy didn't cry.

'He's a child who never cries.'

Brico held him in the trunk of the car all the way to Tripoli.

That night they opened it in the city.

He was lucky that night. Because he found the old smugglers quickly again. They knew he had paid in Niger, and that the last sums would only be released from the money handler, in the market there, once he crossed.

And so they welcomed him back with smiles.

'Things were different in Tripoli.'

It had been quite the city, not that long ago. They weren't hunting blacks here. The war had been easier here. Here, the Arabs didn't buy and sell blacks like they did in the desert. Here, the Arabs had them do little jobs in their homes.

Washing. Cleaning. Folding. Sweeping.

Waiting, that was what he did.

'The smugglers put us in the French embassy.'

The whites were gone from the French embassy.

Someone, or some bomb, had blown bits off the front.

'There were mattresses inside.'

There were maybe fifty people there.

Ivorians. Guineans. Nigerians. There were so many people.

'There was hot water. There was cold water. It wasn't a total wreck.' There was still power, gas, heating – there was still everything.'

That night he ran his hands in hot water.

'And I washed him. I washed my son.'

One morning at the embassy a bang woke him up.

'An Arab had come, he had fought with a youth and he'd fired at his head whilst I was sleeping there. The boy, he screamed. I was sleeping and he was playing. And I woke up . . . and I saw the blood flowing.'

The brain was on the floor: white, covered in blood.

'The Arab, his name was Faslam.'

That week he bought a phone.

That week Brico went on Facebook and posted with a picture of Kris:

> three years he is bilingual and whilst the haters talk about
> his dad they don't know if their children will ever walk on
> european soil down with the haters we go on. You keep
> talking

They lived for two weeks on a mattress on the embassy floor.

Two weeks until they came for him.

Do as we say, they said.

Do as we say, or the police will fuck us.

'I got inside.'

It was a 4×4.

'And I put on a hat. The child, I put him at my feet.'

'And I went to him – *Sit, sit still.*'

The water was far from the gathering point.

They would have to walk ten miles to the water.

To walk again. Again, where he walked before.

'On the shore there was a police helicopter patrolling for mi-grants.'

No, they said.

No, we can't go now.

Dusk came, and they dug little hollows into the sandy earth.

Do as we say – and they threw palm leaves over them.

'That was how we slept.'

That night he lay in the hole, in the cold of the sand.

Thinking over and over.

'This is between life and death.'

'My life, my death.'

—

Night. Water. Midnight.

They shook them awake.

Ta'ala – Come here. Now there were many of them on the shore. There they were. 'They were little lifeboats.'

Bisur'atin – Quickly, they said. *We haven't much time.*

'There was no space. Everybody was standing.'

Standing, he held on to Kris.

'There was such a mix of people.'

When the motor went, they were a hundred and fifty.

Land slipped out of sight.

The water surged. The water gurgled.

'There were waves, there were waves and they scared me. They made a noise like *vrrrrooou, vrrrroooou* . . . And there were people who were crying on the boat. There were pregnant women. There were children.'

Dawn came. They were still on the water.

Between the crying and the waves.

'I closed my eyes.'

Bright, the sun grew.

They were nowhere. There was more and more fear now.

The boatman was lost. That man was crying now.

There was screaming now.

I don't want to die, I don't want to die, they screamed.

Allah, Allah, be merciful to me, they screamed.

'I closed my eyes and prayed for God to save me.'

He held tight to Kris.

'He was sleeping.'

They first saw a dot. Then they saw a ship.

They were Italians, who scooped them out of the water.

'They were nice.'

Shivering, wet – they gave him a croissant with a very thin slice of chicken folded inside it. 'But I wasn't hungry.' Something was wrong. They were almost there, but something was going wrong. The child was shaking. The child was almost convulsing. 'This whole time, he hadn't fallen ill. But as soon as we arrived, that's when he felt the whole journey and he fell ill.'

He was running with diarrhoea.

Black like blood.

—

You are in Sicily, they said, at the dock.

The Italians, the ones in uniforms, began to form them into lines.

'But me, when I arrived, they took me somewhere else.'

They took him to a hospital. Kris was very ill. The machines, they bleeped and whirred. The doctors and the nurses, they fixed him up to a drip. *The boy has fever, the boy has diarrhoea* – they said, again and again.

'I didn't eat anything that day.'

He paced the hospital corridor, hungry.

'I was just an immigrant so they didn't give a shit about me.'

The boy stopped shaking. The nurses said things he couldn't understand. They took the needles out. They took him off the drip. *Seguici* – they said – Follow us, but it was in Italian so he could hardly understand.

They were taking him, somewhere, he was going to live.

The *campo*, that was what the Italians called it, was overflowing. Malians, Senegalese, Bangladeshis. Faces he had never seen before.

Sign – they said, pushing paper at him.

Hand – they said, pushing his fingers onto a small screen.

'I signed. I didn't know what I was signing. But I signed.'

Then they took him to a bus. Kris was still very weak. *Where are we going?* he asked. *Torino,* they said. But he had no idea where that was.

Kris was still very weak when they got there.

Not once had he asked for Blandi.

'They gave us clothes and tokens for food.'

You are free to come in and out – they said.

He was nervous at first, he was worried about Kris, but then he couldn't resist.

'That was the first time I saw a European town. It was marvellous. The light . . . It was marvellous. That was the first time I saw snow.'

'That was when I realized I was truly in Europe.'

Those first few days were heaven. He wandered with Kris to the square with columns and he told him over and over, 'This is Europe, all this.'

	NATIONALITES	EFFECTIFS	Le 12/06/2018
1	CAMEROUN	22	
2	GUINEE CONAKRY	173	
3	LIBERIA	99	TOTAL : 544
4	NIGERIA	88	
5	SENEGAL	31	
6	SIERRA LEONE	09	
7	CÔTE D'IVOIRE	30	
8	MALI	20	
9	NIGER	35	
10	BURKINA FASO	02	
11	TCHAD	02	
12	SOUDAN	07	
13	BENIN	06	
14	TOGO	02	
15	GHANA	08	
16	CONGO	09	
17	GUINEE BISSAU	0	
18	CENTRAFRIQUE	00	
19	GAMBIE	02	
	MAURITANIE	00	

Brico showed him the Europeans: how they dressed, how they talked, how unlike it all was in Abobo. But every evening they went back to the *campo*.

They fed them soup there.

They gave them a little bit of money.

Days. Weeks. That was when it clicked.

How little it really was.

'With €75 a week, what could I do?'

The city was there. But he wasn't really in the city. He walked past shops he couldn't afford to enter. He stood outside huge buildings like a beggar. The men in suits, the women in dresses, they didn't look at him, they hardly saw him, because without money he wasn't even there. Brico stood in lines when he was hungry. He stood in lines that told him *No*.

Becoming frantic.

No, you can't work.

No, you can't leave.

It was like a prison, he thought, a prison in a palace.

Here it was illegal for him to get a job. This was going to be Italy for him: years, in this *campo*. Staring through glass at the minimarket.

Maybe, they would send him back.

He wasn't going to beg like the blacks at the station.

But there was one last hope. *France*. He had to get to France.

'France, for me, it became everything.'

'It's a language I speak, it's the future for Kris.'

Everyone was talking about it. Someone in the *campo* told him there were people who you could pay to take you to France. Someone then told him, *Don't listen to him. Look at this map. Look at these buses. It's easy.*

'Someone told me they gave you four hundred euros a week.'

That was so much more than Italy.

He had to get to France.

Torino – Bardonecchia – Briançon. That was the route. The mountains, that was where people were crossing to France. This is not permitted, said the *campo*, they will throw you back.

'But how could I work? I couldn't speak Italian.'

He had to get to France.

It's comfortable, the others said. *They respect you.*
And if only he got there, he thought, everything would be OK.
'And it would all be worth it.'

They left the *campo*.

Kris walked besides him, all the way to the big station. There were other Africans there. He knew what they were doing, and they nodded at each other, without saying hello. The loudspeakers, somewhere above them, boomed with sounds and names, and as the crowds jostled, the boy started to cry. Until they found the right train. And the train pulled out of Torino.

The air was different in the mountains. The snow was thicker. The sun brighter. There were different smells. And the Africans they met told them where to go. That night they slept on the floor of the small station there. There were people there – Arabs, Africans, Asians –exhausted, tired, hungry. Almost in France.

There was a doctor there, in charge, and a Cameroonian.

No – you cannot go. That was what the doctor said.

She was a woman, and the young Cameroonian translated.

No – you cannot cross by foot.

No – you cannot cross by bus.

'She told me everything . . . *not to go to France.*'

That Europe was not one big country. That only Europeans can go between the countries. That every road is blocked by policemen. And that the only ways open are through the mountains. And that the mountains kill.

'She said, the police, they could take him away, my son.'

Again and again – the Cameroonian said, *They will send you back*. Again and again – the Cameroonian said, *You have no right to France. Go back. You must go back.* The woman was there. Watching him.

He grew frightened of her. She began to make his skin prickle, with tension.

'I knew I was in Italy, where women are like the bosses.'

'I had to take precautions.'

He grew frightened of the doctor with power.

'I told myself, she could take away Kris.'

Yes, he said to her. *Yes, I'm going back.*

Tomorrow, she said. *Tomorrow, a car will take you back to the campo. It's over. Torino, it will be good.*

That night he thought of the camps, and he thought of the desert, and he thought of Blandi. *No*, he couldn't go back. *No*, he couldn't. When he woke up the doctor was gone.

He ran. The bus. There must be a bus.

The others, they said, they were going to walk.

'I couldn't walk. I couldn't walk the mountain. My son was so tired.'

The others, they told him he was a fool.

That he was risking everything and they could take away his son.

He was shaking when he got on the bus.

Br-r-r-iançon, he said, stammering, *la France.*

Neuf euro, said the driver, *s'il vous plaît.*

Then they left. The snow was falling. Thicker, faster than the sand in the desert. The forests, the rocks, the light – everything was white.

'I closed my eyes and I prayed.'

'I asked God, please, please, bring us to France.'

The bus stopped.

Passeports, s'il vous plaît – it was a policeman.

Brico's heart was thumping as he moved down the aisle.

Passeports – checking papers, cards, and little booklets.

Have you got your passports? he said.

'I started to pray.'

OK, please show me, the man said.

'So then I pretended to look for them.'

His heart was pounding like a generator.

Do you have them? the man said.

Yes, Brico said.

Then without a word, the policeman turned and left. The wheels crunched. The bus shook. The man was gone. They were moving.

'That was when I realized . . . We'd made it.'

12 MEURSAULT

It's always on your mind as a winemaker.

You can't stop thinking about the weather.

No matter whether he's in Burgundy, or he's left for a tasting in New York.

Jean-Marc feels he can never really be away from this place. That when you grow wine, you can never forget what the temperature is. You go to bed knowing it. You wake up seeing it. You feel it in your sleep. What it's doing to the vines.

Every day no matter where he is he reads the emails.

His specialist forecast.

The one that comes twice a day.

Jean-Marc sees the number and he knows immediately: *Am I in danger? Will the cold snap kill the vines? Or has, yet again, a warm spell come too early, before the frosts are gone, tricking the vines to grow?* He reads the emails and he feels it so keenly: how there isn't really winter any more, not like there used to be; how they are harvesting a month earlier than they used to in summer; weeks and weeks earlier than they'd done for hundreds of years.

It still feels so strange.

Often his head spins, how different it all is – the tastings in London, the collectors arriving from Dubai, the orders from Singapore and Japan – to what his father had known, let alone his grandfather and before him. They were almost peasants, a moment ago. They never left the village. Now because of global warming many of them are buying land and planting vines in Romania, in Scandinavia, in England or in Hokkaido in the north of Japan.

They are well-known faces in these parts.

Where the grapes will be happier when it's 3°C warmer.

Jean-Marc flies to Patagonia. Twice a year he leaves Meursault.

He drives to Paris, parks his car in the long-stay car park, passes security, waits for boarding and flies south. The night flight buffeting over the South Atlantic. He lands in Buenos Aires, then he flies to Neuqen. Then he drives. East, for an hour, an hour and a half, into the deep valley of the Rio Negro. And there's the estate.

At night, there are so many birds, you can hardly sleep. And at moments like this, he lies there wondering if this is what it was like in Burgundy, a hundred or two hundred years ago; the feeling of nature, the memory of the light, brighter, so much more intense than it ever is in Europe. He thinks about his father, he can see his face in the dark and he wonders what he would have thought about all this. And about how he came to make wine at all.

Jean-Marc told them he was leaving at breakfast.

'I told them I was leaving home.'

'I told them I'm leaving the village.'

He would never forget that morning. Not now – not ever. He could still see them there around him. His father on the left of him. His mother on the right. And their faces. They were stunned. Taken back.

'I told them that I was going to stop being a winemaker . . .'

'And that I was going to be an actor.'

The table fell silent. Their faces only shock.

The breakfast – the bread, the jam, the cheese – paused. Their hands not reaching. The tableware not clattering. And then the grey light. It was no longer summer. The harvest of 1977 was over. The harvest they had done together.

Like they had done every harvest since he was very small.

'They couldn't believe it.'

'They were speechless. They didn't yell in front of me. But I know that for my father, for him, this was a complete calamity . . .'

It was all in his face. Like something was ending. Like something about to be cut.

'For my father It was a catastrophe. An unbroken chain. About to snap.'

Jean-Marc would never forget what he said to them. He could still hear himself. Promising that *Non*, he wouldn't just walk out on them. That *Oui*, he would work in the cellars. But in the spring when it all began again he would leave. It was very simple.

And then breakfast was over.

All day they worked. His thoughts rattling.

'Wine is the life I was offered . . . and I didn't want it.'

There was something else.

It was calling to him as he pulled up weeds.

It was calling to him in the tool shed.

There was more out there. There were other lives.

'I didn't want to be that person, that winemaker, who had always done the same thing . . . I looked ahead and I didn't want that life. I felt like I was staring down train tracks. And there was only work, work, work.'

That's what he saw falling asleep.

The cycle again and again. The plants. The village.

The same bottles of wine. The same habits.

'I saw no place, nowhere here . . . I could tell my own story.'

But it wasn't like anybody had ever said anything.

Nobody had ever given him an order or left instructions; like, we expect you to keep these vineyards one day. Everything in the family had just been assumed. The way people talked and the way people planned. Everything moving towards it. The tradition was so heavy. That Jean-Marc would take over the domaine.

'I was the only son in the family.'

It was expected.

This was how it went in Meursault.

Father to son. The generations never breaking.

The precious work never stopping. That everything revolved around.

'But I didn't want to be a sixth-generation winemaker.'

Jean-Marc didn't want to live his life in the same village, on almost exactly the same patch of land his family had been on since before Napoleon retreated from Moscow and there were still kings in France, making the same wine.

'I felt it inside me.'

A feeling that was finally overflowing.

It had been building for a long time. Because Jean-Marc had long been dreaming. Even then he wondered why this. *Why do I*

want to be an actor? Why not a diplomat, or a journalist, or a scientist?
Or some other kind of dream.

He would catch himself thinking in the fields.

'Maybe it's because I was so shy as a little boy? Maybe because I was so closed?'

A little boy who hid behind his sister. That nobody would make out in the crowd.

A little boy who didn't know how to speak.

'Who'd finally found a place to.'

Then all of a sudden it started to grow. This little dream inside him: of stages and lights and seeing yourself as somebody else, somewhere else – on screen in front of you.

Like he'd found his own key.

Jean-Marc hadn't expected to find it.

Big dreams weren't what people did in the village. Big changes weren't what they were after. They did what they knew. They did it better than anyone else. They kept their secrets. And they stuck together.

'I didn't feel like I'd found a dream . . .'

'That they really understood.'

He found it when he first went away. To the nearest big city. To boarding school in Dijon. Not a fancy thing like in England. It was a state school where the tiny wine villages sent their kids. But it was somewhere else.

'They took me to the theatre.'

'To do things I'd never done before.'

He felt himself changing. He felt happy in drama class.

He felt that thrill in every role – in little plays they wrote themselves.

'I found it then . . . I found theatre.'

'I found this way to speak and to be someone else.'

But at first it didn't happen. In fact, nothing happened.

As planned, he sat and passed his exam.

And then he floated through military service in 1975 at a seedy port town in the south, night after night in the cinema – you could still smoke then and he sat alone – watching thrillers, cop chases, American love stories, wondering if that could be him.

What is it like to do a chase scene?

How would it feel to play a spy?

It was like a promise.

You can be anything.

Then the year turned. First came the discharge papers, then his suitcases loaded onto the train and in little under a day he was back. Back in the limestone village, under the ridge, the village that shone white in the sun. Back to his mother and father and back to the vineyards, back to each *terroir*, each different with their soils or how the wind fluttered through them on a summer's day. And it began again.

Like a great wheel turning.

He applied for nothing. He did nothing.

He went back to the tool shed. Back to his father.

'And I did what I'd always done.'

Another harvest came, they gathered in the grapes, they sang the songs they always sang. And then the year began again: first the frosts came and then came the rains and they clipped the vines. The leaves went green and the grapes came. Then slowly they went through the fields; until they knew the time had come to gather them in. And, like every year, the pickers came. Old people, who loved wine. Young people, students, looking for a little job. People, from the towns, from the village itself sometimes, who took anything that came to hand. They all came to Meursault.

And he got to know them, like he did every year. The summer sun bright on their necks. They would eat together – they fed them, they always did – and in the gloom of the cabins they stayed in he found himself talking to someone. His name was François.

He was studying classical song. And one evening, Jean-Marc found himself talking to him, sharing confidences with him in that innocent, easy way you do when you're young.

'And what he said touched me deeply.'

François listened.

He told him about the routine.

He told him about the long months of prep. About how quiet the village got in the winter, when it was just them, the families who lived here, in the drizzle and the mist and the same corks and the same bottles. Like he was always reading the same novel. How he could see every year of the rest of his life here, all more or less the same.

'How there was nowhere I could tell my own story.'

Jean-Marc stopped talking.

François listened.

Then he leant in, making Jean-Marc look at him, looking at him like he had something very urgent to say.

'He said, *If you want to do theatre you have to do it right away.* And then he added . . . *If you don't do it right away you will never do it.*'

The words hung there for a moment. Heavy.

He was right. That was what pulled the trigger.

You have someone in your life like François.

You met them on a train and they told you to break up. You talked to them online and they told you to quit your job.

Maybe you listened. Or perhaps not.

'I listened to him. I listened to François.'

Then a few days later François was gone. The harvest, the party with all the singing they had on the last night, the goodbyes in the morning. It was all wrapped up. It wasn't a world where you asked for numbers.

He never spoke to him again.

A few days later he told them at breakfast.

'I'm leaving the village. I'm going to become an actor.'

Nothing happened immediately. He was still in the vineyards. He was still in the fields. He was still not there, the big city where everything that he'd ever wanted seemed to happen. And even when he got to Paris – a year later – it didn't happen immediately. One year. Then two years. They were miserable, table-waiting years.

He sold flowers in the market, he taught French to make ends meet.

'But the conservatory was always in my head.'

Until finally, it worked.

The one shot he had to be an actor.

'I was admitted to the national drama school.'

The letters came confirming his place.

It was that autumn Paris really began. It was all swirling fast and through him. The lectures, the classes, the artists, the tiny studio on Rue de Turenne. Through the pale city where each day looked different in a way he couldn't quite explain.

'That autumn I felt my life there really began.'

He had listened to François. He had done it. He was in.

'This whole world that I didn't know.'

And there a professor, Michel, began to guide him.

'His grave and precise voice still resonates in my ears.'

They would be in rehearsals – *not like that, stop, start over* – and slowly he felt himself winning his trust, learning something, learning to be someone else.

'I felt like I was learning from a man who cared nothing more than to help his young actors, not only find themselves on the stage, but to weave their own special relationships with the great plays they practised.

You could be your own Antigone.

Your own Tartuffe.

'Sometimes he invited me to lunch and I think he picked up on some guilt that still clung to me about leaving the family domaine. I sometimes spoke to him about wine, about Meursault, but he didn't want to hear about that. For him it was clear. I had to focus on being an actor. Exclusively.'

And that's what he did. He even felt his father was proud of him – not that he told Jean-Marc, of course – but he'd told his wine-making buddies and they let him know. And now there he was sitting awkwardly at the back of their end-of-year show.

Clapping and smiling at the end.

And then it began to feel far. That meanwhile in the village, the days went on, his father went on, like all the winters before: the work in the cellar he liked to do when the days were short; the work in the fields when slowly, slowly, plant by plant, he clipped the vines; muttering to himself and to them. It all went on. And a year passed.

Then his mother phoned him.

Jean-Marc . . .

Her voice was shaking. That way you already know something is wrong.

That voice anyone would know and everyone has heard.

We were at the hospital. It happened earlier . . . Papa was working and then he had this appalling pain in his stomach.

It just wouldn't stop.

And she spoke faster.

The doctor saw him. He said it's cancer, t-t-hat ...

And she paused, stammering.

... he said he's only got a few months to live.

Then she was only sobbing.

I'm coming, he said. *I'm coming.*

His head spinning, his voice trembling.

I'll get the first train tomorrow.

After that call he sat there for a moment.

He looked out of the window on Rue de Turenne – so elegant, so everything he'd ever wanted – and he could only think.

I've only just got here.

And voilà, *it's now this.*

You hear the news and it's like a Copernican revolution.

You had something at the centre. Now it's a dying sun. You had someone you felt would be there for ever. Now they're almost gone.

That night Jean-Marc smoked.

Watching the traffic. Waiting for it to steady in his head.

You never forget these days of your life. You watch them grow enormous in memory; whilst thousands of days, they disappear.

The streets in Paris empty when it rains.

Like everybody was only pretending to be busy. Jean-Marc rushed for the first train. The one that leaves for Burgundy from the Gare de Lyon: the one that flashes through forests, across dark landscapes; where you sometimes feel like you are going back in time. To another France – a France, a Europe – that refuses to change.

They didn't have to say a word when he arrived for him to know. He would have to come back to help with the harvest. His father couldn't manage alone. And if the vines failed – the family failed.

'Of course I had to do it.'

'There was never even a question.'

And then he went back to Paris.

His eyes looking at her – the river, the monuments, the small *traiteurs* – like he was going to lose her. And then he went back to his great, grand, school on Rue du Conservatoire. Up the steps and up the stairs to the great, grand office of the school director. It was not the first time he'd asked for something. He was twenty-four, almost twenty-five; he'd already had to ask them for an exemption to get in, and now he needed this.

My father's dying.

Jean-Marc stood there, as the director squinted at him from behind the desk, trying to explain to him the thing that defined him. That he was from Burgundy and not only that he was from a wine family.

A domaine in Meursault.

'I stood there and I told him.'

I've worked with my father and I know how to turn the machine. And nobody else knows how to do it. He's sick.

It's too late to train someone to do it.

My mother, my sister can't do it.

The director listened. He nodded.

He moved some papers around. Then a pen.

And then he made a proposal.

Young man. You can spend three days in Paris and four days there.'

Our lectures are on Monday, Tuesday and Friday . . . so if you're here Monday, Tuesday and Wednesday, I'll let you spend the rest there.

Next week the commutes began. The dash to the station. The early mornings. On those trains more times than he could remember. If he was lucky – his head slumped on the window trying to catch some rest. Then the car. Then the village.

The same faces. And his face.

That of his father. The light slowly draining.

The spring came. Then the summer. The school year ended. Now he was spending every hour in the domaine. Doing what he had to do. What they had always done. What they had done for centuries. Men with the same name. Making their wine.

This time alone.

He was never not sweating. Nor his hands clean.

But it was like a switch had flicked inside.

'I couldn't put it off any more. I bought a little notebook and I went up to my father. He was bed-ridden . . . he couldn't walk any more.'

'And I sat beside him.'

He took a little pen.

Then page by page he began to scribble.

'Those were the days he told me what to do. How to manage the great harvest of '82. I wrote everything down . . . and I did everything he said. About our wine.'

Jean-Marc sat by his bedside.

He would close the book as his father dozed, now it had been passed to him, and he would ask himself: *How do I know so much already? How do I know, exactly, how to run the vats? Or fix the barrels?*

Jean-Marc wasn't sure how he'd learnt it. It was like he'd learnt it just watching and without ever wanting to know. Through a habit. Through osmosis. And now here he was in one go. Learning the rest.

'I was obliged. There was no choice.'

The seasons turned. The leaves fell. The harvest was over. He went up and told his father at his bedside that it was done. Everything was fermenting. The village grew empty. Silent. The vines were bare.

'I started to go back and forth to my classes in Paris again.'

He died on 1 November 1982.

'I was here when he died. He died at home.'

'He was fifty-three years old. My mother was fifty-two years old. My sister was thirty . . . and I was twenty-six years old.'

Everything went as it was supposed to.

The coffin was readied. But it did not go far. The family domaine came to an end at the cemetery gates where a jumble of stones and crosses looked out into the vines. The ceremony went as expected.

And everyone was there.

The funeral came and went. Then, afterwards, there was the succession to be occupied with. There was a big meeting at the domaine; the first big one without his father. They were all there apart from him: his mother, his sister, the solicitor, the specialist accountant.

'And sooner or later . . . all eyes turned on me.'

'When the question came up, who's taking over the domaine?'

That was when he said it again.

'I said no.'

They kept looking at him.

I've started something at drama school, he said.

And I want to finish it. I've gone to Paris for good.

They had asked. But on some level they expected the answer.

'We hired Ted, an American, over the phone, we had heard really great things about, to run the domaine.'

That was how they still did it back then.

And Jean-Marc tried to put it behind him: the cutting, the treatments, the pressing, the fermentation, whether the temperature was right in the cellar. No, it wasn't his problem any more. It was the managers. Good people. Quality people.

First the American; then his cousin Frank.

Jean-Marc left again.

He got the train at Beaune and then the train from Dijon. He came back to Paris. To the city and the noise and this world where nobody thinks about where anything comes from or the people behind what they drink. To his tiny apartment on the Rue de Turenne and the women who would wake up with him there. And then he threw himself into the theatre, into the school, into the night.

'I drowned myself in theatre.'

Tartuffe. As You Like It. He shot a film in Switzerland. His hours were suddenly filled. He was on stage next to Gerard Depardieu. He grew used to cameras turning, to the sounds they make. To having an agent, to waiting hours crouched by the phone, replaying old messages, waiting for new roles.

'I didn't look back. I didn't want to look back.'

You never know what's going to happen.

You tell yourself you do. You don't really. You too have one dizzying moment that shaped the rest. Without which everything would be so different. You don't have to think long to find them.

Jean-Marc got a call. It was six years later.

It was Frank, his cousin. He'd been managing the domaine. He'd got a job offer, he said; it was a very good job. He wanted it. The domaine was in Puligny-Montrachet. He was going to leave quickly. No questions asked.

'My mother called me.'

'We had no idea what to do. She came up to Paris and we found ourselves asking . . . *What are we going to do?*'

You don't see this far from the game. But it's very simple when you make wine. When the person who signs the bottle changes every few years; something goes. The coherence. The identity. Commercially something fades. Then the taste.

Your wine slides. Then your family.

What are we going to do?

They talked for hours. And then for days.

'And then I talked to my sister . . . over and over.'

That was when it came down. Not a mania; not a panic. Something deeper. He couldn't sleep. One week; two weeks. He crossed Paris. He walked backwards and forwards across the city, along the empty *quais* along the Seine; under gilt street lamps with glowing orbs of light; until the crowds had faded, until everyone had gone home. He lay there at night, his heart racing, his memories flashing, fading; thoughts, coming and going.

'I wrote. I wrote a lot.'

Notebooks filled up by the side of the bed.

'I saw maybe ten people who were very important to me.'

'Friends. People in theatre. Doctors. This thing was eating me, eating me . . . and they all told me the same thing. *Jean-Marc . . . you have to go back. Jean-Marc . . . you have to leave Paris. You have to be in Meursault.*'

That was when he realized it had all been coming up.

It had been brewing. Growing. Bubbling up for years.

'And that was when I understood that . . .'

'I had never digested the death of my father. That it had run away from it. I had thrown myself into activity . . . plays, roles, films. But you can never escape your grief. You can run away from it. You can delay it. But it will always catch up with you.'

That was what was happening.

He could now see it. It was all still unspooling.

'I thought I was constantly ill. I thought I had cancer. I thought things were wrong. I thought I was sick like him. And now I realize, unconsciously, my desire to make wine had been rising. It had been building inside me all these years. To go back . . . to confront myself, to my past, to my father, to prove something to myself. That was then I made up my mind.'

—

His first vintage was 1989.

He moved that February and before he did he made a promise to himself that he would never stop acting. That if jobs came he would take them. That was what he told his mother and sister. That, and that he was coming back for himself. He kept the flat in Paris. Whenever the phone rang in Paris, it would ring in Meursault. Whenever his agent had a meeting to offer him the next day the answer was – *Of course.*

'I never told my agent, not at the beginning, not for years.'

'I told very few people. I acted like I was still in Paris.'

He wanted to keep one foot in each world.

'Whenever I thought of my father I thought of work.'

'Because I'd seen him work so much.'

The cycle set in. The vines were trimmed. The barrels set. The routines sank in. The clients came. The wine merchants came. And, sometimes, the neighbours came. It was a serious thing in Burgundy: things were never just eaten here. The tables would be set out. The glasses would be arranged. The tastings would begin. Everything measured. Exchanged.

'But it felt odd. Because for years . . . I was offering them a wine I hadn't made.'

The wine his father had made.

That the managers had made.

'It felt awkward . . . *It felt odd.*'

'Until the day came it was mine.'

The wines that he had made not only with what he'd learnt from the family and from the village. The wines that he'd made with also what he'd learnt in the theatre. The wines he'd made with the words of Jacques, who'd been his professor, ringing in his ears.

'To say more, show less.'

The taste changing, until it wasn't the old classical, round flavour, which people expected in Meursault. It was sharper: in pursuit of more minerality and balance.

'The art of almost nothing.'

This is what he brought to the tastings.

The palates of the old vintners. And the people who came to the cellar.

That was when he missed his father the most. Not as a father.

But as a winemaker and taster and carrier of all the family heritage. Because there is something unique that happens when winemakers taste their wines; something electric, something powerful when men and women who do nothing but work this sense of taste and smell, circle a bottle; something you can see on their faces, in their eyes, with every sip.

'The way it can open your head.'

'The way it creates an arrow right between you. It's like nothing else.'

'But my father never got to taste my wine.'

'The wine full of everything I'd learnt in Meursault and outside.'

You know this when you work in wine. It doesn't matter who you are. All young winemakers are the same. They really are. Hunched over your wine. Impatient. That whole year, paranoid how it will taste. And when you do, is it good? Are you imagining things?

That hint, that note?

The only moment you know is at the tastings.

The tension is immense.

The moment exhilarating, crushing.

And that moment had come for him.

'For years I did nothing special. I did a copy-paste of what I saw my father doing. Then, slowly, I started to change. Add a bit here and there. But there was one moment . . . I knew where my palate wanted to go.'

They call them *courtiers* in Burgundy. They always have. The buyers for the big holdings and the wine merchants in Beaune. There was one man who came every year. He could see him now: very small, bald, one of the *courtiers* in the old style. He'd been coming every year, since . . . in fact Jean-Marc couldn't remember him not coming. Every year he came with a *tastevin*; they don't use them any more. But back then he still used one; one of those small shallow cups, with a thumb handle. The kind they had used in Burgundy since the Middle Ages to taste the wine, to smell the wine, to judge it, in those dark cellars. Jean-Marc would never forget the first year he offered his own wine. Not his father's, not the managers', his own.

Jean-Marc watched him lift it and draw in a deep smell. Then taste it, like a *courtier*, flicking it round his tongue. Then he paused.

Thinking. Before spitting it out.

It's good, he said.

It's very, very good . . . It's really your own.

The relief. The thrill. It began to shine through him.

Merci, he said. *Merci bien.*

Like he'd told his own story.

13 STORKOW

The light is grey in Germany in the winter.

It cracks through the blind into the dark room as he lies there. It's minutes before his alarm. He feels something. It's a knot in the pit of his stomach. Then it beeps. It's hard. It's sharp. No matter how many times it still startles. He thumbs it off quickly before it wakes her up. She's sleeping. He wants her to sleep, to be peaceful. And he leaves the bedroom dark.

It's a hot shower. There he loses the last fragments of his dreams. Moments, he's not sure from what. Then it's all gone. He shaves. He knows his face and where he's getting older in it. He squints: *Is this right for thirty-one?*

Dark circles and the first few lines.

He steps back from the mirror. It's almost time. He's in the kitchen. It's black coffee and sugar. Out of nowhere he thinks of his mother. Then, grab it – phone, coat, keys – he's out of the flat, he's bounding down the stairs and outside. A shock of cold. He looks back: she still isn't up. There's the blind in the window.

Will she get up today? Will she get up?

Aboud blinks. The light is pale. Hard morning light and something about it stings. It takes the colours out of the field at the edge of the estate. They're in the last block in town. And there's his van: staring into this thick grassy scrub. It's feels like it might suddenly rain. Quickly, he's in the van. It's those same car smells: crisps, petrol, something stale but he's not sure what. Inside his head: should I text her – *I love you.*

He can't worry. He has to focus now.

Then he switches on the app.

It loads up. It won't stop now till it's over.

Hello from Amazon. And it begins to trill.

Scroll and press: it's his route, it's his packages, it's his day. All planned out. Swipe through; it's now monitoring the route. If you don't do what it says – *Take the BAB 10 towards Potsdam* – they can start calling you.

What are you doing?

Why are you not on the preferred route?

Aboud pulls out of the estate. He turns the bend. The small town in Germany where he's ended up seems quiet, quieter than usual, even though it's always quiet. It's been a few years now. He can speak the language at B1 elementary level but it makes him tired. There's the school where they taught him German. There's the kebab shop where he worked for a year and he realized he'd never be a dentist. There's the church where they gave out food and clothes for the refugees.

He's on the motorway slip road. Then he switches on the Koran. It's chanting. It's rising and falling. It's a part that he knows. He feels calm.

He does this every day. It soothes him as he merges onto the autobahn. He doesn't pray. *I'm almost there*, he thinks. *It's the first petrol station. It's my second coffee.*

It's a routine and he sticks to it. Black coffee and sugar before the depot. Sometimes he twirls the plastic stirrers and thinks of Syria. He's back in the van. He wonders if she'll have a good day. Then it hits him. *I'm going to be late*, he thinks. The app flashes.

It's traffic. It shouldn't be at this hour. He's slowing down.

It's there. It's digging into him. It's stress.

It's at moments like this he remembers how amazing it was when Covid began. *Nobody knows it*, he thinks, because nobody cares what they think. *But it was beautiful what happened that March.* There were three or four months when the BAB 10 was empty. He felt like he was flying down it. There were weeks on end where there would be – *what, twenty, thirty* – packages a day. He'd be done by lunch.

And they'd cancelled all the pointless briefings.

It was not something the customers would ever understand.

He begins to see the signs for Berlin.

It's strange, he thinks. *It's not really like I imagined it. It's not a German city, really, any more. It's full of everyone. It's full of Turks, it's full of Poles, it's full of Arabs. And it's full of crime. At work you can see* it clearly. It's the Germans at the top, you can barely see them, they're behind computers. Then the Western Europeans, the ones who think they are their equals. Then the Turks, they own so much here. Then the Eastern Europeans. Then the Asians. Then the refugees: Arabs, Africans, all of them at the bottom.

That's what he sees at the fulfilment centre.

The Germans don't do this kind of work, that's what he thinks. *Only the people they can exploit like Syrians or Serbians and that kind of thing.* That's not the only thing he has realized. There's a whole layer between him and Amazon. The *Unternehmen*. These are the contractor kings. They're almost all Turks and those are the guys he sees when he pulls up outside the fulfilment centre. They're all mafia. He knows it. He can smell it off them. They're in their Hugo Boss and their Mercedes. They're playing with the car keys as they pay for their petrol. They've got these haircuts and this look in their eyes he recognizes.

They're all liars, the Unternehmen, he thinks, squinting at them

They lie to each other. They lie to Amazon. And they lie to drivers like him.

Of course he's working black-market. That's what a lot of them do. The *Unternehmen* tell Amazon it's a part-time job. The *Unternehmen* run it out so it's really a full-time job. The difference? It's paid in cash. But the benefits, the bonuses, the insurance – they've got none of that – like the boys Amazon has on full time in their data flows.

The van crawls slowly. He'll be filled up soon. Packages for Berlin and Brandenburg. A normal day: fifty to sixty stops. A busy day: seventy to a hundred stops. His mind wanders. He has to be careful today. He has to focus. He can't let anything distract him again. He can't afford another accident.

They're all the same. The black-market drivers live in fear of a bump or a scratch. Scuff an Audi, dent a Porsche, it's all on you. It happened to him on the slip road: there was a hit, they're on the hard shoulder, the guy's screaming about his paintwork. That's how it began: then half his salary's gone for the month when the claims comes in. The *Unternehmen* don't cover it. It makes his skin pucker just to think about it.

The packages are being loaded now. Fifty of them. A pretty good day. *I wouldn't be working in the black*, he thinks, *if it wasn't for the rules.* And the rules wouldn't matter if this hadn't happened to his wife. Earn over a certain level and they take her benefits away. Earn below: they keep them. They don't seem to understand this. But they've pushed him into this, driving paranoid of a scratch into West Berlin.

It's hard to know where the suburbs end and the city begins as he drives in. The houses, the trees, the gardens: it's so green and un-urban. It's here that silly stuff happens. Like that time he rang the buzzer and got bitten by a small dog. There was a little girl standing there – she'd answered the door – and when she asked him, *Did he bite you?* she burst into tears. It properly sank its teeth into him. Or stupid stuff like when he'd buzzed and buzzed on a big white house but he heard the owner round the back. That's when he stepped into the side garden, to wave at them, but the hobbling old man came screaming – *screaming* – at him, until his children ran to him saying, *He's deaf, he's deaf, I'm so sorry, he doesn't know what he's saying.*

Forty-one stops. The app toggles. The line turns. He's passing Charlottenburg. He can see the River Spree. The parks open up dense and thick. But he hardly notices them because the app has the route going red; it's flagging traffic, its time to destination has shot up from seven to eighteen minutes and it makes him sweat. *Shit.* It shouldn't be this jammed on Kurfürstenstraße at this hour. He's grinding his teeth. It's at moments like this everything feels stressful. The app's telling him to stop. It's the middle of Berlin. There are bikes and couriers. He's got to be careful: one moment of inattention and he could send someone flying. He's sweating. He's either too hot or too cold in his work clothes. *Fuck it.* He's just gonna have to leave the van with the light blinking – there's nowhere to park.

Twenty-four. Where's twenty-four?

Shit it's an apartment block.

He can't just leave the package in the hall: he's got to take it to the door.

He's pressing the buzzer. *Buzz. Buzz.*

They're not answering. Finally a long – *Buzzzz.*

The door clicks open. He ignores them hooting at his van.

There's no elevator. He's out of breath with this tiny box. *No, this is the wrong floor. No, actually, it was the right one. Fuck it. Where is 4B?*

Is this it? Yes, OK, time to knock.

Coming, he hears.

He takes his time. *What the hell is it in this tiny box that he couldn't get it himself?*

Danke schön.

Bitte, he says.

He hardly sees them. They hardly see him. The door clicks in his face. Outside, it's not good.

You can't park here, a driver is yelling. He nods.

The app is pinging. He's so stressed he can feel it in his heart.

It's at moments like this he gets flashbacks.

The light dances on the windscreen.

He's in Turkey. He's alone. His wife will come on the next boat. He can see the face of the smuggler. *Fifteen minutes,* he says. That's how long it takes to reach Greece. *No, no,* he says, *you don't need a life jacket.* It's night now. The patrols have stopped. And they're on the beach. They're all Syrians from Latakia. And this is their chance. There are about fifteen of them: there are women and children and cousins of his on this boat. There are too many of them, really, to be out here at night. It's a quick motor. He can feel them moving. The rocks and the sand pull away.

Then he begins to feel it, the water.

No, it can't be. It's coming in. He doesn't want it to be true. He wants it to be otherwise. But they're screaming now. The women and the children. Now the men. *No,* it can't be. It's actually sinking. It's been ten minutes. Nowhere close, but too far from land. The smuggler, he's distraught too, he's telling them to jump. *Don't try and swim,* he shouts. That's what the men, the ones who also know, are shouting as they leap, as they go down.

Lie still, lie on your back.

We need to keep our energy until they can get us.

The splashing water. The wails in between. The children: it cuts right into him as he jumps. The water, it's so cold it makes him shiver and gasp. There's shouting at first. Then there's a horrible sound when the motor goes down.

On his back, his whole face turned up towards the night.

This is really happening. The worst is really here. There's no signal this far out. Their phones are gone or sodden. There's only God but He's not speaking to them. The water's black and purple and it pulls at them, it's freezing them, like it wants them to sink. It's an hour they've been there. The children are quieter. The waters are louder. It's two hours. It's three. There's nothing. There's no light. There's nobody coming.

There are two guys next to him. He can hear them panicking. Talking to themselves. Are those prayers they are muttering? *Aboud.* They are not all together any more. *Aboud, look.* There's a vulture. It's circling over them. Those huge wings. He's looking at them. He's hungry. And that's when you realize. He's waiting for them to die.

The water is louder. The waves are less settled. Then the vulture swoops. He wants to jump up to go after him. But he's got no idea where he's gone. Maybe they've lost someone.

The little girls, he shudders. *The little boys.*

But he can't hear them. It's too loud, the waves.

Aboud, Aboud.

Those guys are close to him again.

We've got to swim. We're going to die here. We're going to drown.

There's land, they can see. They think they can see it. The three of them swim. They swim until they're out of breath. Until they're hoarse. Until they can go no further. But it's got no closer, like it was a mirage. He can't bear it. He's hurting. He can't go on.

He pulls himself over onto his back and breathes.

There's nothing in the night above him.

There's something wrong. He can't move his legs. It's like they're frozen. It's like he's paralysed. Like the nightmares he's sometimes had. It's in his arms now. They're like ice. He can only half move his hands.

Aboud, Aboud, they are shouting.

We've got to go on.

But he can't explain.

He can't tell them about his legs. He can hardly even speak.

Leave me, he yells back or tries to.

I can't go on.

I can't go on.

He sees Syria. He sees Latakia. He sees how it was before the war. He sees his mother. He sees his father. He sees *her*. He wants to tell her how much he loves her. How he's dying but it was all worth it – his life for her.

He speaks to God and he tells Him what He wants to hear.

That there is only Him and his Messenger.

Then he lets go and he loosens.

Aboud, Aboud.

They're shouting but he can hardly hear them.

Laila. He only sees her. When they met. When they kissed.

They never had a baby.

Aboud, Aboud.

There's a light. There's a boat.

He's being pulled in. They're Turks.

There's a flashlight at his face. Police.

Merhaba, Merhaba.

They're trying to talk to him.

Salaam Aleikum.

They're almost all there on the boat.

Have you seen this man? This man Yusuf?

They're asking about this man. Again and again have you seen him. It's his first cousin. But his memory's gone. He can't remember who he is.

No, no.

I don't know . . . Yusuf.

He's shaking under this metallic blanket.

I don't know him.

Laila. He's only thinking of her.

I'll see her. I'll see her again.

The sun is on the windscreen.

It's only for a second or two that he sees bits of this in the van. He's too busy judging the lights. Following the route. Trying to focus.

She's not adjusting. He keeps worrying.

It's not working for her here. It's like she can't recover.

She calls him. Every time she does, his heart clamps up.

It was only a few weeks ago she called him from outside the

driving school. They've been trying. She's pregnant. And that's making things worse. *I'm going to abort it, I'm going to abort it,* she was shrieking down the phone. *I can't have a baby in this country that treats me like shit because I'm a refugee.*

They'd kicked her off the course, for some reason.

But she was spiralling: why hardly mattered.

I can't have it. I can't have it.

This time it's something else. He stops the van. He tells her it's OK. That the baby will be OK. That it's normal to feel sick at this point in the trimester. He talked her off the ledge the other day and now she's having it.

The app chimes.

You're wasting time, that means. *Why have you stopped?*

They'll be calling you soon. He hangs up. Turns right, then left. He's heading south. Past Tempelhof.

She's not been well since they got here.

It was hardly a plan to come to Berlin. They arrived in Mannheim at first, and there was a cousin of hers here, so that seemed to settle that. The refugee centre referred them to the migration Ausländerburo, which referred them to the settlement scheme, which sent them to Storkow for absorption. But it's not Berlin. It's Brandenburg. It's an hour outside in the countryside where everyone's German – OK, maybe one or two Turks at the kebab shop – where everything's silent and every window shuttered after dark.

She hates it. Everything about it. She hates the quiet, she hates the cold, the way they look at her even when they're handing out clothes – *Willkommenskultur.* It pushed her to tears when the host mother – they slept with a German family at first – asked if she knew what the toilet was, or how to flush it, like she was a Bedouin. It happened again when someone in the church group that was always giving her food said Aboud shouldn't go to mosque – there were all kinds of terrorists there.

She was fragile. It's made her brittle, he thinks.

Leaving Syria. Coming to this. To this town where she knows nobody where there's nothing for her to do. She's like a plant, he thinks, *without light.*

It's been years now she's been in this depression. On this medication.

It's been years and it's not getting any better.

The arrow wants south now. *Why can't it stick straight?*

They're in Zehlendorf.

There are the shisha bars where the mafia clans hang out in. You can see the Palestinians, the very dangerous ones, in the Moncler puffers. They're a little darker than Syrians, he thinks, with smaller eyes. Then the Turks, like the *Unternehmen*. There's so much crime in Berlin, he thinks. But that's how the Germans like it: they don't want to know it's happening.

That's it. He knows that shisha bar.

That's where forty black drivers, like him, had to surround that Iranian *Unternehmer* who wasn't paying them. *No, no, next week, you'll see it,* he'd kept telling them, with the pipe half in his mouth. They hadn't been paid in months. That's when one of them gasped – *the clans, the clans* – we have to go see them. The black drivers, mostly Syrians, went to one of the Arab gangs, at one of the cafes, their own cafes, where they hung out in Neukölln and explained the situation.

A few days later they surrounded that Iranian *Unternehmer* at his little table. He dropped his pipe and they told him – *We're not going until you get our wages.* The Iranian froze. He could see the mafia hovering in the back in the Moncler puffers. He knew what it meant – the forty of them there – and what back up they had. The *Unternehmer* was begging them now – *Just a few more hours, just a few more hours.*

They laughed about it, the other drivers.

That was quite the day.

Fifteen packages left.

Direction Kreuzberg. The app is trilling.

He's been separated from the route by a mistake. But there's no way to tell Amazon. They'll be calling him if he can't re-join. At moments like these – it's stress. It pulses behind his eyes. The traffic is blocked. Somebody's hooting. He can't understand what the app is telling him and his eyes are getting heavy. It's been hours already. He opens the window for air. It's at moments like these he wants to abandon the van here. To just leave it. And walk out. Leaving them beeping at it and the app pinging and the *Unternehmer* screaming. Like the Pole who wasn't paid and drove his van to where he came from – texting his *Unternehmer* – if he wanted it he'd have to come and get it.

Karl-Marx-Straße.

He hates East Berlin. He hates the huge buildings and these huge corridors and these neighbours who refuse to take packages.

No, I don't know him.

Danke schön.

Bitte.

The door shuts in his face.

Every time this happens it's his time they are taking. He's got to come back. He's got to do it today or tell the app and do it tomorrow. Those corridors are so dimly lit. He feels like he's walking for miles. He's aching by the time he's back in the van.

He presses the app.

Delivery failed.

Three packages remaining.

Let's hope it's not another three buildings.

It's getting cold. In a few weeks it will be even colder. It's on evenings like this he thinks of Syria. The sunset over the sea. The smell of fish barbecue on the beach. The bright coloured lights they hang over restaurants and cafés. The sounds of children playing.

Tour completed.

He stops. He breathes.

He's on his time now and the first thing he does every day is he calls her. She answers quickly. He'd be worried if she answered slowly.

Habibti, I love you.

That's what he tells her every day.

It happened after they got here. He didn't understand what it was at first. What was hurting her. Why she couldn't get out of bed. Why she went silent for hours.

Then cried herself to sleep.

It was a very serious depression. The doctor had told them it would require medication and it would require time. *These things are not easy*, he said. *They can be latent or they can be provoked by the kind of things you've gone through.*

This is why she can't work. Every few days she Zooms with a psychiatrist in Syria and every day she tells him she wants to go

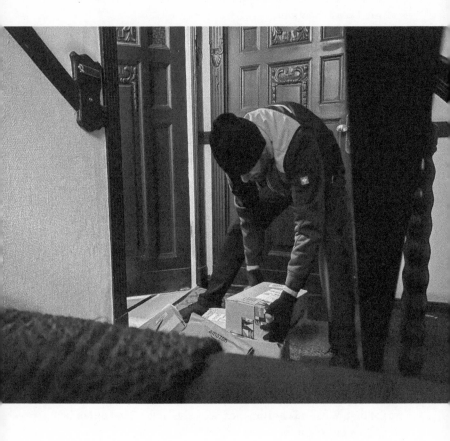

home, she wants to go back to the Middle East, to Turkey where her sister is, or even to Dubai.

He asks her about her sessions and she tells him. There's this nightmare she's having again and again. That's she's on the plane, that she's in the airport, that she can't fly, that they're pulling her off. *It's trauma*, the psychiatrist told her. It's deep trauma from when immigration threw her out of the airport the first time she tried to fly in Greece. They took one look at her and knew it was a fake passport.

Then there's this nightmare that he's dead, that he never came back, that he drowned that night in the water, that she's all alone.

That's what she tells him.

I'll be home in about an hour and half, he says.

I love you, habibti.

Then he drives to Hermannplatz. It's a filthy place and he hates it. *Why are the junkies and the dealers left like this in Berlin? It would never happen in Dubai,* he thinks, *or a country like that where they keep order.*

He picks up dinner at the Arabic supermarket.

Kibbeh. Pitta. Manaqish.

There are sometimes people he recognizes here from Latakia, from the camps, from the Balkan route north. They didn't have enough when they reached Greece for them both to fly on a fake passport. The money in his pockets had disintegrated in the water into the tiniest bits of paper. Hundreds of dollars, gone, that night he almost drowned. They were running out of time. Everybody knew the border was about to close.

She would fly, they decided. He would walk.

It all passed in a blur. The mountains. The nights with the smugglers. The days trudging by the side of the road. The last few days it was almost a stampede. The borders, they all knew, were closing on the fifteenth. That was the day Germany had said it was enough. He could hardly sleep. Every step, he forced himself to do it. If he didn't make it he would be stuck in Hungary or Austria or somewhere worse.

And Laila would be there – alone.

That last night, his body so stiff and his feet so sore, they found a group of journalists on the road, who filmed them into Germany.

Gawking at him. Trying to catch him at his lowest. He was relieved to see them snapping his ruined face. Nobody would do a thing, no one would beat them, or turn them away with them watching.

Aboud arrived hours before the border closed.

He puts his shopping bag in the van and pulls out to leave.

There's the mosque. It was supposed to be the happiest day of his life, he thought. They had only been in Berlin a few days when they decided to get married. They came here, to this mosque full of Turks, with her cousin. The one who had said to come here. But they didn't know anyone else so when the imam asked for a second witness they had to pick someone they didn't know – he couldn't even remember his full name – from the crowd there for the prayers. It was just the four of them. Aboud. Laila. Her cousin and this total stranger who looked awkward being there.

They did nothing afterwards. They didn't celebrate. They went back home that night and she cried. For hours, she was crying, because this wasn't how it was supposed to be.

Aboud likes to think about how he first saw Laila.

How he saw her: her face, her hair, her beauty and how he knew he was in love. They were so much younger. He'd finished school the year before, but he'd seen her in the final class. He'd spotted her when he went to the sandwich shop. It got hold of him, like nothing had ever got hold of him, that he had to speak to her. That he had to find some way. He already knew about her: her name, her status, her father – not just any old doctor, but a doctor in Latakia who had studied in New York.

Aboud could think of nothing else. He waited for her class to break and watch them milling around the sandwich shop, for it to open. *Yes*, that was it, he'd ask the owner if he could work there, just to have the chance to speak to her. That's how they met. That's what he remembers. As he drives to Storkow.

And it fills him, that smile.

There is less traffic at this time, as he sets out of Berlin. It's before the rush hour but it's over, his shift. It's no longer bothering him, the app, his mind can finally wander. The city falls away. He's on the A113 and he begins to dream. He's got a friend in Dubai.

He's in bathroom fittings. He's like his brother: he'd do anything for him. He's telling him to come.

Glass skyscrapers, glinting in the sun. The beach. Arabic all around him.

She'd be happy there. She'd be happy with the baby.

The slip road. Past the kebab shop. Storkow again. The roundabout. The afternoon quiet. The estate. His heart flutters. They're there when he parks the van. There in the field. The deer that come every evening to the edge of the block. The mother and the little ones. Their fur a ruddy brown. Aboud goes very quiet and tries to get a picture.

But they're suddenly gone.

He looks up. The blind's open. She's up.

Sometimes he comes upstairs after work and she hasn't left the bed all day. When it's bad she'll hardly say anything at all. He'll have to open the blinds. He'll have to be there, really be there. He's exhausted. It's like he's left work but he's come home to another job. It's all right today. It's not too bad. She isn't crying. She's just quiet. He's so drained from Berlin, he lies down on the sofa and within a few minutes – it's like something's pulling him down – he's asleep in his clothes. It's only a moment, or maybe a minute, or fifteen minutes, but he feels worse afterwards, like he's groggy, like he needs a glass of water.

On nights when she's too depressed, he cooks. But normally she does. It's cheap stuff, from the Arabic supermarket, but it makes him think of home. Syria. It would have been so much easier if this had never happened. He'd have kept his job at the port. He'd be working in an office. Working in a suit. He'd not be on the regime's wanted list, meaning he can now never go back. Instead he's here in Storkow, watching the football, trying to remember what season that player had and his team. Trying to care.

Sometimes she's so depressed she doesn't speak when she eats. She can be silent for a long time and if he says the wrong thing she implodes in tears. He doesn't know what to say or what to do some nights. He just eats and tries to get through it.

It's so difficult.

—

She paints most of the day.

She won't show him what she's been doing.

Canvases of severed roots, of boats, of figures trying to reach another shore. The paint is dark and anguished. The therapists said it was a good idea. He wants to believe she can do it. That she can be a painter people recognize. He encouraged her to do this scheme he saw in Berlin for 'refugee artists'. It seemed like a fantastic idea. They accepted her. They exhibited her. He drove the canvases from Storkow in his van. At the event she was nervous and held his hand. He knew even then it wasn't going well. The drive back was bad. When they finally got in she became hysterical, she started attacking the paintings, the whole thing had made her feel like a circus animal – a 'refugee artist' – for them to gawp at in Kreuzberg.

She's so alone. When she's not on WhatsApp with her sister. She knows nobody. She doesn't want to know anyone here. She says she's heard them saying bad stuff about Islam. She just doesn't think she can do it alone: a baby – this far away. His friends say they should move to Berlin. *But there's no point*, he thinks. He knows it's different there: there are Arabs, there are shops, centres she could go to. But it's not about that. *It won't make any difference*, he knows, if they do that.

He's watching the news.

He's not vaccinated. He's not sure about it.

He doesn't understand it very well. But some people say it might be dangerous. She doesn't want to get it now she's pregnant.

It's bedtime.

He's close to her. He can feel it.

There's a baby in there. It's everything he ever wanted. It's a feeling he's never known before. It's like vertigo, knowing how much he loves them, how lifeless he would be if he lost them. He sleeps. He dreams.

She's screaming. It happens every night.

She's sobbing. She's shaking from nightmares.

He's dead. It's the airport. They won't let her fly.

Hold me, she says. He does, until morning.

The light is showing. It's another day.

14 TBILISI

It was one of those evenings when Nino came home worrying about the orchestra. That the pianist wasn't good enough. That they were missing violins. That after all the work she'd put in at the conservatory the music still didn't carry her somewhere. They just weren't *there*. It was one of those evenings that Nino got home and tried to forget about it.

There was her daughter, her beautiful daughter, making tea.

She's my whole world, she thought.

It had been years since her husband died.

For years it had been just the two of them.

In this small flat, almost filled by the grand piano. Their whole crooked city of pompous marble, wild dog alleys and wooden balconies jumbled outside.

Sometimes, Irina didn't want to talk. She had plans. Academics to meet, seminars to organise. A life built around flaking stucco avenues. Purpose found in echoing lecture halls. She was busy. But this was one of the times she stopped. It was then she told Nino about Gogi. That she'd been seeing him.

Her mother's ears pricked up.

Curiosity, concern, a touch of relief.

Her daughter was almost thirty.

Nino's problems with the cellist were a long way away now.

It was always a surprise when Irina, who kept her distance, mentioned anyone.

It's not easy to find someone in Tbilisi, she'd kept telling her, for all of her twenties.

It's not like Paris or Moscow.

And now she was talking about someone.

He's a bit older, she said, *he's in his forties.*

He's an intellectual. He's studied abroad, at Harvard, even.

He had some job in the Ministry of Education.

Gogi was the nephew of her very first English teacher – *Mummy, don't you remember* – the one she had when she was very small. But that wasn't so important. What mattered, Nino thought, digesting this, was that she seemed to like him.

'She trusted this man, and within five months, they were married.'

Mummy, Gogi's lost his job.

That was the first she'd heard of it.

His great mission, setting the curriculum, was gone. He said he'd left it, of course. But neither of them believed that. They'd only been married a few months. He'd been full of promises about where they would live, about where they would go, of what he would achieve. But now he was in their flat, living there too. Waking up looking lost, unsure what to do with himself, this balding man, who held himself like a cross between a gentleman and a playboy, right down to the expensive cognac Nino saw him swill every evening.

'It was then this strange personality became very difficult.'

It started one of those evenings.

The scales and the trills, still running through her head from work.

They were both rushing, Nino and Irina, as tired as they were, to have everything ready for dinner. They knew he expected to eat properly. Nino's mind, as she chopped vegetables, was still back at the conservatory – *Professor, what did you mean by that?* Her daughter's, she could tell, as she stirred the pot, was still at her job at the university. They dashed to set the table. The great bourgeois sound of the orchestra on the stereo. One of the great performances, which she knew almost by heart.

That's when Gogi would sit down, having done nothing. The conversation, his conversation – the one he wanted to have – progressing nicely until someone disagreed. Then he would stop, like something had shot into his eyes, his tone suddenly rising – out of disagreement, into aggression, into anger, into a yell – until there was suddenly silence.

'Like *there's my point* and nothing else.'

Then came the monologues, like he wouldn't stop, like only he should be speaking at dinner. The table, his seminar, his voice all urgency to educate you, to make you learn. His mood swinging violently if there was the slightest hint someone wasn't paying attention.

'It didn't matter what the topic was.'

It could be about traffic circulation or Russia.

It could be his theories of making soup or history.

'He was always the same.'

It was those nights she went to bed worrying.

The strays, you could hear them barking in the street.

Then, louder now, she could make out their muffled arguing.

This isn't right. They shouldn't be like this . . . just a few months married.

The cars passing until she fell asleep.

You find yourself with your child in the kitchen.

You are confidante, counsellor, carer.

You both can and can't say what you really think.

You are close, but not quite, a friend.

These moments that she needed her, came more and more often. That confidence that came from Irina's degrees, from her English, her Russian, her German, sapped from her. Nino didn't need to hear that those outbursts – or those long arguments in the middle of the night – were upsetting her. She knew Irina was becoming someone she wasn't, anxious and worn down, in the questions she asked her – *Mummy, what am I supposed to do?*

She could see it in her face.

Her brown eyes had stopped smiling.

Nino tried to soothe her – *It must be losing his job*; to tell her they had to be as calm as possible. That they couldn't give him the slightest hint they were nervous or upset he was unemployed. That would only make it worse.

Not like that made it stop.

'It was like it was a necessity for him.'

'For us to say how handsome and intelligent he was.'

Things will get better, Nino told herself, as she left the conservatory every evening, leaving those rounded windows and pale yellow pillars, near the point where you could see the pine ridge that ran along the city, as if up into the mountains, so clearly.

Sadly, she thought, *there are a lot of men like this.*

In our part of the world.

Those moments of calm wouldn't follow her home.

They had been there, in the apartment, wrapped up, away from the city with all its troubles, where her daughter couldn't spend an evening without listening to classical music.

But the sonatas were now punctured by his eruptions.

The meals got worse. Finger-wagging, the man at the end of the table, snarling to get his point across, until she started to see him as the exact opposite of how he wanted to come across, like he was gripped by some sort of complex.

'That he hated himself and wanted us to treat him like a prince.'

It was exhausting her and it was exhausting Irina. She caught herself – once, or twice – feeling resentful as she opened the door knowing what was in there. That man, agitating her daughter. That angst, making Irina a different person.

'I felt like I was the one supporting her . . .'

'In this difficult situation that has happened because she wanted it.'

You worry differently about your child.

You worry completely. You worry helplessly.

It started with vomiting. Irina was pregnant. Then it didn't stop. The retching in the bathroom. The fights with Gogi getting louder and louder across the apartment until they started to break out in public, him screaming at her in the car to the hospital – *all doctors are thieves* – that she didn't need another costly examination, until suddenly, her perfectly calm daughter seemed to snap, flinging open the car in traffic to make him stop.

'Of course, *he* wasn't paying for anything.'

'But for Gogi a second opinion was too expensive.'

They were still in the hospital, after Tsotne was born, when he really lost it. The baby hadn't turned in time and Irina was so weak from the caesarean, she was lying there, quietly, when Gogi began to spiral. Everything he said twisted him deeper into a rage, until he was hollering – *Babies mean nothing to surgeons, you can't give that man a thank you gift, it's my son and my first born, I'll have to spend the money then.*

That's when Nino reached for the baby.

No, put him back! yelled her son-in-law.

His ageing face ugly and hysterical. But also weak.

'And at that moment I thought *no*. I said, *No, Gogi, it doesn't only belong to you. It's our baby and I better go with him to take a walk in the corridor. He's crying.*'

It was the first time, she realized, she'd said no to him. This man who Nino never really understood at all, who had come from nowhere to take over her life.

It happened a few days later when they got home: he lost his temper, he skidded off track into rage, until he was in a place he couldn't seem to hear, he couldn't seem to think.

'Then he simply left. Like the baby was too heavy for him.'

You never forget your first days with a new soul.

Tsotne was so small when Nino held him, his skin almost red, his eyes wide like he had travelled far, as she walked him around the apartment showing him the pictures of all the composers in his family, her daughter resting, the house finally quiet.

I'm a grandmother, she kept thinking.

I'm Tsotne's grandmother.

It was on his eighth day that Irina told her it was over.

I want to get divorced, she said. *I can't go on like this.*

That she would write Gogi a letter, full of kindness and tenderness, thanking him for their son and their time together and telling him that it was time to live apart.

'I never told her there's one right decision.'

Even as Irina sat writing it, her mother could tell something wasn't quite right. That this wasn't a firm decision, that she still had feelings for him, almost maternal ones, excusing him, indulging him, like she felt all women did, when they were still in love.

'It wasn't long before he was back.'

His arrival interrupting the piano Nino played in the evening.

Gogi seemed chastened, almost frightened, when he came back

to the apartment, at first just to visit, to see the baby. Then, after this courtship, to spend the night. He seemed to show interest, at last, in Irina's Ph.D., in the work she was doing on the Georgian Church, in what she had to say about the monks and the mountain monasteries far away.

'And again he charmed her.'

You don't want to say the wrong thing.

You know words wound. That the wrong word can scar.

You're an outsider watching something you can't control.

I'm pregnant, is what her daughter told her, full of nerves.

They had not been back together long.

He was still living with his parents.

'And all I said was – *Very good*. Because I had this sudden thought, *I want her to keep it*. And so that's why I said – *This is good, very good*. Because I was worried.'

Everything was repeating, like they were stuck in some loop. They had barely arrived at the hospital, but this man was screaming again, his voice turning into a screech as her daughter's hands began to shake, her body already in labour.

'That summer he decided to come back and live with us.'

'To show he is the one who rules all.'

Those first few nights she lay there fretting.

Her daughter, her grandson, now her granddaughter. Baby Niniko wasn't sleeping well. Always wanting to be held and walked around, the little apartment that now felt so overcrowded. At night, Gogi and the boy in one room, Nino and the baby in the other and Irina on the sofa bed in the living room. It had been another caesarean, but she wouldn't rest, waking up in the middle of the night to come to Nino's room where the newborn was sleeping, telling her mother to sleep, that she could handle Niniko. Those nights, it seemed to grow hotter, the whole city seemed to be baking. And Nino lay worrying, one fan not nearly enough, the sweat creeping over, until her anxieties started to play with her dreams.

'And then one of those mornings he erupted and finally left.'

Mummy, look.

It was Irina who first noticed him, little Tsotne, sitting upright, like he was listening to the opera she was playing. Then, just to see, they switched the music off to see if he would react.

The three-year-old looked at them as though he'd come out of a trance.

'It was then he learnt to tap on the computer to make it start.'

These were the things she learnt about him, her grandson, as Irina played little games with Niniko, the flat filled with music again now Gogi was gone. He would stop, as though suddenly he wasn't a little boy at all, as his mother listened to her favourite agitato, his eyes almost rapt. Then, like she had to be sure it was really happening, she would play him Tchaikovsky.

Tsotne, she'd ask.

Tell me when the violins are coming.

Then, like he'd memorized it, he'd pause.

Granny, I think they are coming now.

And as they burst through the flutes, she smiled.

You know music is like a language.

You know there is part of it you can never teach.

They moved so fast when she first sat him at the piano, when she first taught him how to hold his hands over the keys like dancing spiders, through the notes, then his first pieces, like he was much older than five, like he knew it all already.

Mummy, wouldn't it be wonderful if he could at least play jazz? said Irina, excitedly in the doorway, about to head off, back to her office at the university.

The best pianists, you know, are all still men.

And then she laughed on her way out.

She was still seeing him. On again. Off again.

She'd decided to divorce – they'd even gone as far as signing some of the papers – but, once again, he'd reeled her back in. He'd begged again. Just for one more chance. Gogi was teaching English now, as a tutor. This man was full of promises again, an off-plan apartment and various schemes. And they had some kind of arrangement, where they saw each other, but they lived apart. The children spending two nights a month with his parents.

'It was such a light, bright day.'

It was Niniko's third birthday.

The table spread with tarts, treats and *khachapuri*. The little ones eyeing the big sugary birthday cake – the one Niniko had wanted to have little footballs on, just like Tsotne, her big brother. As she lit the candles and they all started to sing. The musicians and the professors, her friends and Irina's, the faces she knew well and those who she could see in their children, they were all around them, their whole little world.

The phone ran a few days later.

It was Irina, on her mobile. She'd just left work.

I just want to say thank you, Mummy. All of my colleagues are telling me it was a wonderful birthday for Niniko. Thank you very much.

Then she was gone.

She was going to work in the archives, then she would stop by Gogi's where she liked to have tea and eat sandwiches out of her tupperware, before coming home.

'It's not very often you say thank you in our culture.'

'Not to a mother you live with all the time.'

Tsotne was on the clavinova when the phone rang.

Nino was standing over him, teaching him how to play.

Nino, Nino. It was Gogi's sister.

Irina's unconscious . . . she's unconscious.

Nino, her voice was breaking. *We can't make her conscious.*

In that second, before she answered, she saw something. It was Irina being hit by a car. It was every crash she'd ever seen on the streets of Tbilisi. It was her body being thrown through the air. The screech of wheels. Flesh gashed by tarmac and metal.

But it wasn't that.

She's on the floor. She fainted.

Come, please come!

Nino scrambled in an instant. Telling her grandchildren to stay with the cleaner, that she'd be back soon, her stiff, ageing legs aching as she rushed down the stairs. Thoughts flashing – *If it wasn't an accident, what it could be? And how can I help her?* – as she flagged a taxi. The grand avenues of Tbilisi, clogged like they'd never been before, barely seeming to move.

Her nerves – jangling, scratching – were unbearable now.

She had to phone her brother.

She's unconscious, Nino said. And then, yelling, *Do something! Do something!*

She was almost there.

Her legs in pain, when she finally got there, at the top of the stairs.

Then they opened the door, these red-faced crying women, before rushing her through the living room, into the bedroom, to the crouching paramedics.

'And I came here and I saw her dead.'

It was like the face of her husband, her mother and her mother-in-law.

It was like the face of her aunt and all these people who'd died in her arms.

It was a calm face, a white face, her body half-undressed, for resuscitation.

Her eyes already closed.

'You can always see death on a face.'

'It's a stillness. And that's what I saw.'

Gogi's mother was hysterical at the doctors, shrieking, flapping her arms wildly like a pigeon, like it was her disaster, her daughter. But Nino didn't cry.

She had never, she thought, been a woman who cried. Instead she walked over to Gogi's mother, with perfect poise, as though she was the medic here, and sighed.

Don't speak with them . . . everything is finished.

Don't speak with them . . . be calm.

Then she left them with the body.

She walked into the kitchen and closed the door.

The agitation and the voices, on the other side, growing louder.

'And in there, I realized. That this was my earthquake, or my volcano. You don't cry at the moment when there is an earthquake and everything starts collapsing, or when there's a war and bombs start to fall. You feel adrenaline. Your mind working very fast.'

'I couldn't cry at all.'

In that little space with the fridge and the oven, she stood.

She could see Tsotne, then Niniko. Her mind was working very quickly.

I have to keep them, she kept thinking.

I have to do everything to keep them with me.

She could see their whole lives, without a mother.

And then she could see herself, ever older, and everything she had to do.

'That I had to keep working. That I could never stop.'

It was then she knew, she wasn't only her, she was all the people that went into her.

She was all their strength. She could see her grandfather, who they'd imprisoned in the repressions. She could see him, being dragged down that corridor, when they shot a man in front of him, the agents trying to frighten him, trying to break him with that blood. She could see all the women that had made her – *her*.

I didn't kill her.

It was Gogi standing in front of her.

His face aged almost into an old man.

Then her brother arrived, as white as paper, followed by her sister.

They said it had happened suddenly, that Irina had come round straight from the archives, while Gogi was teaching English in his room and his mother was teaching Georgian in the living room. That she'd been waiting in the bedroom, until he brought her tea. *I'm not feeling well*, she'd said, her face perfectly normal, like nothing was about to happen. Then she'd collapsed.

Nino didn't leave that room.

There was the sound of people arriving.

The sound of them taking the body away.

There were a lot of people at the apartment when she got back. Musicians, colleagues, men and women from the orchestra crowding in on her. The children had been taken elsewhere, to one of their relatives. These people surrounded her, offering help and condolences, but she could hardly hear them, there on the sofa, cramped by the piano.

I have to work.

Her mind was running in circles.

I can't stop working. I have to work because now we're alone.

We're alone without Irina. We're alone with the children.

It was at the moment she started to scream.

Irina, come back . . . come back!

We can't live without you. We can't.

And quickly she was given a sedative.

Her legs heavier, like lead, until the pill rolled over her.

You feel grief.

You feel it physically.

In your body. In your brain.

Those first few days Nino could hardly eat.

She was hardly drinking. She could hardly sleep.

The condolence visits. The people in the apartment, coming to pay their respects. Irina's friends, the faces she hadn't seen since her wedding, now there to say goodbye.

The doctors told her it was thrombosis.

Blood clots had stopped her heart and lungs.

'That it was instant death.'

Please take me to work.

That was what she begged her friend, a few days later.

Please take me out of the house, I beg you . . . I need to get there.

'Because I was so scared of missing work.'

'We couldn't live without the money.'

Not once did Nino let herself cry.

Not in front of the children. Not when she was alone.

'But when I could, when nobody was around, in the toilet at work, or in the bathroom at home, I would go and bang my head over and over against the wall.'

The days passed, then the months. The visits thinned, then stopped. Then slowly, people forgot to ask. They smiled strangely, or tried to talk of other things.

He was still there, Gogi. She still didn't understand him.

He appeared at the apartment, saying if she cried even once that he would take the children away. That when it came to Irina, there shouldn't be so many photos of her. That when a man was a true intellectual, it should only take him one day to reset.

He was drinking.

He was supposed to spend a few nights there a week, for the

children. But really he was wandering around throughout the day. Only coming to her apartment to sleep. Gogi was never drunk but there was the smell of wine and gin on his breath. He began saying strange things, like now his life could now begin, that he was even happier than he was before.

Nino hardly played music any more.

She'd stopped teaching Tsotne.

She'd even stopped playing herself.

It was then Nino realized.

'I had no feelings that I wanted to live.'

'I didn't want to live. I had the feeling that I had to. But it wasn't really an emotion. It was something rational. That I have to protect the children and help them to grow up.'

It was a year later, in the dacha in the hills, where the smell of pines filled the house, that she started teaching Tsotne again. Nino leaning over him. The little boy at her old electric piano, about to play those first simple melodies that had followed her – that had lived inside her – almost her whole life.

Then they kept going.

They kept going through his first Mozart, first his sister watching, then her brother, until they tried Wagner. They kept going until he started to improvise, the sound filling the warm summer air. Until she started to notice something. That when he was alone – that when he was playing, his eyes lost in concentration, his fingers like they were casting a spell – it was his own language, his own fantasy, his own sadness that was coming out.

He wasn't imitating.

'It was then I started to see it.'

'That he could be a real composer.'

'That was when I started to feel, again, that I wanted to live.'

In time, they gave a little concert, for Irina, and printed little fliers.

Nino's sister telling her: *He's a genius.* The professors from the conservatory saying: *He's truly exceptional.* This was something so wonderful, they were saying. But as she closed her eyes, the harmonies surrounding her, Nino felt only pain.

'Because when I listen to him it's like she's there.'

'I'm listening with her. I listen to him with Irina.'

15 BERLIN

Haidar unblocked the German. He wasn't sure how they'd connected at first – maybe he'd sent him a friend request, or maybe he'd sent it – but he knew why he'd blocked him. His boyfriend had made him do it.

Rami would change in a flash.

That German guy? The one that goes back and forth to Beirut?

You've never even met him. And you just DM?

Haidar would try and explain. He'd made these friends online, with gay men, in Europe, in America. It gave him hope, being in Syria.

I want you to block him, Rami would snap.

I don't trust him. I don't want you talking to him.

It was like his boyfriend was two different people.

And they both could make him go limp. Rami had made him give up on studying the arts and choose English as his degree. He'd made him block so many friends. He told him who he could see – even after they tried to draft him, even after he'd fled the country, to get away from the fucking war – Rami was monitoring his every move. On Facebook, by WhatsApp. Then video calls.

Are you at home?

Prove it to me you're not lying.

He'd want photos or voice notes of Haidar's mum.

Are you walking my dog?

He'd time how long it'd take him.

That should take ten minutes. You hiding something?

He was scrambling his head.

He was making him beg.

Tell me the truth.

Rami was hysterical. His brain eating itself. Then he'd phone and cry, on the edge of collapsing completely, wailing to Haidar

– *another fraud, another one* – that he'd been swindled out of thousands of dollars in Turkey and the sea – *it's so rough* – there was no hope of crossing it this winter.

'He was trying to get to Germany.'

'And I was trying to keep a light face for him.'

'And, you know . . . for us.'

This is what he said. It was late at night. It was early in the morning. Haidar, always on the phone, pleading with Rami – *I'm coming, I'm trying to get out* – he kept repeating the same thing, on those calls that went on for ever.

'Then I would try and live my day.'

The war killed any chance of studying in Damascus. And there was no chance of a real life there. The war hadn't swallowed Latakia yet. But it was worse than ever. The parties, the private venues where they could meet, laugh, have a drink, the old guys and the young guys – the gay world, if you could even call it that – was dying. Everybody was leaving. Or trying to leave. He'd walk along the sea, it was beautiful there in the evening, thinking, feeling – there had been another gay suicide – *I've got to get out.*

'Because, basically . . .'

'That's going to be my only chance to live.'

You could hear the war out of the window: it was getting so much worse, with the *mukhabarat* spreading rumours – *the Alawites are gonna kill you, the Sunnis are going to get us* – that were rippling through the city. The graffiti on the wall – *the people want the fall of the regime* – the booms of MiGs at night.

Over the mountain a city had fallen to ISIS.

'It was around then I saw the videos.'

Young gay men thrown off high buildings.

'I remember watching those videos in despair.'

'I felt my heart and soul ripped out when I saw them.'

He was in tears. *I have to get out of here.* The horror felt like nails digging into him. *I have to get out as fast as I can.* This was panic. Not the kind that spikes and falls. But the kind that never goes away completely. Like a big red emergency button had been pressed inside him. Non-stop bleeping.

Haidar was crouched in his bedroom, the one from his childhood, thinking, *I can't go on like this.* Every gay text message, every conversation that even hinted at it – he deleted them. But it still gave him the chills whenever his brothers as much as touched his phone. Everything he either did, or wanted to do, was a secret.

'A secret that could have me thrown in jail.'

'Or God knows what.'

And his secret – Rami – treated him like shit.

'I was in a cage, really.'

'It was like I couldn't breathe.'

It was like he was sleepwalking, not fully alive, anything that could give him that jolt, to really live, was almost impossible, here. One false step and you could be beaten – even by your own brothers – until your face ran red.

'Hardly anybody knew.'

Just one member of the family.

'Everything. It was constant precautions.'

Late at night. No one could hear him.

Haidar would be on the phone with his boyfriend.

'I knew staying meant no life, it meant no future.'

'So I told Rami, either I flee now and I follow you along the Great Route of Death, as we call it, or I try and find another smarter way.'

He knew his parents would never let him go like that. Across Turkey, over the sea into Greece and the Balkans. Everyone had heard stories so terrifying they still struggled to believe they were real.

'I needed a plan that was actually legal.'

But even then he knew his family would never support him. Financially. Emotionally. The idea was just absurd.

'I had this concept in my head from Western movies, that I can do what I want. That I can get out.'

That's when he remembered.

Toufic: his childhood friend.

hi you're in Germany??

New message from Toufic.

i've got a student visa, yeah

Toufic is typing.

for people with degrees like you

Haidar's eyes widened. There was the way out. He started Googling it frantically: he'd need a passport, and he'd need to apply to

study somewhere in Germany. His mind was growing lighter: he could see it now – another actual life. Then he found the catch.

'This was only open if you had a big fat bank account.'

A student visa needed an €8,000 bond.

'Not even my parents could pay for that.'

Rami's voice would be cracking on the telephone. In Turkey, it was getting worse. That's when Haidar brought up the German.

'That's when I said, *I have a friend in Berlin . . . Philip.*'

'I said, *I think this is the only guy that can help me.*'

'*I know you're jealous*, I said.'

'*But this is the only way.*'

You can unblock him, said Rami.

That's when they started talking again.

There was a lifeline, if he could grab on to it.

'So I unblocked him and I started to explain why I had blocked him and stuff again and I told him, by the time he called, I need, like, I need to get out.'

They were talking every day now.

I can help you get to Berlin, said Philip.

I can help you.

Philip was telling him everything. Then he said the incredible.

I'll lend you the money.

They call it the melancholy of departure.

But the worst moment wasn't when Rami said he would out him – he'd finally snapped, he'd finally woken up and dumped that psycho – menacing those pictures and texts that he claimed to have on his phone. The worst moment came right after the best moment. It was morning.

Haidar was holding two letters that had just arrived.

We are delighted to inform you that you have been accepted . . .

'I immediately went into crying mode.'

It was like he'd seen the mountain. But instead of starting on the peak he felt suddenly like he was drowning in a stream in the valley below.

'I thought now I must tell my family.'

He'd been longing to tell her, his mother, for months – as he did

VISAS التأشيرات

Visumantrag
vom 20.02.16 in Beirut (D) 155924

it all in secret, as he got the passport he'd never had – knowing he could break her heart.

'Those days I really wanted to come out to her as a gay son. I wanted to open my heart and soul to her and say I'm leaving for a better life.'

'A life I deserve.'

You'll never survive outside your family's arms, she'd once told him when he raised the topic. *Your place is here.* He'd look at her and he'd think for a moment, maybe it was.

'I was the ultimate mummy's boy.'

The worst moment came when he gathered them round, his mother, his father, his brothers, to explain what he'd applied to do, why he had to leave, because there was no point studying for five years just to become a vegetable-seller, there was no future here, only the risk of being drafted.

'Then it got heated.'

His father had got upset. His brothers said he'd insulted him. The next thing he knew one of them had smashed his nose and was pinning him down, yelling at him not to talk like that. It was only his mother that got him free.

'The emergency alarm button in my brain was reactivated.'

He grabbed his stuff, tears streaming down his face.

'I opened the door and ran as fast as I could.'

'I knew exactly where to go.'

He had a plan, like every other queer person in the Middle East, he thought, for where to go if shit really hit fan in the family. They would help. Haidar's nose was bleeding in the taxi there. His mind flashing with a hundred reasons to blame himself. Only when he got there did he see his full black eye.

'It was a few days later that my mother sat in front of me.'

It was when she saw his swollen face she started crying. Soon they were all crying: Haidar and his mother, his friend and her mum. *I can't go home until they respect my choices*, he said. *You need to let me go.*

They stood and they didn't hit him, this time, his father and his brothers, when he got back. They treated him with respect, maybe it was right, they said, he should leave the country and go to Berlin.

Now he was counting days.

It's a strange thing to say goodbye, it takes over everything you do. Your last moment with friends. Your last party. You're always thinking – *When will I see this again?*

And then it had come. The last night of the last day.

'The funny thing is we spent it like any normal night.'

They were all there, all the extended family and they ate and they talked – *You're going to grow, my son* – and laughed – *You should watch out, my son* – and everyone kept their emotions almost sealed. The suitcases were packed. And suddenly it was almost midnight, it was time.

Haidar held his mother. He kissed all of them.

'And then all of the men of the family went down with me to say goodbye. And there was nobody in the neighbourhood. Just us . . . crying our asses off. My dad, my brothers, I've never seen them like that.'

And then the city, the only one he'd known, slipped away.

He WhatsApped Berlin.

Message to Philip.

i've left

They were on the motorway now.

Nancy Ajram was playing on the radio.

My life has begun, he thought in the taxi.

This is it. It's beginning.

They drove south through Syria, for several hours, until finally they saw the border – that jolly little green cedar on red stripes on the Lebanese flag.

They passed Tripoli and the towns in the north, passed the bay of Jounieh, which still had it, a little bit of glitter from before the civil war, until he was in Beirut, that city under the mountain, that city he loved from the voice of Fairuz, where the poster faces on the walls were so different.

In Latakia, in Syria, in government areas, there was only one face – his, his long head, his thin moustache – or maybe the face of his father, the same eyes, but greyer, thinner hair and that more bulbous head he could recognize instantly. Those were the posters

he knew. But here the faces were dizzying: the Maronites, they had this cherubic, long dead, black and white face on their posters; the Sunnis, in their streets there were these men with thick eyebrows; and the Shia, they had this bespectacled man in a black turban on theirs. And things he never thought he'd actually hold.

Starbucks and Dunkin Doughnuts.

And then there was him.

The first man he'd kissed.

Standing there in front of him, helping him with his bag.

Habibi, you're finally here.

He was his first boyfriend, in a sense, though he'd never slept with him.

'It was a stealing hands situation. We were both kids. It was a virgin love. And we couldn't take it further as then he left for Beirut.'

That night they did it.

In his student dorm, by the university.

'It was very intense. It was hectic.'

The street lights dancing on the ceiling.

'Because it had been waited for . . . *for so long.*

And then it was almost time to fly.

The plane was boarding. It was cold, colder than he'd expected.

Then a muffled announcement.

Boarding complete.

A stewardess was suddenly there.

Have you fastened your belt?

Haidar grimaced. So it was actually happening.

'I was afraid. This was my first time on a plane.'

The trembling on the runway. The roar on the ascent.

And as he felt the ground go beneath him, his skin crisped and Haidar clasped on to both the arms of his seat. It only took a sudden jolt – like something had given – and his mind flooded with movie clips: the flames from 747s hitting the tarmac or the screams if they suddenly plunged.

Nothing's going to happen, he muttered, again and again. *Nothing's going to happen.*

It bounced, it rattled, like they were on water, getting hit by the

waves. Then it seemed to flatten and calm, until it was as smooth, or smoother, than a train. Only anxiety and excitement still making ants and butterflies inside him.

Haidar breathed. And listened.

It was light, the drone from the engine. That was Arabic all around him. Some people were laughing now, whilst others were whispering to children. And that accent, he knew it, he'd heard it before – *That's Iraqi* – on almost all of them. He listened harder. There was hardly any German. He caught a little bit, here and there, but not enough to get used to it. It was then he tried to chat a little bit with the guy – *Right, he's also Iraqi* – sitting next to him.

But just questions poured out of him.

So what's it like? What is it like out there?

'Because he was, like, abroad before me.'

The Iraqi fell asleep. It was dark, the night blank, like they were flying through a tunnel. The lights were dimmed. Haidar sat squirming in his seat. *I'm going to Berlin*, he kept thinking. *So I'm really going to Berlin.*

'But it was one of those moments when time just slows down for you.'

You feel it insufferably. You feel like you've never sat for so long before.

You've felt it too.

'It was only three hours, but it felt like three years.'

Ladies and gentlemen, welcome to Berlin Schönefeld.

Local time is 2:14 a.m. and the temperature is −3°C.

He'd done everything he could not to imagine this. Not to have any expectations. *Passport, bitte.* Not to have any images of arriving. *Danke schön.* None. Because then he'd only be shocked or disappointed. Like he was when he first went to Damascus. *Never imagine Berlin.* That's what he'd said. But now he was at the carousel, this new language everywhere, on everything – trying not to think about it – trying to be as stony-faced and indifferent as everyone was else in that moment, waiting for their bags.

Then he stepped outside.

'It was super super cold.'

It was almost 3 a.m. when he left the lights of the airport. To meet Philip. His old Facebook friend had written it all down, so meticulously. How to get out of the airport. How to get the first bus. How they'd get the second one together from this to that in the city. And his number, of course. He'd left nothing to the slightest bit of chance. Haidar was only following the messages.

The city began to appear. *Can't be long now,* he thought. *But I've never met him before,* he kept mumbling, now the moment was getting closer. *Three years of friendship. Everything he's done for me. Just . . . I've never actually met him!*

And there he was. At the bus station. Steam from his breath.

This angel in a winter coat.

Hallo?

Haidar, in that moment, he wasn't Haidar.

Because Haidar wasn't like this. Haidar was a social person. But in that moment he was so shy he could hardly look at him. He was so – I guess you could say timid – he could hardly talk to him.

Haidar?

They were both there, on the Berlin *Nachtbus*, heading to Philip's place. And it was strange: because even though he'd told him everything – every secret – on chat, a long time ago, he had no idea what to say.

It was night in Berlin. It was all out there, somewhere, he didn't yet know.

They arrived in Prenzlauer Berg.

Then at Philip's apartment. They had a snack, like they'd been living together for years, talked a little about the flight, then slept.

Haidar woke up in Berlin. Somewhere deep into the morning. He could hear the street, a different kind of street, outside. That was the tram. That was something he didn't quite know the sound of. Philip was going about his daily chores. And after Haidar had showered, but before he'd touched his bags, it all suddenly burst. He was happy. He was giddy. He was laughing hysterically. The next moment he was crying.

'All those emotions they just . . . came up.'

Philip was frozen, with no idea what to do with him as Haidar sobbed and then suddenly lurched into questions.

What now? What shall I do?

It was all pounding through him. The exhilaration. The confusion of arrival. That knowing there would be no going back for a very long time. That was what he felt. All at once. But Haidar did leave the house that day – the trams passing under the elegant facades and past the trees of Prenzlauer Berg, the crowds walking faster, more concentrated than they did in Syria, nobody ambling – and then it was like he didn't stop. To school, to get documents, to the immigrant Ausländerbüro, it was all – *Hey, I'm here, let's start.*

'I didn't want to waste one second of my life.'

'I had this urge to like . . . *get it, get it, get it.*'

Philip told him everything. How the metro cards worked. How the gay world worked. Which clubs were open late and which ones kinda sucked. That there was anything he wanted here – he just had to turn up for it.

You can do anything here.

And that was when he began to search: *sauna.*

Haidar went alone.

He'd been in Berlin about a week before he went to Boiler. The rooms and the pools were in red and purple: it was all neon. There was a bar and a garden and steam-room lit blue. Men were kissing. Gays were relaxing. People were doing stuff in this place. And when he put his head under freezing water for the first time Haidar felt something: something that felt like freedom.

'You know . . . I never felt a culture shock.'

'Because I'd never allowed myself to imagine it. I had no expectations. I kept my mind empty, I zeroed it, because I knew coming to Europe, my whole life is gonna be turned upside down. You might find it odd but that's how I kept it open, fully adaptable and ready to be free.'

It had been so long.

Never imagine Berlin.

He felt it again two months later. That was the night he went to St George. It was a party called Unshaved and it was a party for Bears – *So that's what they call that kind of rugged hairy gay here.* It was like a bunker in there and under that red exposed ceiling – metal piping, stark lights – Haidar could feel himself sweating as he began to dance. It felt so light – *It felt like . . . like I didn't know how I could feel* – and it felt right. And they were moving. There were Daddies and Muscle Bears and Daddy Chasers everywhere. There were colours, on their clothes, in the strobes, on their glitter. They were kissing, and *yes*, that really was a blowjob in the corner. And as the music got louder and he danced faster and people came over he suddenly felt something at the Gaga anthem.

Oh my fucking god, I'm super fucking happy.

That night Haidar didn't actually do it. What they were all doing: like it was the easiest thing in the world. He was in Berlin, RuPaul was playing, the Bears were dancing, now all around him. But even when they were in front of him, these beautiful men, he was frozen: it was like he was still in Syria, like he was still afraid of it. To actually do it and kiss a man in the open.

'It was basically my first openly gay party ever.'

That night he left with three friends.

The streets in Kreuzberg, like they were smiling.

'I met someone . . . I was so strongly attracted to.'

Haidar moved out from Philip's after three months. Then, shivering at night, he slept on the thinly covered conservatory balcony of some guy he'd met on an app. At least until he found a room in Wedding. And then, just like that, Haidar found his friends. Bob from Lebanon and Adeed from Homs. His fellow gay Syrian. They would be fooling around, when it started, putting on their friend's makeup and her mascara in the mirror.

'And that was how it began.'

Think for a minute.

You might have felt like this once or twice in your life.

You find yourself free. But you know you haven't really let yourself be.

You start wondering – who could you be?

You start noticing things about yourself.

It's good like that, Berlin.

'I knew it, that I still wasn't really me.'

It's a feeling that follows you always, when you feel it.

He'd been in Berlin for six months but it was like he'd been born to be here. It was good, the German-language course. It was working. He could feel those long looping sentences beginning to form fully in his mouth without falling apart. He was learning. But what he lived for was the night. He'd be there in jeans, Nikes and a white T-shirt. There in front of him, it would open up like a parade.

'That's when I started seeing the drag queens.'

They would be there, singing, performing. And what came off them: it hummed, it thrilled. It felt like everything that was just impossible. He'd go home with them in his eyes.

Their songs in his ears.

'It happened slowly.'

The way the biggest things often do.

Now, a few months later, he was starting to speak. *Freut mich.* He had found the scene now. From Kreuzberg to Mitte: it was all opening. He had his Berlin. They would go to Humana – Bob, Haidar and Adeed – and they would spend hours in that huge vintage and second-hand clothes shop, laughing and giggling as they tore through that huge pile of eighties and nineties chic, putting on the frocks, the boots and the wedding dresses. Playing until Bob and Adeed said they really had to buy something.

'It wasn't just a game.'

He was there in the changing room.

'Club culture was touching my personality. It was making me question my gender more and more. It was making me question my sexuality more and more. I was starting to explore it more and more.'

'Making me the person I became.'

His people in Syria.

He'd be in the U-Bahn, thinking about them. He'd be on the bus after class and he'd text his mum. Then his friends in Latakia. They didn't know anything about this back there. That things were possible here.

They were dancing the night he met Judy.

It was one of those nights Haidar was practically spinning, the way he danced: throwing his all into it, throwing it all into it, everything it had taken to get here. His clothes were drenched. There were drag queens that evening. There'd been singing, there'd been dancing, and then one of them was suddenly there in front of him. He'd never seen one come down like this to the people.

Floating there in the crowds.

Hello, who are you?

She had fabulous thick mascara.

The wig was incredible, like an eighties mane.

And she was speaking to him. Just him.

I really enjoy your vibe, said Judy.

I think you would really enjoy my show.

'And then we discovered I'm from Syria and she's Jewish from Israel-Palestine. And we were like – *Oh my god!* The fact that we came from two countries in conflict made no difference to us becoming friends.'

Will you come to my next performance?

All that week at the language school he kept thinking about that moment. Thinking of the night when he could see Judy again. And when it happened, she was stunned to see him. She hugged him and squealed – *You actually came, most people never even remember, but you did!* – and then, that night, she really performed. Lip-synching something he'd heard so many times in so many places; but never like this and never here. It was Nancy Ajram. The star of Lebanon. Her greatest pop song. And it was in Arabic.

'I flipped out.'

There were Arabs and Jews, Germans and Brits, and all kinds of gays that night. The magic was rising and at that moment his heart raced.

'It was all there in that moment for me. Because I never thought: *Oh my god, there's a drag queen singing in my language in Berlin.*'

It was never a question after that that he'd be back.

We've got to do this again, right?

At first it was social. Then it became part of the act.

Let's do something for our culture! they said, the big Middle Eastern one they were both part of – and weeks later they were at the Axel Hotel. There was a little stage by the bar and kitchen and Haidar was dancing with Judy – as a belly dancer. It was Tuesday night. *Who went out on a Tuesday?* But that's the thing. This is Berlin – you can even go out on Monday – and on those nights he began to feel something as he danced.

'I began to feel a little constricted.'

'The clothes I was wearing. They were overheating me . . .'

You might have felt it.

The moment you realize – I don't have to do it this way.

You might have heard it like a bang or more like a whisper.

Haidar would be getting ready and it would be like a flash.

'I decide.'

'I'm the one in control here.'

He'd be watching Judy getting her makeup done.

And then he'd just do it. He'd throw that thing off.

'It began with me wearing less clothes. Then more feminine clothes, like heels, to the club. From there, gradually, I started learning that I am able to wear whatever I want. Be it masculine or feminine.'

'Because this is how I felt at my best.'

It started with skirts and hip scarves and coins.

He'd be dancing, he'd seen them, rapt, watching him and he'd feel it running through him – the pain and the joy, the war and the city, the journey and the moment of home – and he'd throw himself further, further into the dance, the way only dancers know how to do, until the song peaked, it ended and then the flutter, tingling through him, of applause.

'It was nothing but liberating.'

He'd be dancing, like his mother, like a woman, like himself.

It was like he'd crossed something, some invisible bar.

'That was the moment where I felt I was actually in charge.'

'Where I was free to be me.'

He'd be having a drink afterwards. The people, the gays, the queens, the community, would be coming up to him, stunned by what they'd seen.

'It was gone . . . the conflict in my mind.'

'I was being applauded for being me. For representing the real me, for getting into myself and finding myself . . . I was being praised for it. It was like nothing I'd ever felt before. This is a feeling I think everyone should feel.'

On those nights it felt like everyone watched.

And if you didn't know him, you didn't know what it meant to be Haidar, you'd think he was just doing his shows. But it wasn't quite like that. Every time he danced he felt like he was claiming more freedom. He felt finally, he was learning his worth. He'd be exhausted, back in his room in Wedding, the images of the night flooding past him and then he'd suddenly stop and think.

I am my own. And I can create whatever I want.

And be anything that I want. Here.

It was around then something else crept in. It came through WhatsApp and Instagram. Rumours from Syria. That they'd been talking about him. *He's gay.* He'd never posted anything, well almost anything, that might arouse their suspicions. But they were still talking about him.

'That was the breaking point for me. I said, *I'm gonna start from scratch. Because if I drag my previous life into this new one, with this new freedom that I've created, it's gonna clash.* And I didn't want to . . . I just didn't want to have to explain everything, everything, every time.'

'How gender works, what trans is.'

'What my life is.'

He imagined trying to tell them, if they saw a reel from one of those nights. *No, that woman is not a woman, and no, that man is not a man; it's a form of art, of expression, and no, it doesn't mean that. No,* it would just cause too much pain for him, trying to explain it to them, over there. There was only one thing for it. He started blocking them. Everyone. All of them on Facebook and Instagram. Even people who were close friends.

And then he began to post as himself.

'I couldn't live half there, half here.'

'I couldn't half be me.'

He had wanted to come out to his mum but not like this. Not by phone, at a time he hadn't chosen, when he was so far away. But none of it should have happened like this. The car crash in Latakia that killed his brother's fiancée. It shouldn't have happened. The text messages that they found in her phone: telling her about Berlin.

They shouldn't have found them.

what you think of this cute guy???

The text messages telling her what he was doing. Telling her who he really was. And then his photos. It happened quickly. His brothers' grief in Syria hit like artillery. And it fell on him. Their words pounding on him.

this is disgusting.

this is your life. this is your choice.

They were shouting. They were threatening. These brothers, his brothers, in their country at war. And he was here: cramped in his little room in Wedding, his friends at St George or getting ready for Tipsy Bear, trying not to crack, trying to say it calmly.

This is who I am.

Trying to make them understand, as their denial filed their voice.

You can do whatever you want, said his brothers.

You can choose this life.

But if you do, we won't choose you.

You can only repeat yourself so many times.

You can tell them and you can tell them clearly.

And then the rage cools and it's almost worse.

Fine. But if you choose to be this way . . .

We're not your brothers.

And then the line goes dead.

Haidar was shaking. For a moment there was nothing and then it all flooded in. How could they be like this? They had gay friends – in their social circle. They'd caught him red-handed. *How could they think it was just a phase? They were educated people. But they were there, in Syria.* It was night in Berlin. He was almost crying.

'They didn't even want to listen to me.'

That's when he called her.

'Because at that point I realized, if I don't tell my mum . . .'

'I don't want her to find out from texts.'

There are moments when you see it all, what got you there.

It was like his whole life, from the moment he first told his friends – *I'm gay* – was there behind him at that moment, helping to build the confidence to tell her. She picked up, she always did. Ever since he was a baby they'd always said he was exceptionally close to her. And that's when she heard it.

It's not true, is what she said at first.

What you're feeling, what you're saying, it's not true.

It was denial, in her voice. It was there the next day, when he came back from the language school, and the day after that.

'She wanted to listen.'

'She wanted to understand.'

And they didn't stop talking. She didn't hang up on him. She didn't cut him off like his brothers. It was like a horrible rollercoaster:

up and down, emotions that came crashing and the moment they'd calmed they shot up again. At first, he was trying to explain it to her, literally all the details. *This is what it's like here.* And at some points that got too much, when it became too intense. He blocked her – just to have some time out.

But it was never for long.

Listen, said Haidar, *you are important in my life.*

I want you, no matter what, in my life. I know you might never fully understand my style of living, but I hope by trying, you can understand more.

He'd been in Berlin almost a year.

He was vogueing. He was dancing.

He was performing with someone born in Israel.

He'd found his stage name: The Darvish.

Now he'd found work in the fashion world.

Haidar was trying to tell her everything: who he was, what freedom was. And then he'd lie back, exhausted, after they'd been fighting on the phone, and he'd be overcome with a painful empathy.

'Just how difficult this was for her.'

'Because she'd grown up in a completely different country, with a completely different mindset, it was just so different to this.'

And then he'd think of his brothers.

'You're losing me. You're losing me over this. I gave them time to understand and assess and I thought, *Maybe they'll come back to their senses.*'

He didn't at first, after what they'd said; but after a while he made sure he always would ask her. *How are they? How are my brothers?*

My dad doesn't know.

I can't believe he still doesn't know.

It was about a year later that he first did drag. Not a bit of makeup, but the art. Haidar had the dress, he'd spent ages finding it, and the wig, both in his bag. It was Halloween. The night itself had not yet come. But there was already that feeling there, on the bus, that you could wear things, that you could be things, in a carnival moon, that normally – in the streets – you couldn't quite be.

It was a special night in Berlin. The night a lot of people do drag for the first time. The sloppy vampires and slutty witches all around them on the U-Bahn making them feel safer, braver, not alone, because we all want to do this – making this a night where no one gets attacked.

Haidar arrived at his friend's on Frankfurter Allee. He was a makeup artist and he gasped at how perfect the costume was.

'And I told him, like please give me Cinderella.'

'My favourite Disney movie.'

They blocked his eyebrows. He sat in the chair like one of his stars. The princess was appearing in the mirror as they painted. And after he got tucked it was like he'd transformed when he put on the dress. They could hardly control themselves looking in the mirror – *Oh my God! Look! Haidar, look!* There were the second-hand heels from Humana, sparkling under spray paint silver, and there was the €3 mirror with the big blue bow, like Cinderella too. And there he was: a Queen.

They felt giddy as they stepped outside.

There was that tingle on the street, when you know it; you and the city are going to have an amazing night. They skipped and hopped like children. They passed the station and the bridge like the world was smiling at them. It was at Monster Ronson's karaoke by the U-Bahn station.

He'd been there so much.

He'd changed so much.

Halloween in Berlin. There are nights when everyone seems to be going over the bridge to Kreuzberg and tonight was one of those. The queue was so long – and so colourful – but Haidar didn't have to stand in line. He was in the loop. He knew the bouncer and he blew kisses and curtsied at the cheering gays as he passed. Then he swung in the door.

Cinderella!

At first they didn't recognize him. And that only thrilled him more – *I've done it, I've transformed.* And as the music started and the dance floor filled, Haidar found himself there in the mix, astonished how many were in a look under the pink light: scarecrows and devils and cosmonauts. As these wonders began to dance it started to rush through him.

All that love and art and inspiration lifting him up.

'I thought of everything Philip had done.'

'Of everything I've given up, and sacrificed, to be me.'

'That Berlin was where I was meant to be.'

The songs got higher and wilder. The bar was crammed. The dancing faster. Then the moment came when it was thinning. And it was gone.

'I didn't want to go home. I didn't want the night to end.'

They were laughing by Warschauer Straße.

'Thinking, *This is only the beginning.*'

It was long past midnight.

'I remember being so happy I was prancing in the street.'

The cars passing. The last revellers smiling.

'It was a joy that I cannot express.'

'I felt so happy in my skin.'

16 HATVAN

The hardest part of working at the LIDL was the trucks.

They would bleep and reverse in the morning and Szilvia would be there trying to work out how to unload them and telling people what to do.

Tamás, can you lead the frozen meat?

Kriszti, can you take the vegetable crates?

Then she would bend down and pick up those boxes too until her back ached and her hands were sore. Then she would go back inside.

It was air-conditioned in the LIDL.

Everything was bright and sharp and smooth. Sometimes, it felt to Szilvia like she could be anywhere. Not just in Hungary. Especially not just in little Hatvan. Then suddenly she would hear a shriek. The wild dogs had got in again and the customers would be screaming they were raiding the sausages.

The announcement system trilled.

Da-da-dam. Cashier manager required.

It was a sound that could follow her into her sleep. The sound that meant the assistant manager had to come urgently to help with the customers.

Madam, I need to return this. This is out of date.

Excuse me, madam, I want my money back.

They came in two kinds, either they were really nice, so apologetic, like they'd always known her, or red-faced and frustrated, yelling about refunds and returns. Simply refusing to understand it wasn't her who was the LIDL, that there was a whole system here that they couldn't see, and a procedure they had to follow.

Those were the days she felt tired.

And the time couldn't come soon enough to close the tills.

She'd cycle home, back to her daughter – she couldn't believe Dzsenifer was already thirteen years old – back to make dinner, hoping tomorrow someone else would get to be floor manager and she'd get to be a cashier.

Not to be run off her feet.

It only took fifteen minutes to cycle home: the bridge over the railway that went to Budapest, past the old church and all the pubs and the bakeries; but it went past almost everything she'd ever known. Places she'd been with her daughter's father, before that all fell apart. Places she'd been with her ex-husband, until those seven years ended for good.

I've not been so lucky in love, she'd sometimes think.

She might be watching TV, when those great love affairs came on, when she was finally alone, late at night. Or she might be cycling to the LIDL on one of those intense summer mornings, the sun yellow like it was already midday.

I'm on my own now, she'd be thinking.

This is what it's like to be free. Maybe something will happen.

Maybe something will happen to me.

But nothing happened.

The summer festivals came and went, when the squares were full of teenagers, sneaking into the LIDL to buy booze, pretending to be eighteen; more stray dogs braved it past the glass sliding doors; more birds flew in and lodged themselves in fear on the tops of shelves under white ceiling tiles.

Then the cold nights and the bare trees and the mornings of mist and frost she would find when she cycled to work. That daily meeting would come; she would be floor manager again; then the big deliveries would come again: chocolates, wrapping paper, fairy lights, all for St Nicholas' Day.

The scanner bleeped.

The cash register rattled with change.

It was her day at the till. There were old women with very little, counting the change. Mothers with huge piles for dinner. Men, who must live alone, with just a few basics like beer and cheese and then, standing there, holding a St Nicholas chocolate pack, was a face she recognized.

József, hi.

It was a face she'd known since school. But with deep lines now, a widow's peak and a kind of gravity that hadn't been there. A strong face.

He suddenly pulled a half-smile.

Szilvia, hi.

These are for my nephews, he said, pointing at the pack.

It's really nice to see you.

He was smiling at her, lingering at the till. It took a moment for him to go but once he did, he suddenly turned his head, and looked back.

You know this look.

You've given this look.

You knew exactly what it meant.

It made her feel goosebumps. It made her feel wanted.

Then he was gone.

That night she cycled back faster than normal and after she'd fed her teenager and they'd chatted about what was going wrong and right at school she went on Facebook. There was József. They were already friends. Then she spotted it. A couple of five-year-old bubbles with his words in them. He'd kept messaging her and she'd never replied. Then it flashed. That man was still liking her pictures. He looked muscly in his. Grown up.

She didn't hesitate.

hi :)

It was only moments before he wrote back.

hey :))))

That night they started chatting. József said he worked pretty near the LIDL, actually, at the petrol station, it was hard work sometimes and it wasn't great pay but he liked the people. And then they kept chatting; into the next day and when she had a moment on her shift. It was then that he asked her out.

do you want to have a coffee at the pastry shop???

Then two days later they met. He said he would pick her up in his car and drive her there and right home afterwards and now he was sitting there, smiling at her, in a way that made her feel good, a way that made her feel happy.

I like you, he said, smiling with his pastry in his hand.

And she was smiling too: but in that moment it all came back to her, how it hadn't worked with her daughter's father, then how it hadn't worked with the man she married after that, how she'd only ever had bad experiences with men, how she didn't want to believe in them any more, or to be hurt.

'I was putting a wall up between us.'

'I knew what he wanted but I was creating this distance.'

'I wanted things to go slowly.'

But József didn't seem to mind. He drove her home, well in fact almost home, as she didn't want him to know where she lived exactly. And then he became a regular customer at the LIDL, buying sausages, beer and a little cheese, looking for her when she was the floor manager and smiling.

'And he kept on asking me for coffee.'

And they kept talking, as if they'd been waiting their whole lives to start talking, about Hatvan, about their families, about all the things that had gone right and all the things that had gone wrong and that was when he told her.

I've had two brain tumours, he said.

The first time it happened it grew so large it was pushing the vein of his eye, so forcefully he almost went blind in his right eye, his head pierced with migraines, all confused and angry, thinking – *Why me, why now? It's not fair.*

I had a week to live, the doctors said. But they saved me.

He told her about the surgery and how scared he'd been, then about the treatment, the steroids he took every day and the testing every three months.

And it means I can't have children.

The doctors had spent years telling him this. They'd even given him a certificate.

And I'm telling you this, well . . . this is me.

This is part of me and you have to get to know this.

József made a serious face and he said the last time this had happened, the last time he'd liked someone and they'd been together, he'd told her – well, maybe he'd told her too late; *Hey, babe, I've had these operations, it means I can't have children* – and then one month later she'd left him, probably because of this. And then he smiled.

That doesn't bother me at all, she said.

I'm just happy you're better and you're still here.

And they kept talking, as it got colder and colder in Hatvan, until the snows came in January and the children fought with snowballs and made angels on the white banks by the LIDL as their parents rushed in and out.

I'll drive you home.

He always said it but it had become a routine.

József parked the car and quickly, like a gentleman, jumped out and opened her door. It was one of those nights that were so cold you could see your breath, lit orange in street lamps, and as she stepped out something happened.

It was like a flow.

Like one thing to another. She was holding him.

They were kissing. Like there was no way to know who initiated it.

Good night, he said, smiling.

Wanna have coffee at the pastry shop tomorrow?

And as she turned to walk the last corner to her house, she could feel herself beaming, her hands trembling, her mind fizzing. *Is this a new life? Or just a little adventure?* And then she caught herself and thought again. *Maybe it can be a new life and a little adventure? Maybe, maybe, this is finally him.*

They went fishing a few weeks later.

Szilvia, József and Dzsenifer. They both liked fishing; the calm, the fluttering wind on the water, the excitement of a tug on the rod. They both felt it was important that her teenager got to know him.

That was how they told her they were together.

'It felt like it was important.'

That's when they started walking together, more and more often, into the woods near Hatvan and the forests, to catch a glimpse of the deer, breathe in its smells and rustling silence and to talk about their dreams.

She told him how she loved nothing more than the holiday she took with Dzsenifer to Greece every year: the beaches, the people from all over Europe, the smell of suntan lotion and grilled meat.

'Then we started meeting family.'

He was at the LIDL every night to pick her up now. They were no longer a hidden couple in front of their friends and all the other women on the tills – Csilla, Noémi, Ági – now knew who her József was. It was around then, when the spring had come and the hares were boxing in the fields that led out of Hatvan, that he started talking about a home.

How nice it would be if they lived together.

'Then we started to look for a house.'

They didn't pay much attention to the news of the virus from China. To the numbers they kept citing on the news. She didn't feel so worried when the panic started. The state of emergency and the first cases in Hatvan. The LIDL mandating old persons' shopping before noon. Then one morning she started throwing up.

She found herself retching over the toilet bowl at work.

It would suddenly grab her, in the aisle, at the till.

Then she would have to run.

The swallows had come back.

They were darting through the orange skies at dusk as the heat faded.

She told herself – *Maybe I've got Covid, maybe it's something worse, maybe it's because I'm too overweight.*

You have to go to the doctor, said József.

Especially, after everything that had happened to him.

Szilvia, hello, the doctor got up from the desk and greeted her.

And welcome to you and your new baby.

At first it was like she hadn't heard him.

Baby? What baby?

Then suddenly her mind was boggled and confused.

I'm pregnant? But I can't be . . .

The doctor laughed as she sat down.

But how do you know I'm pregnant?

I can see it, he said. *In the gleam of your eye.*

You feel cold. You feel hot.

You begin to shake. You can hardly speak.

You can't go back to the moment you were in before. You only feel this once or twice in a lifetime. A moment of complete surprise.

Szilvia rushed to tell József and when she did his face crisped and his tiny eyes almost seemed to disappear, like he was trembling, thinking, *I'm not the daddy.* Then he stepped closer, he looked into her eyes, he saw everything that was in there, then another face entirely came over him and he hugged her.

We're having a . . . a . . . a baby?

He was almost stammering with shock.

I can't . . . I can't believe it.

It began very prosaically.

A friend had mentioned loans you could get from the government if you got married and planned to have children; as something practical, something theoretical, was how he started talking about marriage. He asked about it and she answered, again and again, in a way she knew he could read as yes.

No, no . . . not here!

József was on his knee in front of her in the car park outside the doctor's. He'd been waiting for her on her second pregnancy visit and there was the ring.

No! Not now! Not in the car park!

It was awful, she thought in that moment, that men never paid attention to things like that.

Then came the moment he went down again, as traditionally as he could, in front of her parents, the way it was always supposed to be.

'It was a colourful wedding.'

They stood there in Hawaiian shirts and flower garlands, just their parents and their two witnesses, in the registrar's office. Szilvia had always dreamed of a beachfront wedding by the sea, but with Covid rules – numbers, borders, masks – this was the closest she was going to get. And, anyway she thought, when it's your second wedding it's not traditional to wear white.

Maybe we'll have a big party eventually, he said. Though there was something about the way he said, driving on their honeymoon to the thermal springs nearby, that betrayed he thought maybe they most probably would not. It's expensive, that kind of thing.

'We didn't have a chance to go anywhere else.'

They found the name soon after the scan.

The X-ray like a photo of a ghost. Then a tiny party again, for her gender reveal, just the two of them, two friends and her Dzsenifer.

They played the game they always play in Hatvan.

Scribbling down names of boys and girls.

Her daughter had written Napsugár.

A name that means sunshine.

It's so strange, she told József, that night in bed.

It's so weird. I've never told her that's my favourite name.

Then she's our Sunshine, he said, *that's her name.*

It was a strange summer, the world suspended.

It was a worse autumn. The newscasters became frantic. The graphs that popped up on the TV had gone in the wrong direction and Szilvia, the baby moving, feeling first a flutter, then the first kicks, kept going to the doctor.

Your baby's growing but you're losing weight, they said.

Then they sent her back home, worrying, to the new home she had moved into with József and her teenager, but outside everything had gone crazy. Her daughter's school was already closed. The restaurants had closed; for pick up only. There was a curfew now; like a city at war.

'Then I started to feel lightheaded.'

They had only been in the new home a few days when, surrounded by boxes, by everything in its wrong place, Szilvia started to cough. It was light at first, like a little irritation, nothing more, but the next day it had built up.

You have to rest, for the baby, said József.

The next day she started to wheeze.

You feel it piercing your lungs.

You feel it pressuring you. You feel you can't breathe.

It'll pass, it'll pass, she thought, but there were now chills, there was now a trembling running through her and a confusion, forgetting things, unable to focus. *I can't have it, I can't have it*, she kept repeating, her hand on her belly.

You've got to go to the hospital.

Szilvia didn't protest as József helped her into the front seat, then she strapped in, aching, shivering, with beads of sweat on her forehead.

She could hardly see the doctor's face behind the mask.

Just have lots of rest and take plenty of Vitamin C, he said.

Nobody thought to test her.

The system was like that here.

That night it only got worse. Like she couldn't use her lungs: every breath shallower than the last, until she was gasping, until she could hardly think or feel, outside of this bundle or aches and pains, her teeth chattering. *What about my baby, my Napsugár?*

That morning she struggled to walk.

József held her, his wide face pinched with worry.

She could hardly speak. This time they tested her.

Positive – Covid-19.

I'm sure you know the rules by now, they said. *You need to quarantine inside for fourteen days.* Almost immediately József phoned the school to tell them her daughter had been exposed. Then they drove home.

Fuck, said József, the moment they got in.

The doctors didn't check the baby.

Szilvia wheezed, in pain, pierced, like she was full of glass. She coughed like it was going to rip through her. She fumbled to put on her mask back at the hospital.

Those men suddenly looked very serious.

Your wife has to stay with us, the doctors said.

Her breathing was failing. But the baby was still there.

There's no way she's going home. She's in real danger.

Then behind their masks they told József he had to leave.

I'm so sorry, these are the rules.

It was after he kissed her goodbye that things began to fog; the bright lights and the faces leaning in, the tests and the machines, them heaving her onto the bed, her mind only able to think one thing: *What's going to happen to my baby, my Napsugár?* The doctors shouting. Somebody running. Then the mask strapped over her face, the oxygen that rushed in and dried the corner of her mouth.

Szilvia, Szilvia, can you hear me?

The doctor, whoever he was behind his mask and goggles, was leaning in. *You've got pneumonia. You're going to go to Budapest. You understand?*

You can only nod that you can still understand them.

You're empty now. You're numb. You're hardly there.

You no longer see one moment leading into the next.

Szilvia saw an ambulance and then there's a gap.

She saw masked women taking off her necklace and then her rings. They leaned in. *We've got to clip your nails*, they said. But when she tried to say something – she wanted to say – *I can do it myself* – but nothing came out, she couldn't speak, she'd become so weak.

Then it breaks down completely. There are only pictures. Little scenes that might be memories or dreams. The ventilator. The iron lung. The doctors calling József, twice, to say he should brace himself – because his wife, because his baby – won't make it through the night.

She sees the beds around her.

An old lady next to her drops a glass of water.

Again and again, a woman is writhing in the bed next to her.

The trolley rattling somewhere. The nurses peering over her.

Moments looping. Then nothing.

It's all black.

She opens her eyes.

But they're so heavy, they're dropping, she can hardly hold them. There's something in her mouth. It's a mask. It's a tube.

It's making this rasping sound.

Then she realizes she can't move.

This time, she manages to open her eyes.

Then her head slumps back. She can hardly move her arm, but she wants to see her hands, and when she finally does she sees they are wrapped in tubes.

'I couldn't believe those were my wrists.'

'They were like the wrists of a skeleton.'

The first memory.

Szilvia?

It's the doctor.

Happy New Year! he says.

I'll be back at midnight with a glass of virgin champagne to celebrate this!

Then he disappears.

Light again. She keeps trying to move her hand, to lift it, just to raise it but she can't, like it no longer works.

Another moment. The nurses are there.

Goggles and masks. Moving her. Wiping her.

She heaves and she tries, with her whole mind, with her every strength, and she lifts her arm and she points her finger at her belly.

When? she wants to say. *When's it happening?*

But only rasping comes out of the sides of the tube.

The nurses look at each other, touch her gently, as though to calm her down.

Then one of them leans in.

You've already given birth.

Your mind can't work when it comes out of a coma.

You can't remember things. You can't sort things.

You've already given birth.

Those words lie there like a code. Like a foreign language.

Something that she can't understand.

When?

Struggling, she lifts her finger again.

Rasping again, she points at her belly.

Then she's gone.

You can't sort day and night when you come out of a coma.

You don't know if you've been here for weeks, for years, for a thousand years. Or the difference between a minute and an hour.

The nurses are asking her questions. She can't answer. They are holding a piece of paper down on a board in front of her. They pass her a pen – *Write, write,* they say – but it slips from her fingers.

She's horrified by those wrists.

They come back. Is it days or is it weeks later?

They have print-outs. They pass them to her. She peers long and hard and she sees the form come out of the haze.

That's your baby.

'They kept saying it but I couldn't understand what they were saying. I haven't given birth. How can that be my baby?'

Slowly it happens.

You start to feel again.

You start to think again.

I'm in the hospital. I'm all alone.

I don't know where my fam . . . my family is.

'I kept trying to speak. To say . . . Where's my baby?'

The nurses move close again. They pull out those print-outs again.

You gave birth in the coma by c-section.

The baby's doing nicely.

The picture is there. They're showing her.

It's several months old.

Then it's like a dam breaks.

'I was sobbing. I became hysterical.'

'I kept trying to pull the tubes out of my arms, out of my mouth.'

They strap her down. The nurses hold her. They wrap rope around her like a prisoner. Then she lies there sobbing and eventually she falls asleep.

Szilvia is screaming through the tube.

I want my baby . . . I want my baby!

She's strong enough to speak now.

The nurses keep repeating.

Your baby can't come here because there's Covid in the hospital.

And your family can't come here because of the rules.

And it only makes her sob, louder and deeper.

Like a wounded dog, a beaten one.

Days pass. Weeks.

She can sit up now.

Then they tell her. *Your husband's here.*

It's József. Then there's this woman. She sits up, breathing through the ventilator, blinking, trying to make her eyes focus, until, a few minutes later, she recognizes her.

That's my best friend. That's Zsuzsi.

The nurses pass her a pen and pad and – *Where's the baby?* – she writes.

József is emotional, but he holds it back, he tells her how the baby was born by c-section, that very first night, when they induced a coma. Then, that things had got worse. József told her about the blood clots, about the internal bleeding, about the calls the doctors had given him saying she might die, that she didn't, that she's still here. He says that at one moment, the doctor thought he might lose her, but she lifted her head and smiled at him, like she'd received a message, or maybe some strength, from God. József says that the baby is back home and he took her there, himself, alone. That her

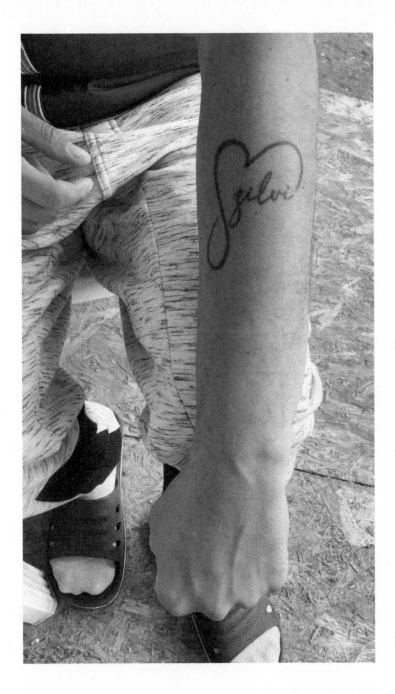

mum is looking after her as he's at the petrol station all day. That she's beautiful.

That she's sunshine.

She's her Napsugár.

Szilvia sits up and, at one moment, touches the back of her head. There's a cold rush of fright.

It's gone. Where's my hair?

You were losing a lot of blood, says József.

The easiest thing, and with cleaning you, was to cut it off.

Then it's all too much. They still won't let her see the baby. And she begins to cry.

The next days she gets stronger, then the next weeks.

The nurses help her. They help her stand up, though the first time she falls. József and her brother help. They show up with matching tattoos of her name. The doctor makes her start trying out a wheelchair. And she becomes less afraid of the bruises and blotches on her arms and legs from lying still for so many months.

And then one day, they tell her, she can come. Napsugár.

Hi, Sunshine.

She's waking up. She's not so little, actually.

She's almost four and a half months old.

Hi, Napsugár.

She meets her in a corridor, waiting to be let into a little room, where they say she can hold her. Szilvia is in her wheelchair. Her baby in her carry cradle. Waking up and rubbing her little eyes. They pass her to her.

She's never held her. Her baby starts to cry. She starts to bawl. There's nothing she can do to calm her. József comes and takes her. There's a pang of pain, of confusion, of wanting what isn't yet there.

Two psychologists are watching them.

She can feel the clock ticking. She's only got one hour.

Hi, Napsugár.

She's looking at her, at her little face, at her little soul, and inside there is only one feeling building. One enormous feeling. Stronger than any other.

I'll get better for you.

I'll get better for you, I promise.

17 HOMYEL

It was a beautiful house.

It was a beautiful garden.

And if she closed her eyes she could still see it now. The sun creeping through the sitting room in the afternoon. The light catching the icons in every room. The cat asleep on the sofa. You might not think it was anything special. The heaving bookshelf and the piano. That this was just a regular house at the edge of Homyel. That this was just another family home somewhere in Belarus. But that's not how Natasha saw it.

It was here she'd raised her children.

It was here she'd had her routine.

Life, almost rural, at the edge of town.

Mornings: with the roosters crowing, telling them to get up. German, her husband, pulling himself out of bed to get to feed the chickens, then the pets, before tending his bonsai, as she got the young ones ready for school. Afternoons: the door ringing in the little store they ran in town, selling herbal teas and remedies. Evenings: knitting, in front of her detective shows, thinking, *At last it's me time.*

'There was always church on Sunday.'

The three kids who still lived at home came with them.

The other two were already grown themselves.

That summer things were getting better. The election was coming. That's all people would talk about, drifting in and out of the store. The election wasn't going to be the same this time, that's what people kept saying online.

Mum. It was Tanya, who showed her some of the posts first.

Mum, look.

She was twenty, that's all people were talking about at university.

That's all people were talking about at the manicurist where she worked.

Mum, people are volunteering.

That's when she felt it.

You know this feeling too.

You know how it feels when all around you, all these disparate, busy, disconnected people suddenly join together and want one thing. You see them registering. You hear them chanting. You hardly hesitate.

It's the easiest thing to join them.

You've always wanted that too.

I've got too much on, thought Natasha, driving out to the villages, near where her grown son Pavel now had a farm. She'd registered as a canvasser. But all of sudden so many people had registered, there wasn't any need for her in Homyel.

I've got to get back to feed the pigs.

I've got to get back to feed the kids.

It was coming. The day everything was supposed to change. The day they wouldn't just let him steal it once again. The volunteers were everywhere. The internet was full of them. There'd been a rally – even in Homyel – with flags and chants and white bracelets: the kind of rally that everybody is so caught up in they want to walk home with the crowds. She was busy with the shop when Tanya called her.

Mum, they've switched off the internet.

Natasha froze.

What? They've actually switched it off?

Then she tried to get back to her tasks – walk the dog, pay the rent, get the eggs, water the tomatoes – but she couldn't focus.

They can't do this, she thought. *They can't go against this feeling. It's everywhere. It's too powerful. You can't just bottle it up.*

Then she began fixing dinner.

The vote was all they could talk about as they ate.

We should march, said Tanya.

Then she looked at German and he nodded. *Let's go*, he said and they got in the car leaving their youngest, Matvei and Agliya, who were too small, at home.

It was always a short drive in.

They'd done it thousands of times.

But that night Homyel didn't look like Homyel.

It didn't look like home. They'd hardly even got there when they first saw them. The OMON. Those riot police filing past in their scary helmets.

Mum, they're everywhere.

Then they saw the protestors.

Not too many. But not nobody either.

Are they coming towards us?

Now the police were circling.

Their loudspeakers were blaring.

Please return to your homes. This is an unsanctioned gathering.

But before she could even think about whether they should stay, the OMON were right in front of her. And then one of them grabbed Tanya.

Do we take this in?

The man yelled through his crash helmet at his commander. Natasha shrieked and pulled at her daughter: limp with fear. Then the moment was over.

The officer let go and with everyone else they ran.

But they weren't afraid.

The next morning they went out again.

They kept walking. They wouldn't stop.

They kept scrolling. Natasha always on Telegram – *German, look, the police are wavering. – Tanya, see, the workers . . . they're heckling him –* her mind like it was galloping.

Yes, he really is falling. Yes, it really is happening.

It was night. She felt so electric watching those clips.

German was on Facebook, liking and posting, he clicked attending and then he actually made it. He went to Minsk, to the rallies, like it was one of the most important things he had ever done, to march with the people.

It was bright. He felt so strong and powerful in that crowd.

Like it was all building.

Tanya kept scrolling, she kept seeing what Homyel had to do – new posts, women in white, proving they were peaceful, not foreign agents, new vids, women giving flowers to the OMON – and she rushed downstairs. *Mum, look at this* – minutes later they were in the garden cutting the roses for the marches. It was a warm evening. It felt so close as they did this. Like they could touch it.

That's what they felt in the crowds with the flowers. They could see it all around them. It was growing: the flags and the balloons. It was growing even in Homyel. The feeling. It was something they all felt that summer and deeply – as they walked, as they shouted and waved – that sense of inevitable victory, that the crowds, that the street, would simply prevail over that evil.

They could see it in each other's eyes.

Natasha, German and Tanya.

And then, slowly, it faded. It began to drag on. The weather was turning. The feeling had darkened. Now it had paranoid twitches. Nobody sure who was winning. Nobody sure what was happening. If his grip was withering or tightening. And then the horror stories – the rapes in Minsk, the mass arrests, the beatings – filling their timelines between mayors wavering, the reports the old man was flagging, that he knew he was done.

And they kept walking.

But we weren't getting any results.

The flowers were all gone from the garden now. They'd cut them all. They'd carried them all to the marches. The weather was getting colder. Their minds were getting sourer. There were days they didn't feel like going back into Homyel, back to the crowd. There were moments now, as they were thinning out, that they thought, *No, this isn't going to happen, is it?* Her husband was losing hope and Natasha, she too, was getting tired.

It was getting cold.

We've gotta keep going. There are people out there.

It was Tanya who was the initiator, always.

We can't stay at home when they're there.

And she would convince Natasha to let them march.

If my daughter was going, then I was going too.

That was how it started on that September day.

The light already autumnal, the air fresh and crisp.

They drove to the centre. But there were really not that many people when they got there. And it felt to Natasha, as she walked –

like it hadn't felt before – like the government had finally occupied Homyel: its streets silent and subdued. And they began to feel small, as they marched chanting, towards the OMON out in force, their crash helmets glinting in the sun. There were too many of them.

Natasha was one of the first who noticed it.

A phalanx was forming.

We're being blocked off by the police, she realized.

The ranks were closing into line.

They've blocked us . . . they've blocked the road.

Like an army in black balaclavas – the ones the OMON always wore – they stood facing them. And their megaphones began to blare.

Citizens! This is an illegal disturbance.

You are being ordered to disperse.

But there was still something lazy about it. The way it always had been in Homyel. Like they didn't believe in what they were doing. So they tried to move forward, towards the OMON and their shields. They usually gave way. The protestors chained up: locking into each other's arms. Their chanting got louder – *Free Belarus!* – and then something happened very fast. Suddenly there were hands on German. Grabbing her husband.

An OMON was trying to rip him out of the chain.

But he was half-assing it. Because my husband was able to push him off.

He wasn't really enthusiastic about it . . . not really.

They pulled back and then they pushed forward. German in the front row. Natasha and Tanya just behind him. Then something changed. A movement came over the OMON: like they had received an order – *Firm up! Take position! Forces . . . Prepare to fire!* Nobody needed to say anything. Any wavering was gone. Now they knew the OMON were serious.

German, Natasha and Tanya were at the very, very front now.

The visors of the OMON five metres from them.

There was a flash and a crack and they fell back stunned. Then another one. They were firing noise grenades right at their feet. Their ears were ringing. Then a blast. They were choking now. That smoke was tear gas. Black troopers lunged forward with pepper spray. Their faces were burning. Natasha could hardly see. Tanya

screamed. The OMON were advancing. They had never done this in Homyel before.

Natasha, stunned, grabbed on to Tanya and found German. As they were coughing the shock felt as strong as the pepper spray. They'd done nothing wrong. They were peaceful. This was Homyel. It hardly mattered at all what happened here.

But they were hitting them like it was Minsk.

You might have felt a moment like this.

When something that is not supposed to happen does.

You feel like you've been hit, you move slowly, stunned.

They staggered, rasping, to the car. The protest was broken. Everyone had scarpered their own separate way or got out in their cars. Natasha blinked. That whole way back in the car felt different. Their eyes stinging. Their faces still burning.

They couldn't get it off, the tear gas, when they got home.

Scrubbing it off in the bathroom only made it worse.

But it was all over at least.

And then they had to do the normal stuff they had to do: to check the animals, to get dinner, to make sure the younger ones were doing whatever they were supposed to do. Then after dinner they sat around talking like they always did, with stinging eyes. There was a knock at the door. *Strange of the neighbours to drop by this late*, Natasha thought.

Then a thought.

They've come for us already, Natasha joked as she got up.

No. That's not what it is.

This was Homyel. That kind of thing only happened in Minsk.

And then she opened the door.

There were two police cars there. The blue buckets flashing on top of them. And on her steps were eight police officers. There waiting for them.

Can we speak to your husband?

They filed in and stood there looking at German.

You participated in a civil disorder tonight.

They looked at him. It felt stupid to deny it.

I was at the protest, said German.

But I did nothing wrong.

The men had filled their hallway. They were perfectly polite, those officers. They made it clear to German that if he came – right there and then – there would be no handcuffs. He only had to get in the car.

It's just going to be fine, Natasha thought, as they marched German to the car.

They don't just arrest people like this in Homyel.

The officers looked at her and, grimacing, said she was expected at the police station tomorrow to write up her own participation in the disorder.

You also participated in this disturbance.

The car pulled out, away from the family home. But from the way they were treating her husband Natasha knew it wasn't just going to be a fine. That he might have to spend – *just a night or two* – locked up. *He hadn't done anything wrong.*

No, she thought. *Nothing at all.*

Natasha woke up.

The first thing she felt was German wasn't there. But as she rushed to feed the pigs, the cat, the foster dog and water the bonsai she told herself she wasn't scared.

I can't just stand here, Natasha kept thinking.

My husband's in prison. I can't just go home and make coffee.

She had a whole morning before her own summons to the police and without thinking twice she drove to the pre-trial detention centre.

There were loads of people like me.

Mostly women – dazed mothers, ashen wives and girlfriends – hanging about by the walls, waiting for the scrape and clink of the bolt on the small metal window to open with any kind of news. But it never did. For a moment or two they heard some steps behind the gate. They rushed to bang and call at it, at whoever was there, but nothing. One woman said the cases were at five. A journalist handed her their business card.

Then, like pulling herself out of a stupor, Natasha left.

She found herself driving straight to the police station.

'My character is that I'm always composed and during these kinds of critical situations . . . I'm never crying or anything.'

But the longer she sat there, waiting, one, two hours ticking away, in the small neighbourhood bureau, in that locker-room atmosphere, the coppers smoking and swearing, she began to feel more and more unsettled. *They are behaving like yobs*, she thought, *Not like officers of the law.* Like this whole office was the result of decades of unnatural, authoritarian selection, to reach these very nasty specimens.

Then finally they called her over to process her.

Do you really believe this?

Natasha was overflowing with indignation.

That we are paid provocateurs? That we're prostitutes or drug addicts massed by some foreign power? Or brainless, brainwashed idiots?

You know us. You came to our house.

They stared, smirking back at her.

I've been sitting here for two hours.

I've got kids coming back from school—

That was when the case officer cut her off.

It's because of . . . disgusting creatures, like you . . . that we're working overtime and we never get to see our own bloody families!

That was when a clammy feeling came over her.

This was going to be much worse than expected.

We're prosecuting your husband under the criminal code.

Natasha's hands began to feel cold. The thought flashed: that meant jail time. Papers were pushed at her requesting her at court for her participation.

Then the man smiled.

You see how we're treating you? Like people of culture. But imagine how they're going to treat . . . your beautiful daughter . . . because she's going to be arrested and charged with criminal offences. Like everyone else we have on camera from the protest.

Natasha sat frozen.

Every report from Minsk rushed through her. Police were raping women with their truncheons there. They were stripping them naked. They were forcing them to do things.

The officer was grinning at her, chuckling quietly.

In a way that told her exactly this is what he was alluding to.

What if they rape my Tanya? She shuddered.

Even if they lay a finger on my Tanya, she'll never recover.

A hundred moments flashed through her – a hundred memories of how she'd been fragile since she was very small – until they all came together into one thought. Them shattering her baby. Natasha in that moment felt swallowed – swallowed by horror.

The streets of Homyel flashed past her as she drove.

As fast as she could to make it to the courthouse.

I need to get my husband out. I need him. Now.

And at the courtroom it was the same scene all over again.

Families begging, rapping on the door to be let in, waving their passports, shouting their names, that they were the next of kin of those accused, and she joined them. She too stood and shouted – *I'm German Snezhkov's wife* – until finally they let her in. The corridor was packed. More relatives. Human-rights activists. Lawyers. Cops.

After work Tanya joined her and then she saw him.

The detainees were being made to wait their turn for the courtroom and in that confusion they let her sit next to German on a small bench.

They're bringing criminal charges against you, she said.

It's not a fine.

Anxiety crumpled his face.

A policeman was shouting: *Snezhkov, German.*

Her husband got up and Natasha slipped in behind him.

And there was the harried judge, who read the charges, then began his run of show with nobody but a flustered secretary trying to keep up with him. After a few seconds, this man called German to the dock and then – exasperated and overworked – gestured at him to come over to his computer.

Mr Snezhkov, watch this.

It was a video of the OMON trying to pull him from the human chain. Natasha sat on the bench watching him; her gentle, thoughtful husband, looking so crushed and confused as this man pulled his computer to the side and began to read the sentence.

Disdain. Then pity. For a moment that's what she felt towards that judge.

I hereby sentence you. The man was hardly looking up.

To fourteen days' detention.

A criminal offence.

She felt it physically, first rage, as they took German away and let her quickly peck him on the cheek as he passed, then a feeling like the ground was moving, slipping away underneath her feet, like she was dizzy.

I'm waiting for your daughter tomorrow!

A fat, pig-eyed officer was yelling at her.

German was being pulled down the corridor.

There's no warrant, what are you talking about, she said.

But this squat man only started grinning. Like he was enjoying it.

You want the OMON to come and pick her up at yours, then?

I want her tomorrow . . . at my station!

Then her husband was gone.

That night, the house silent, in all those ways it was when German wasn't there, Natasha tried to talk to Tanya about escaping to Kyiv. Thoughts of what they were doing to the women in Minsk rushing through her: beating them, violating them.

We can't let you go into detention, she said.

She was just a baby. Sitting there, hardly twenty. And she was telling her that if that policeman was serious, she might have to go to Ukraine, just for a little bit, until it all calmed down. Tanya nodded, nervous.

Mum, will it be soon?

Natasha shook her head.

In that case I'll quit my job tomorrow and get ready for it.

She hugged her. But all Natasha could think about was how they had no one in Ukraine to look after her baby – not a friend, not a family member, unlike in Russia – but it would be madness to flee there. Tanya went upstairs to her room and switched on her music. Natasha sat there alone, Pippa the cat asleep on the sofa, twitching slightly.

It all suddenly felt immense.

Vladimir?

She called their best friend, from across town.

Can you come over?

He was there as fast as he could, as stiff and awkward as always.

They talked quietly so nobody could hear.

Hypothetically, would you take my daughter to Ukraine?

He answered briskly like he always did.

Hypothetically, I agree.

Natasha heard the door click and rattle.

Then Tanya's steps on the porch. She'd gone.

She'd woken up and told her – if it was only a matter of time – she'd go into town to the manicurist and tell her she'd quit.

It seemed harder that morning, with the animals. There was only her: feeding the pigs, fixing Pippa's kibble, fetching their foster dog's breakfast, thinking, *This weekend I'm going to struggle to make it to church.* Then Tanya called.

Mum?

She wasn't there, Tanya's boss, she wasn't coming. So there was nothing she could do but leave the keys on the table. Tanya's boss wasn't even going to pay her now she'd quit.

Can you come and get me, Mum?

The door clicked behind her.

It was the same old road to the centre.

Worrying about things she'd never imagined.

Does my husband have enough to eat?

Is he warm enough in prison?

Does my daughter have enough time to flee?

The road back was faster as they talked. They'd have some lunch and then quickly they'd find a human-rights lawyer from one of the NGOs to tell them what to do.

Maybe there was some kind of legal appeal Tanya could make.

The door clicked behind them.

Then Natasha did something she'd never done, that they never did in that quiet street with the trees and the children coming and going.

Almost without thinking. She locked the door.

She cracked the eggs over the frying pan and as the butter began to splutter she heard Tanya calling her upstairs to the computer. The eggs were done. She left them to see what lawyer Tanya had found. They'd not been back ten minutes.

Then there was a powerful knock at the door.

Then at the window. Then at the back.

There was knocking, angry, a man's knocking, coming from all sides.

They're knocking on everything.

They crept up to the window and then they saw them. The plain-clothes policemen and their car right outside.

Mum, it's them.

There was a rush of cold right through her. Then their phones began to ring.

Both at the same time. It was them.

Tanya!

But in that second Natasha knew what to do.

They powered off their phones and, in a flash, they flew to the attic step ladder that had long leaned so lazily at the top of the Snezhkovs' stairs. The moment Tanya was up there, she shut the hatch and grabbed it and shoved it under the bed.

Please, please don't guess there's an attic.

She lay there, thoughts flying, on the floor of the upstairs room, which had been Tanya's room for so many years, her daughter in the attic above her, as the men knocked again. They knocked everywhere.

And she waited. She waited for them to kick her family's door in.

They might not see it.

You can't really see it . . . the attic hatch.

And they waited some more.

Time seemed to hang and slow surrounded by her daughter's things.

They could rape her.

I'll do anything to save her.

Then time moved. Twenty minutes. Thirty minutes.

Natasha peeped out of the window; they were still there.

Forty minutes. Then she peeped again.

Sixty minutes, maybe, but it was hard to say.

They've gone . . . haven't they?

Natasha finally stood up.

She couldn't see a car.

It was only when she stood up she felt it.

How scared she was.

They must be coming back. They must be coming back with something to break the door open or maybe they've gone to get a search warrant.

Natasha powered up her phone, full of their missed calls, then without a moment's doubt she called him: Vladimir, their friend.

She spoke as fast as she could.

They were out there.

Come round the back.

Over the fence between our neighbour's plot and ours.

But he must not have understood as he came knocking at the front.

Natasha, he said, gawkily.

They're still there . . . just further up.

It rushed through her at that moment. The fear. Then she spoke again as quickly as she possibly could, so they might think, if they were watching, that he'd just knocked at the door and found nobody there.

Will you help us?

Yes, he said quickly.

Yesterday you agreed, hypothetically, to take Tanya to Ukraine.

Will you do it now?

Yes, he said, stunned.

Give us ten minutes. Meet us out back.

Vladimir nodded, then without blinking, he calmly turned around and walked to his house, like he was simply running an errand. Then Natasha ran, she grabbed the step ladder, she threw it up where it belonged, then she burst open the hatch.

Come!

Quickly! Quickly!

We've got five minutes.

Tanya came down and then she told her.

You're going to Ukraine. Now . . . with Uncle Vladimir.

She stood there, her beautiful daughter, and then it was as if she froze. She began to shake and shiver, until Natasha grabbed hold of her.

We don't have anybody in Ukraine.

Nobody. No relatives, no friends. Nobody.

Natasha just took her hand.

'I don't understand how my brain worked. Because I had to do so many things. And I did so many things in just a few minutes. I instructed her to disassemble the phone. How to take the SIM card out as she mustn't be followed when she gets in the car. There mustn't be any phone traces.'

And then she was sweeping things into a duffel bag: One of everything, almost at random, just what she could find: a jumper, some jeans, one pair of socks.

Come on! Quickly!

Tanya was so scared she was stumbling. She could hardly move straight as Natasha pulled her down the stairs into the garden and over to the fence. It had seemed like a good thing for such a long time to have this thing almost two metres high. Now it stood towering between them and Uncle Vladimir.

There was a barrel and she pulled it close.

Tanya, step on it!

But she couldn't. In that moment, the stress was so complete it was like her body had turned to cotton, like she was in one of those nightmares where it's coming, it's after you, but you can't get away. *Mummy*, she whimpered, *I can't move my leg.*

Aggression, that second, flashed into Natasha.

Don't you understand? They can enter any second?

But then Tanya froze on the barrel again, her hands shaking as they touched the fence. Then, her heart thumping, Natasha just grabbed her, she pushed her hands up underneath her ass and heaved so she toppled over the fence.

On the other side, Uncle Vladimir caught her.

She flung the duffel bag after her, then ran back to the house.

'So I would be there . . . facing them when they came.'

Natasha stepped into her empty house.

Her husband was in jail, her little ones were in school, her daughter, who knows where she was by now, and she tried to breathe. As she tried to steady this, as her heart was pounding, because there was too much adrenaline in her body, and it was making her tremble and gasp. And then nothing happened. Her body stilled. Her thoughts slowed.

The sun had crept further along the sky.

It had been more than an hour when she stepped out with Balloo the foster dog. Trying to make it seem as casual as possible. Like they were just going for their afternoon walk. She unlocked the door. And nothing. First she looked left, then she looked right. And as Balloo was straining at the leash to sniff something, she saw that it was all clear.

The car and the agents were gone.

Balloo was messing in the dirt when she turned. That was when she heard the engine. It was Uncle Vladimir's car. Then the shock hit her. It was Tanya sitting in the back.

I forgot my passport, he said.

The window was rolled down.

I forgot you needed it to cross . . . and I just remembered that it's actually expired.

Tanya was looking at her confused.

Just wait there, snapped Natasha.

I'll get my passport and I'll be the driver.

In less than a minute the dog was back inside and they were driving again, Tanya lying flat on the back seat, Natasha trying to call people who knew about borders on Uncle Vladimir's phone. *No,* they said. *You can't just drive his car to Ukraine.*

It's not the same country any more.

You need to be on the car's insurance.

Then they powered down the phone. It was thirty kilometres to the border, past the military encampments they kept massing there, for some reason she tried not to think about, until the long line of trucks and cars, clogged at the crossing. There was only one thing to do. Natasha jumped out, took her daughter, and went up one by one knocking on the hauliers' cabins.

'So I wasn't lying to these men. I was straight, I told them straight, that she's . . . *a political* . . . that there's going to be a political prosecution and that she needs to flee the country. Will you, under these conditions, knowing that . . . *take her to Ukraine?*'

The first three said no.

The fourth, he was a Belarusian guy, about thirty to thirty-five, he looked at her, he looked at Tanya, then he said – *OK, give me the bag.* Natasha only had the time to give her a quick peck on the cheek.

In that instant, she saw her very clearly, Tanya. Like only a mother can. Looking so small and scared, like a child lost at the fair. Then she ran, back to Uncle Vladimir, back to the car, to drive back to Homyel.

They had to get away from the border. They had to disappear as fast as possible.

The forest and the fields flew past until they were back at the edge of the city.

And Uncle Vladimir switched his phone on first, just to check.

It was a call. Natasha's little boy, Matvei.

Uncle Vladimir, where's Mum, where's Tanya?

She heard him. She heard his voice. And in that moment her blood froze. Had they got to him, the agents, and made him call? Uncle Vladimir looked at her and as laconically as he said everything, told Matvei – *Back in three.*

The dog was barking, she was home, as she tried to figure out why little Matvei had called Uncle Vladimir – who'd just then driven off. But it seemed he'd done it all on his own. Then she finally switched on her own phone. A flood of missed calls. And with a start a new one coming in. It was the vice-rector of the kids' school. She spoke haltingly and jarringly, saying that Agliya had been taken out of class, that there were security operatives in the school, and they were talking with the social worker and with her now.

The worst was right in front of Natasha.

They say they are going to take Agliya into care, said the vice-rector.

Natasha stuttered. *They should c-c-come and find me here*, she said. *I'm at home. But they should stop terrorizing my eleven-year-old daughter.*

She hung up and, as she did, she felt swallowed by this overwhelming feeling that these iron claws were ripping at her family, rapping on her windows and clinging to each one they caught. Natasha's hands were shaking as she called Pavel, her eldest son, out on his farm, to come here now. They'd already taken her husband, now she needed backup. Then in a flash she remembered the journalists she'd met outside the prison and she found the business card and called them. She had nothing to lose.

Yes, come now!

And then with a shiver she saw a surveillance car was already loitering outside. There was a knock on the door and then a brief moment of relief broke the fear: it was Agliya, stiff and tearful. Not the police. They'd told her to go home.

Then the journalists arrived. But they'd only just finished setting up and started filming when there was a knock on the door.

More of a thud, the thud of a fist.

Are they there already . . . ?

Matvei, open up.

Then another thud.

Mrs Snezhkov?

There were about twelve operatives, standing there behind a young captain, his eyes full of anger and authority, as the others looked away, towards the floor, like they were ashamed of what they were doing.

We've got a search warrant.

And then methodically they set to work, opening drawers, upturning pillows, searching cupboards, their hands running through sheets, even riffling right at the bottom of their dirty clothes bin as they grabbed everything they could that was electronic: modems, phones, even the ancient dead Nokias buried at the back of the wardrobe.

What are you looking for?

She asked them again and again. But they wouldn't say. *It's a job*, the men kept repeating, whilst their captain scowled, his eyes narrowing to slits, as he wrote down what they were confiscating, his underlings trying to smile and be down to earth, like they were removal men or something, just doing an unpleasant task.

The sun was setting.

Am I staying at home?

Or am I coming with you?

They wouldn't answer.

And the deeper that silence the more she realized it was for the worst.

Where's your daughter?

The eyes of that captain, with that horrible glow, were fixed on her.

I don't know. I don't know where she is.

Call her now, he said. *Or you'll regret it later.*

No, I won't. She didn't pick up earlier. I don't know where she is.
Then he smirked and scowled at her.
She's at the border . . . Call her now! Or you'll regret it later.
For a split second, Natasha felt like she was falling, through the floorboards, through the basement, into something deep and bottomless.

They must have got her.

The sun had set. It was dark. It was past the hour they'd normally be feeding the animals. They'd pulled her through every room in the house, as they'd picked through them; her little girl was snivelling in the living room, her little boy up in his room.

You're coming with us, said the captain.

His voice thrilled, full of enjoyment, full of this power.

Can I bring my stuff?

No, he snarled, *you're coming with us.*

Then his men went to get her children.

There was a feeling now, rising in her throat that this was going to be really bad. It wasn't just going to be her. They were going to take Matvei and Agliya for sure. There was a commotion as they pulled them all outside: the neighbours, they'd gathered a few of them as witnesses, to sign their protocol, and they were all shouting over one another.

Uncle Vladimir had turned up in his car. And now so had Pavel.

You don't have to take the children!

Leave them with us! We can look after them!

For a split second, Uncle Vladimir grabbed her and whispered.

Tanya called . . . she's crossed the border.

The two cars were waiting for them, when something started to bubble up inside her, something like rage, hot in those first chill of the night, and she grabbed her crying Agliya and held her close. Then she raised her voice to all those officers.

Look here, like an actor, like she was in a film.

Every one of you thinks of himself as a good person. And after this you'll be going home to your families and you'll be hugging your children and putting them to bed.

They'd all gone silent.

And in that moment I want you to remember the face of this eleven-year-old girl with tears in her eyes and to remember that you broke up this family. That you think that you're good people . . . but you're doing this, at this moment, to this family.

There was only silence. All the agents looking away, ashamed.

Then the captain said, *Let's go.*

For a moment, she held them, Matvei and Agliya.

It's just for a few days. Don't worry. I'm not far.

Get in! the captain snapped.

And then, brusquely they grabbed the children, and bundled her into another car. At first, alone in the back seat, it was like her brain wasn't working any more, like she couldn't keep up with what was happening, like she was sitting in the back seat not feeling anything at all, like she was the cut half of a lemon squeezed out on the counter.

Get out!

They'd arrived.

They were at one of the precincts in the centre of town, but when they left her there, with no papers, no instructions, nothing, the police had no idea what to do with her.

Who is she?

What's she in for?

So they locked her in the line-up room, with only one chair and a table, and a half window to see the suspects through. She was alone.

I've done nothing wrong!

Natasha shouted, she shouted again, but nothing. She begged for a pen and paper to write a declaration of innocence. And when they refused to give her anything, she found what she needed in her handbag and she tried to write it anyway.

I have an over-eighty-year-old father who is unable to take care of himself alone due to his advanced age therefore I am requesting not to be detained overnight according to my rights under the law.

But they pushed it away.

Dead eyes looking right through her. Then she just sat there, waiting for hours, in that cramped space, until an officer stepped in and told her to follow him.

They made her strip when she arrived at the detention centre. Then they threw a mattress at her and told her to dress. They took her stuff.

Then the guards pushed her forward into a solitary cell.

The door slammed behind her. There was a very high ceiling that made her feel very small, no windows and a small air vent. Only a single bunk under a harsh, bright, clinical light. The kind it was hard to sleep under, that stung your eyes, as she lay there.

That's where she collapsed, her ears ringing, her mind racing, her head thumping; Tanya, Matvei, Agliya and German flashing in front of her eyes; repeating to herself, *It's my court tomorrow, it's my sentence tomorrow.*

Get up! I said, Get up!

Had it only been a few hours?

She wasn't even sure. Time was so confused and sticky. She was half asleep under that painful light, under her coat that still stank of pepper spray, when they came to get her, to strip her again, to make her take off her tights, then pat her down and send her back to the cell. So tired at this point, she followed them like a robot.

Then they came again. She did it all again.

Do you want some calming valerian? asked an officer.

No . . . I just want it to stop, she mumbled as she stripped.

And then they took her back to her cell.

As she lay there, she found herself mumbling: *My husband, he's here, somewhere in this prison, and he doesn't know I'm here, but I've got his glasses in my handbag and I brought the Svetlana Alexievich book he wanted to read.* And she lay there, until they came again, a few hours later, to strip her and search her, her eyes red and runny with exhaustion, so there was no chance of sleep, no moment to slip into that other place inside her head, until they came banging at the cell in the morning.

She had no idea what time it was when they drove her to the courtroom, when they fingerprinted her and when they left her in the paddy wagon, muttering it was going to be difficult to get her in discreetly. There was a rap on the smeared window.

A man appeared.

I'm the lieutenant-colonel.

About forty, bald, a stocky build.

Quickly, he told the others to leave, got in the back with her, locked the door. Then without stopping, he dismantled his phone, took out the SIM card, and rolled it up deep inside his coat pocket. Then he spoke in a very low voice.

If you mention to anyone what I'm going to say now . . . I'll deny everything.

She nodded.

My proposal is this. You plead guilty and you refuse the right to an attorney, and you'll go home with your children. If you don't . . . you won't. And your eldest son won't be getting them as the guardian. They'll go to the orphanage.

He seemed so uncomfortable.

Like he knew he was doing dirty work and he didn't like it.

I agree, she said.

And then it all happened very fast. They took her to the courtroom, somehow the activists, from the movement, from the marches, had managed to get an attorney there, but she said – *No, I don't want these services.* Then the judge spoke.

Do you plead guilty to taking part in an unsanctioned mass action?

Yes, she said, *I plead guilty.*

The judge was a tense, unhappy looking young woman. And then the lieutenant-colonel came for her. And he kept his side of the bargain. He drove Natasha in his car to the school buildings for the documents he needed to get the children released.

It was their town.

It was her town.

But now it all felt so different.

You know, he said.

There will be a criminal case no matter what.

The full force of what he had said settled on her. That this was only a reprieve. That they would be coming back. And everything – prison, losing the children, those hands rapping on the window – would be coming back.

She fell silent for a moment then looked him in the eye.

How long do I have?

He knew exactly what she was asking.

How long do I have to run away?

She saw his face in the light.

You have about three days.

The children grabbed hold of her like never before. And the

lieutenant-colonel drove them home, or what used to be home. He hovered on the doorstep, making chit-chat about the situation, like he'd been brainwashed.

How did it happen. That ordinary, regular, good people became enemies?

He turned to go but Natasha asked anyway.

Did you ever think it would end up like this?

All the beatings? All the extrajudicial arrests? All the rapes?

No, said the lieutenant-colonel and left.

But with a look in his eyes that said, I know what your plans are, and what they should be, to flee, and I hope that you succeed.

Pippa and Balloo were there when she got inside, finally. The volunteers had fed them, and she sat down on the sofa beside them thinking – *I don't know anyone abroad. Don't I need a visa to go west? Can I even manage this? What about the kids?*

But before it could overwhelm her the volunteers started appearing, ten, twenty, thirty people, with packets of food, with advice.

We can take care of Pippa kitty.

We know a new foster for Balloo.

We'll water the bonsai.

It was like everyone she had ever known was there.

Like it was a kind of wake: friends, neighbours, church people and faces, suddenly, from earlier in her life, like the son of acquaintances who'd long ago emigrated to St Petersburg, saying – *We're here for you* – or her eldest's old classmate, who lives in Russia now, who sent someone with money for them – *because we know you'll need it.*

That was when she got a call from Minsk.

It was a woman from one of the opposition fronts. *You must go immediately*, she said – *Lithuania has just allowed you to claim humanitarian visas on the border.* She explained that when they made it across, there would be help in Vilnius for her and her kids.

The last of the volunteers left.

Natasha was in her bed, alone, her body twitching, unable to sleep; tossing and turning until it was time to feed the animals and rush into town as quickly as she could to the lawyer to sign papers for Pavel, giving him power of attorney over the property.

But it seemed that absurd.

That's what they'd told her to do.

She was driving back when her phone buzzed.

It was the police.

There are documents you need to sign, they said. *You need to come in now to the station.* But the more she told them – *No*, the harder they insisted, letting it drop they knew what street she was on, like they'd bugged her car with a GPS.

Well, if you can't come in . . . we will come to you.

Then you'll sign the documents.

The tone of voice said it all.

Natasha was panicking.

The moment she got home she found the children and said, *Pack like you're going to summer camp.* And as they filled their back-packs she called Uncle Vladimir.

Where are you?

I'm at work, he said.

How soon can you get here?

Forty minutes?

Please, she begged. *Please.*

The moment he arrived, he didn't even have to be told. She grabbed the food bag left by the volunteers, she grabbed Matvei and Agliya, and said drive – *To Lithuania.*

Her mind was fraying in the car. Homyel disappeared. The road north opened up, across the whole sad country, the one she'd always called home. Repeatedly, she switched her phone off and on. The opposition had said they'd message her with more information.

But instead it was the police who were there. Bombarding her.

Her official summons had popped up as a message. A woman with a sexy pic of herself in a red dress was pinging her saying she was handling German's case. And then there were the unknown numbers, calls she took just in case it was the voice from Minsk.

Again and again it was the sexy lady.

I'm handling German's case, she kept saying. *He told me to call you, to say he needs to meet you, to discuss something we can't speak of here.*

No, Natasha kept saying. *No.*

It was cloudy, the afternoon slipping away.

Finally, a call from the voice in Minsk.

There were Covid rules, they said, then there were other rules and it meant you couldn't be let out of Belarus so easily.

Tell them, they said, *your children have an emergency appointment at a clinic in Vilnius and that they'll issue the visa on the Lithuanian border. Then,* they explained, *you cross and you claim humanitarian assistance.*

You can feel them.

You can feel them closing in.

It was dusk when they arrived. The queue at the border post.

Uncle Vladimir dropped them, then in a second he left. With Matvei and Agliya, holding their hands, she moved towards the line. Natasha was so frightened she could barely walk, when the guard took their passports, when she told her lie, when the men in uniform told them to stand outside and wait there.

They stood there, by the wall of the kiosk on the border. The bright lights of the frontier glaring, the ground no longer feeling solid beneath her feet, like an abyss was opening, to devour them all. *Pray*, she said. Natasha looked at Matvei and she looked at Agliya and she said one word. *Pray.*

'We were praying for help.'

The line slowly passed behind them: truckers, families, whoever they were, who went back to their cars and drove. Time slowed, until she could hardly feel it at all.

You're free to go.

The guards gave her back the passports. Then they crossed on foot over the border, under those flood lamps, to the Lithuanian side. *I'd like to request humanitarian assistance*, she said, bloodshot eyes, almost in a daze. The Lithuanians were shocked, worried, they told her to sit down, to have some tea, to have some soup for the children as they worked out what the hell they were supposed to do in this kind of situation. Then, there in the night, a feeling swept over her, like running water.

I'm safe. I don't know where my husband is. What is going to happen to me . . .

Or my children. But I'm safe.

18 AVIGNON

You remember where you were.

Mahjoub was on holiday in Tunisia. He worked too hard. It wasn't easy running a French mosque and it was good to see family. He loved having fun on the edge of the desert. The kids were enjoying themselves: camels, 4×4s.

Big red sunsets.

'I was happy, I was relaxed.'

'Because you know, *I work* . . . I work a lot.'

He didn't let it distract him. This thing in China.

They were still talking about it when they got back to France. It was a small town they lived in. In the south. Bagnols-sur-Cèze, near Avignon.

They were still talking about it.

'You know what I thought?'

'This is never going to come to France. The Spanish flu and all that . . . it's finished. It's not our generation that deals with these things.'

You felt it too.

You heard it getting louder and louder. You heard it crowding everything out.

You remember a feeling. Fear.

'Then it clicked. It was coming.'

It was when Mahjoub realized half of China was in lockdown. Then a few towns in Italy. Then all of Italy. His messages were becoming a frenzy. They were looking at him, the Muslims, at Mahjoub, their imam.

Is it going to happen to us?

What happens when it gets here?

They had no idea what to do.

Mahjoub was at the mosque when the order came in. They knew the President was going to speak. They were almost certain what he was going to say.

But they couldn't quite believe it.

It was a Sunday evening. People were already arriving for the final prayers. But he wasn't downstairs, in the hall, where they were gathering. He was in his office by the screen.

The President was talking.

They were heading into lockdown.

They were just a few there, the people he worked with. Their phones were pinging with messages, but Mahjoub didn't answer, he made straight for the door. There were almost a hundred there, waiting.

'I went straight downstairs and I said . . .'

These are our last prayers together. We don't know how long it will be . . . whether it's one month, two months or three months. Only God knows.

The mosque will be closed.

They were all looking at him.

Mahjoub was trembling.

Here we are. It's a divine decision. And as believers we must accept that this comes from the will of God. We have to ask ourselves why.

God isn't happy with humanity.

There were tears in his eyes.

Epidemics, my friends. Humanity has encountered them before on its journey. And now it's our turn. Yet all of this is the will of God. There is a lot that's wrong with the world. We've seen it before . . . and now it's our turn.

He was crying.

There will be no more prayers.

Until the authorities decide it's over.

Those hundred people, they looked at him.

They looked at him in a way they never had before. They looked at him with fear. He could see each of their faces very clearly. There were people crying. There were men who looked angry. And then the shouting started.

What do you mean no more Friday?

How are we going to manage . . . what about Ramadan?

Mon Dieu! The mosque has never been closed before!

Mahjoub could hardly speak through the emotion.

Here we are, he said.

This is where we are. We can't question this.

They prayed. They prayed quickly and with an intensity he had seldom felt before. And then it was done. He took a key and he locked his mosque.

Mosque Closed – his hands shaking as he hung this sign.

You remember it too.

The moment everything stopped. The moment you found yourself at home. Not knowing what to do with yourself.

Mahjoub had never found himself at home with the kids like this. He'd always worked hard – too hard, maybe – and now there he was horsing around, playing little games with them, helping in the kitchen.

There was a strange pleasure to it.

His phone flooded with messages.

Because people still needed their imam.

did allah really want this???

monsieur l'imam, don't you know it's a plot ! ! !

They kept calling. Then the first one died. Aissa had been in France longer than he'd been alive. His nephew phoned him: *Monsieur l'Imam, he's dead. It was an old cancer. It's not Covid I swear. He'd been in a coma.*

'And I knew I had to go.'

'Who else would go? I'm still an imam.'

He was paranoid when he stepped outside.

Mahjoub left in fear to the hospital. His hands gloved and his pockets full of sanitizer. He'd heard people were dropping in the streets in China. He shuddered. He kept thinking: *Will I catch it? What if I touch something? Am I going to die?*

He waved his pass to the police – imams were still allowed to work.

Who else would wash the bodies?

The streets were deserted.

I'm a diabetic, he kept thinking.

Everything, everything was closed. Like everyone had disappeared.

I had a pulmonary embolism . . . I was hospitalized.

I've got pre-existing conditions. But I promised . . . I have to, I have to. The big hospital in Avignon wouldn't let him in. They had the body in the morgue, they said. They promised there were no Covid cases there.

That was where he worked.

Mahjoub washed Monsieur Aissa and sang to him. The way that a Muslim is supposed to be readied. He remembered him. Just before the lockdown. He'd been at his bedside telling him not to fear. That life was the first passage and now it was over. That *–Yes*, everything would be left to his wife. He was always at the mosque. He remembered him, as he scrubbed him, the tears in old Aissa's eyes as he read the suras of the narrow bridge they say we all have to cross into paradise.

Will you wash me? he'd asked.

Aissa was yellowed, his eyes hollow.

Small, bundled, in the sheets.

I promise, said Mahjoub.

Whatever happens.

A calm filled him. The washing was done.

Then carefully he wrapped Aissa for the coffin.

'And then I phoned the police.'

Can I even bury him? Can I have ten people there?

That night he hardly slept.

Was that Covid-infected?

Thinking of everything he'd touched.

Was this it? Will that get me?

The day after, like for all Muslim funerals, they gathered.

'In all my fifty years I'd never seen a sight like it . . .'

Four times he spoke over the coffin.

Allahu Akbar. And then he turned to bless them.

What I saw is burned into my eyes.

This image was a horror . . . horror.

An imam knows funerals. He knew about death. That's what he does. But there were only ten people there. There should have been two hundred. All separated, standing far apart, at the moment they needed each other. All shaking, wrapped in scarves and make-shift masks. And as he began to speak of how He was with us, of how Aissa's hour had come in these awful circumstances, his mind flicked back and he began to ask himself how he had ended up here, an imam, in France, his voice on the edge of a sob.

You rip a child out of its mother's arms, you rip it again. As with the umbilical cord, the energy bond, the life force. The child screams, it howls, like it did the day it was born. This is what happened to Mahjoub.

It happened a long time ago.

'My first memory, the first image I have, is my father's family ripping me away from my mother. I remember them . . . *ripping me out of her arms.*'

It felt like it happened yesterday.

'It felt like a total breakdown. I was a child . . . they were ripping me away from my mother. It's over, it's finished, I can't see her any more.'

'She's gone.'

This is the thing about something like this.

It starts happening, all those little things making it happen, years before. Somewhere, long before, the moment comes and goes, making it inevitable, which will make people do what they will do. Murders begin where lovers are still in each other's arms. Families are torn apart when they are still sitting and laughing together.

Nobody gasps, nobody notices, the moment passes.

In 1971, a man left Tunis for France.

The basket-weavers in the streets, the beggars in the souk, the diners in the halls in the new hotels, the donkey carts behind the shiny new buses, the cries of the morning hawkers; everything went on as before, like nothing had happened. The man was Mahjoub's father.

And he had a simple plan: a few months, travel, a little work. Savings, commercial expansion, some time in France would help everything back home. How could it not? France was France. The great country, *la Métropole*, where everything happened, where everything came from. Apart from him.

Mahjoub imagined him like this.

He turned heads, he was finely dressed, as he left that day. He was not like the others with stains on their djellabas and dirt rings behind their nails. Mahjoub's father was a man who worked inside, a man who owned things, and he left in a suit and tie. Like a French-man. Behind him, he left his two spice shops, he left his business, he left everything he owned, in the hands of his brother. Then, he kissed his family goodbye, picked up his suitcase and left the city. His name was Aamar. Aamar, his father.

And he was respected by everyone.

'When he came back the shops were gone.'

His brother had sold them.

'It was a shock, a trauma, he couldn't accept it.'

He stood there gawping. Gone.

The shops, the money. It was all gone.

He had been completely, utterly robbed.

'They were family possessions, so he could do it.'

The whole of Tunis collapsed in on him.

It was like a nightmare. But it didn't end. It wasn't going to end.

'He had nothing left, so he went back to France, to work in the fields, even though he was always a man of class, well dressed, wear-ing a tie.'

Mahjoub, he imagined his father on the boat, looking back at the white city, cursing that thief, who called himself a brother. He imagined him, as the passengers flooded at the docks in Marseilles, with nothing but a suitcase. He imagined him, rolling up his sleeves in the dirt, picking grapes, pulling vegetables, sweating in the heat. This man in a tie.

But he remembered none of this.

He remembered none of his father's rage as he learnt what his brother had done. He recalled none of his shock, as he stood trembling in the street where the spice shops had been. Nothing of his face as he realized that if he was going to be a hired hand, he would rather be in France than in the markets and the fields here.

'He never accepted it.'

Neither did Mahjoub remember his mother, the distress running from her eyes, as she took him and his baby sister to his grand-mother's village, in his father's country on the edge of the desert. And he remembered nothing of his uncles making their decision. The one he would never forget. That his mother must return to her village. And he must remain here, on the edge of the desert, in his father's country. He, little Mahjoub. He was theirs.

'I remember . . . I was at my grandmother's house.'

It was inevitable, back then, what happened.

'I can see it now . . .'

'My uncles, they had come to take my mother away. And my father's brothers had come to take me because in their heads, unfortunately, in the old ideology, the boy must always stay in his father's family. And this is what I remember. I remember them ripping me from my mother.'

He's our son, they said.

He holds our father's name, our son. He's ours.

'I remember crying.'

'I remember howling as they pulled me away.'

This is what he could still see. His mother screaming as the uncles bundled her into a car. Hands, grabbing him. Yelling. Hands pulling him back, holding him. The car pulling away. More screaming. Her voice disappearing. The car vanishing. Him beginning to scream.

Mahjoub was five years old.

He did not see his mother again for a year.

'My next, vivid memory is when they took me to her.'

The memory was faded.

He was in a little pickup truck. His uncle was driving. It was hot. There was a winding road, cactus and countryside. It was the harvest. There were piles of yellow wheat in the fields and figures gathering it in.

'And I can feel joy . . . joy that I am going to my mother.'

The road continued, it wound to its end. The land began to change. It became greener. The fields became bigger. There were cattle now. And this, his uncles said, was how they knew he was in his mother's country.

'I can see her there . . . in a long skirt.'

'Then she sees me and she starts running towards me.'

His mother was holding him.

'It felt warm, it was my mother, holding me.'

His mother's country was not like the edge of the desert. There they slept in a house made of mud with a floor covered with straw.

All of them together in one room; his grandmother, his cousin, her cousin and him. Under one rough blanket they made every year with what was left from the wool.

'My mother's house was very different.'

The walls were painted. Made of bricks not mud.

There was a shower there and they even showered every day. Not like in the south, where there was nothing like that, where they went weeks without being able to wash, sometimes, if they were lucky, warming some water over a fire.

His mother held him and his uncles, they brought him butter and milk straight from the cows. They spoiled him, before he went back to the south.

'They told me about my father.'

'I knew he was alive.'

'I knew he existed. I knew he was in France. When they said *Papa is in France*, this is what I could see. A richness, lots of money . . . lots of things, where *Papa* is, a man with a car, a man with a tie.'

'I felt like I was the son of somebody.'

'All my images were like this.'

'I imagined high society, I imagined cultured people. I had seen French people, you see. I was maybe seven years old and whenever I saw them, French people on holiday in our markets, I would run up to them and say . . . *Bonjour* . . . and then I'd run away because I didn't know French.'

'I looked at them and all I wanted was to go there.'

'There where *Papa* is.'

Mahjoub's mother kissed him, and said she too was going to France. But she would leave him here, with his sister Salya, in this country. He would go back to the south. But he would not be alone. *Mahjoub*, she said, *I promise, I promise . . . we will be coming back*.

The winter came and went and she did.

'I knew my father existed because I saw him.'

The men in the village, they looked at him with awe when he came back. The elders, their teeth had fallen out, and they wore long hooded cloaks, not like his father.

'But I saw very little of him, even when he returned.'

His car, his father's French car, threw up dust as it circled. He was busy.

He saw the important people, he saw the big men, he saw high society, he saw judges, always in his suit and tie.

'Nobody had a father like mine.'

They waited for him. They longed for their parents to come to the village every summer, where the water mostly came from a well, where most people didn't have electricity and the dogs barked, angrily, nervously, every night, when there was the moon.

'They hadn't decided what to do with us.'

'Whether we would come to France. Or stay here.'

It was the summer of 1985 that they told him.

They were excited. They were full of joy.

'My father was sitting there, and he said to us, *If all goes well, next summer you will come join us with your sister.* And in our heads, at that moment, it was like a movie. And for months we were like, *How does it take off? How does it do it? A plane? What is it . . . France? When will it be? What will we see . . . on the other side of the Mediterranean?*'

But the wait, it seemed like for ever. Mahjoub and Salya made a little notebook together at school. And they crossed them off one by one: one day, two days, five days. And every day they looked at the date on the board, waiting, waiting, for 15 June.

'That was the date. Our deliverance.'

That night they got ready.

But they didn't get ready with any bags as they didn't have any bags. They didn't take any clothes as they didn't really have any clothes. All they had was two dresses for Salya and two pairs of trousers and a few shirts for Mahjoub.

'That morning my uncle drove us to the airport.'

'And all we had was one bag of Barbary figs. And the moment we got to the airport the bag tore, it ripped, and the figs . . . they flew everywhere. And I was so ashamed, I pushed them all into a corner, until someone came and said, *You can't leave this here.* So I got on my knees and began to gather them up.'

They were full of fright as the plane took off.

They couldn't believe what was happening as they flew to great heights. The aeroplane was already like another world. The women in little red hats brought them food and drinks. The trolleys were filled with all kinds of treats that kept moving through the aisles.

'And then it landed . . . it landed in Marseilles.'

There was a commotion, as everyone got up, and suddenly they didn't know what to do, Mahjoub and Salya, until the women in little red hats came to them, smiled and took them by the hands, speaking to them, it must have been in French, because it was something they didn't understand.

They took them, holding on to as many figs as they could, through the lines, through the lights, past all kinds of things they had never seen before, to where their passports got stamped. And then, there he was, the one who meant everything, the one they hardly knew.

'It was our father. He was there, he was beautiful, still young.'

The first thing they noticed were buildings, the buildings were different. And the cars, there were so many more cars, everywhere, as *Papa* drove. And even the countryside was different, everything, apart from the heat and the light. Then they arrived, where they could scarcely believe their eyes.

'We had gone from a mud hut to a castle. It was a château.'

Mahjoub's father took them in to meet le Monsieur.

'And there were two little dogs with la Madame. I couldn't believe it. Back home a dog lived outside, it ate rubbish. And here were two little dogs being combed every day in little butterfly knots on a little leash.'

Their eyes were wide, Mahjoub and Salya.

Their eyes were on their every movement, le Monsieur et la Madame. The way they stood up and the way they lay down. They listened to them and they watched them. The way they spoke and the way they dressed and the way they ate. It was so different from his grandmother, in the mud hut surrounded by sheep; the chickens running everywhere where they put their feet.

'There were things we had never seen before.'

There was marble and ceramics.

The water flowed all by itself.

'And then father took us to his . . . *his own rooms.*'

That night Mahjoub did something he had never done before. He lay in his own bed. He was alone in bed. He wasn't on the floor. He was sinking into what felt like springs. He was under something that was soft.

'I never felt anything like it before.'

The next day his father took him to the fields to see the men. This is what his father did. He said: *Do this, do that.* They were Arabs in the field, they spoke Arabic like him. But they were Arabs he had never met before. Algerians. Tunisians. They spoke differently. They looked a bit different too.

'I was happy, I was so happy.'

And when the sun reached its highest, when the midday meal came round and the Arabs, they stopped for their lunch, his father came back to the château for his own lunch. And it was like nothing he had ever seen. There was meat on their plate, there every day. There was fruit, in a basket, there every day. There were things they said were peaches, but Mahjoub had never seen anything like them before; never imagined they came in such colours before. And then these other fruits.

'*What are these?* I asked.'

'*These are called strawberries*, they said.'

And they showed him things that were apples, too.

'I never knew they could be red.'

They had a bathroom, their bathroom, all white and tiled.

They had a dining room, a kitchen, a terrace, everything.

'I felt . . . freed, my frustrations over.'

The dogs were eating with their masters, they were carrying them.

'I was in France.'

And it was summer. Le Monsieur, he walked around in sandals and a short-sleeved shirt. It smelt like summer. Everything was straight, or smoothed out. Everything seemed to glow.

'We were in another world. It was not our own.'

And then it was over.

'We went back to Tunisia, with two little suitcases stuffed with clothes. It felt like we were leaving another planet. But we had hope. Because *Papa* told us, *If all goes well next year you will come for the holidays.* But it was very long. Until our parents came back for two months that winter.'

'*Wait for the summer*, they said. *Wait.*'

'And then we went back.'

'And we began to grow used to the château, to it all, and then when the month of September came before returning to Tunisia our father asked the question to me and my sister, *Would you like to stay here? In France.'*

You've felt these moments.

You've had them too.

These moments of pure happiness. These moments when it seems to swell up and burst through you. You've had, in your own way, the unbelievable come true.

Mahjoub was speechless.

'It was something that we couldn't believe. It was something that wasn't possible. And I said to *Papa, Yes, I'm staying,* and I felt, I felt . . . *joy.* For the first time inside my head, I'm thirteen years old, and I tell myself, *Finally, my family is united for ever. I've lived a period of my life with no father, with no mother, I saw them occasionally. And now finally, there is* Papa, Mama, *my sister and me.* And I say to myself, *This is good.'*

'*This is what it means to have a family.'*

There were not many Arabs at school.

They would come later, as the migration grew. But when Mahjoub found himself in class in France there were only a few. And they were different from him. They knew how to speak French, they knew all the codes, they knew how everything worked. But Mahjoub hardly understood what the teachers were saying. Every time he tried to speak his words came out mangled. And everyone laughed at him.

'I felt this savage rejection.'

Nobody respected him. Not one.

The guy back home everyone had wanted to be.

'And when I say *savage,* I mean it in the sense of being aggressive. I wanted to impose myself by force, I started fights, I was fighting at school.'

Almost all his grades were 0/20.

And Mahjoub felt worthless, as whole classrooms cackled at him failing, cackled at his cheap clothes, cackled that he didn't know the difference between Adidas and Nike, whipped themselves into hysterics that Mahjoub was so dumb he thought Nike was an Arabic swear word, an idiot flinging himself into punch-ups when people asked if he was wearing Nike.

'It wasn't an easy period.'

The teachers contacted his father.

His father arranged for someone to tutor him after class. But still the words weren't coming. Still he couldn't make himself understood.

'And then my father changed his face towards me.'

He was thirteen, he hardly knew him.

He didn't know this was also him.

Mahjoub's father began to beat him.

When he heard about the grades, when he heard about the fights, he took his belt, he pinned him down, and he beat him. And it didn't stop.

'I regretted having accepted to stay in France.'

The beatings grew so savage they frightened his mother.

'So here I was, lost. A teenager, who couldn't find his place in society with a father who was too harsh. And I said, finally, *I should have stayed in my own country because I was freer there.*'

It was written all over his face, what was happening.

He was not well. His mother could see he was not well.

'Because I was discovering another father, authoritarian and harsh.'

It took him a year to finally speak.

Slowly the words come out of the fog, then whole structures, verbs and patterns; until what he could see he could hold on to. He started repeating things, then more things; until he knew what they meant.

At nineteen, they held him back a year, and he dropped out.

With no qualifications.

'I could speak really well but I just wanted to work.'

He got little jobs here and there and on building sites.

'I was a fan of Michael Jackson.'

'I had long hair, a black hat. It was the Michael Jackson era, the album *Bad*, I had tumbling locks, long, baggy pants and I danced like Michael Jackson. I was a fan, a fan of Michael Jackson.' He was twenty years old and went everywhere in a red Peugeot 205 GT.

His Peugeot 205 GT.

He hardly ever prayed.

Sometimes, but not very often.

'I was always with French girls.'

'I was the nice boy, so nicely dressed.'

He dated Carole first.

'I thought I was in love.'

The summer came and they would hang out. They would listen to music and they would dance. And they would drive to the beach at the weekend.

It was a Moroccan friend he used to roll with.

'I was clean-shaven at the time.'

The whole gang would get down there with their cars.

It was easy. The sun, the water. The glint of sun on the bonnet.

'There was a Moroccan girl who told me about Elisabeth.'

She was her friend and she told her about Mahjoub.

He sang all the Jackson songs that summer.

I Like You The Way You Are.

'They were telling Elisabeth, *There's this Tunisian . . . his father's rich and he's got a nice car, this boy. He's Michael Jackson. He's the guy.'*

You don't forget these moments.

You remember seeing who you want.

She entered the room. Mahjoub could still see her, still so young, standing there, the day he met her. They were in a living room by the beach. He started talking to her. He couldn't stop himself. He started flirting with her.

Then he asked her to come to the water.

'I took her hand and we left for the sea.'

That was how it began.

Carole found out about it and the breakup was ugly.

But Mahjoub didn't care.

'I stayed with Elisabeth . . . she had her own apartment.'

Her parents were pieds noirs.

Whites from Algeria, who had fled to France.

'They were people who didn't like Arabs at all.'

And when they found out about him, they thought it was a disgrace.

'With my father it was a catastrophe.'

And Mahjoub was banned from his house.

'Because I was with a woman . . .'

'Because I was following a woman. That wasn't acceptable. He was frightened, my father . . . what they'd say about him.'

But Mahjoub didn't care.

'I only felt joy.'

Mahjoub didn't care that she was banned from her parents' house and he was banned from his parents' house. Because he had money and a car and Michael Jackson. He had a woman and she had an apartment. He didn't care that she was five years older than him. He didn't care that she was French.

Or that she already had a daughter from another man.

'I decided to work and to accept her as mine.'

They were alone.

But it's only when you live with someone you get to know them. With their mess and their little moments. She noticed him praying at first.

Why do you put your head like that?

'I would say, *I'm submitting to God.*'

But who's God? she asked.

'*It's not Jesus,* I used to say.'

How do you see Him, God?

I can't see Him, He's bigger than we can see.

But how do you know that?

'And that's when I tried to show her the Koran.'

Mahjoub went to buy the Koran in French and Arabic.

'But I didn't know it myself.'

He wanted to show her. He wanted to explain it all to her.

Something. But he wasn't sure what, exactly.

'I wasn't very educated in Islam.'

It crept up on him slowly. Then totally.

When you fall in love you just know. You wake up. Light enters the window. You watch them sleeping. And you know it. That you could never let go. They got married at a registrar's office. They had a son.

His name was Yanis.

'After she gave birth, her parents did go to the hospital.'

'But never to the house.'

Mahjoub was taking little jobs here and there. A little bit of bricklaying, a little bit of that. It wasn't easy. But then he found a job in the fields of the Domaine Sénéchaux, where they make Châteauneuf-du-Pape. Because time was ticking on.

And they couldn't be alone like this, for ever.

'I told her, Elisabeth . . . *We have to see your parents.*'

You know the worst thing about losing someone is knowing they are still there. They're not dead. They're not gone. It's you that's lost them. It's them that's lost you. You come in, hang your coat up, all you want to do is call them. But it's not so easy. That thing that just happened: you want to hear it – what they would say, how they would laugh. But you can't. It pulls at your stomach. And for a moment you're just standing there. Knowing you'll have to find them again. Elisabeth called her parents.

Mahjoub, she said, *they said yes.*

He wanted to do everything right.

'I didn't want any shock when she invited her parents. So when she announced her parents had accepted I bought some wine from Châteauneuf-du-Pape.'

Mahjoub put the bottles down in the middle of the table. He put them between the meat and cheese and everything you can imagine to make it as nice as possible. Everything was in its right place, there as it should be, in France.

'But I didn't drink them.'

He just put them there.

'I didn't have a beard or anything. And with their daughter, you couldn't see the Islam on her. She was a civilian woman.'

He looked at his wife. He looked at her parents.

'We ate together and I felt happy.'

They kissed each other on the cheek.

'I felt happy as they left that I'd tied this knot.'

And that was when they began to speak again.

'They finished by accepting me as a son-in-law, despite themselves.'

'But they never accepted the Arabs.'

It happened slowly, around that time.

She was still wearing jeans and T-shirts. One day she asked him:

How do I convert to Islam?

'I was so happy. In our tradition, as Arabs, when a man marries a woman who isn't Muslim and she becomes Muslim, it's paradise, it's joy.'

And with that their lives went on.

'It only started later.'

'What made me an imam.'

The day to day. It all went on.

But something had changed. That joy had gone.

That light he had felt in the days he met Elisabeth.

'I just wasn't well.'

You know when you're not well.

You know when you're not in a good place. That you're not yourself.

Sometimes you only realize you were not well months later, when your friends say, *Oh, you were in a dark place.* That you seem so much better now. That's when you smile nervously because you thought you were fine. And you suddenly feel worried, worried they knew and you didn't.

'I just wasn't well.'

He was married. He was working in the fields. He was working for Châteauneuf-du-Pape. He was a father, the father of Yanis. His boy, his son. But there was something wrong. Mahjoub, he wasn't himself.

He wasn't well.

It hovered over him at work. He felt it, when he was distracted, when he was slow to reply. I knew something was wrong, but he wasn't sure what.

That was when the news came about the Kabyle.

'He was dead.'

He was a Kabyle, a Berber, not an Arab.

'He'd gone into the hospital, he'd been in fine form . . .'

'And he'd come out dead.'

The Kabyle was always around his father's house. He was really a friend of the whole family. They came to him. He came to them. He was a friend of his father, the Kabyle, a big chicken-wholesaler, to be more precise.

'It was this moment that made me really latch on to prayer.'

That evening his dad came in his car to pick him up. The body was still in the hospital. He drove with his father to Marseille. That night in the car on those long winding roads and onto the motorways they talked. About this man. About who he was.

'He was somebody respectable.'

'He was someone who'd been to Mecca.'

But at that time Mahjoub didn't know very much about Islam. They arrived. They climbed up a long flight of stairs into the apartment and there it was.

'The grief.'

There was his wife and there were his children. They were spread out on sofas and their faces were red with tears. That father was dead. He was gone. They embraced them, Mahjoub and his father, as they sobbed and cried into their arms.

'Each one of them did.'

They were reading for him, for the Kabyle, because he was respectable. There were learned men, on the sofas, reading, almost singing, in a singsong voice. They nodded forward, they rocked back and forth. They were imams. It was Arabic, they were singing. The pages they were turning; it was the Koran.

'The body was at the hospital.'

Then Mahjoub began to feel something he had never felt before.

'I felt the fear of death.'

That was when he felt it happening.

'Something unlocked inside me . . . that this world, it will pass away.'

'That I have to be a good Muslim. That I have to practise . . . that I have to be frightened of God, to fear God.'

'That I am going to have to change my life.'

In the Kabyle's apartment, as they wept, as they prayed, Mahjoub began to feel fear, rising inside him. The fear of it all being over. The fear of the days passing. The fear of his face ageing. The fear of the sun going down.

'The fear of dying a bad man.'

Something was creeping over him, he felt it, he felt it physically, he felt himself beginning to realize something. That this was it. Where it all ended.

This was the first time he'd felt it.

'I'm not so young any more.'

You know this feeling too.

Imams sang and the women cried. Then they spoke and they all listened. And Mahjoub listened too, in that apartment's gloom.

'You see death,' they said.

'This world passes away.'

The next day the body was washed. Then they wrapped him in a shroud. They took the body to a mosque in Marseille. They turned and prayed around him. They said things to him, the family, by the coffin. As Mahjoub was there they said goodbye, hoping he could still hear them. Then the time had come to take the body away. A car came and with his children they drove the coffin to the airport.

'And after that, straight to Algeria.'

A few months later, a Moroccan arrived in the village. He was different. They began to talk about him. Mahjoub heard more and more about him. He drew close to him; and he drew him closer. Abdel Hamid was his name and he was learned; he was an imam. They began to meet more and more. To talk, about everything, about Mahjoub.

And they became friends, of a sort.

He was really quite something this Moroccan. Then, slowly, Abdel Hamid began to say, *I see something in you*, in Mahjoub. That he saw something spiritual, something gentle and kind, in him, in Mahjoub. One day he said to him, *Mahjoub, I've got something for you. Something which will go well with your spiritual sense, with your gentleness and your kindness.*

That was when Abdel Hamid told him that he was a Tablighi.

What's a Tablighi? asked Mahjoub.

A group that goes into mosques, said Abdel Hamid.

Oh la, non, non, said Mahjoub. *I don't want any of that.*

He was suddenly frightened.

I don't want to be like an Iranian, me.

Those were the only ones, Mahjoub knew, who went into the mosques.

But no, chuckled Abdel Hamid.

He could see that he was frightened.

These are spiritual people . . .

Who will show you the practice of prayer.

You'll find yourself, said Abdel Hamid, coming closer.

He trusted him, Abdel Hamid, and Mahjoub calmed down.

What do I have to do? he asked.

That was when he told him.

There is a group that comes to the mosque and, in general, this is what they do. They go away for three or four days, to pray . . .

And you will go with them.

It was around then that Mahjoub began to realize.

'That I was an empty man.'

It's often the same.

You know that finding a religion is so much harder than losing one. So much harder to explain. You find yourself struggling to explain why. They give you baffled faces and strange grins. But you can't make them feel what you feel.

It's an intensely personal thing.

You're all on your own.

You find yourself with different people. People who've lived their whole lives with rules and codes you stumble over and forget like learning a foreign language. Hoping they'll accept you. Sometimes they do. Something they think you're strange too.

The first time Mahjoub went with the Tablighis he went to Marseille.

They took him to a mosque, in that dirty city, where he knew nobody. Where everybody had a beard, apart from him. Where everybody wore white, like they said a Muslim should, except him. Where everybody knew what they were doing, apart from him. Mahjoub sat down. He felt so far away, so far away from being a real believer. They slept there, they ate there. On the floor of the mosque.

'I would see them at night, sometimes I would wake up and I would see them, not in a group, but alone . . . one would be praying, another would be reading the Koran . . . and I would tell myself, *I'm so far away, my faith, she isn't here . . . I'm still full of doubt.*'

But he went back, for three days, then for ten days.

It was after this he decided to grow a beard.

'Because, I told myself, I can't be around these people without one.'

So it started to grow.

A little beard at first, then a big one. But Mahjoub, he still didn't dress like them, until he decided to wear their robe. It was white,

it was comfortable, his djellaba, but at first he couldn't leave the house.

'I couldn't go out because I kept telling myself . . . *The French are going to look at me.* I was ashamed and I walked with my head looking down.'

The Tablighi he met were kind people.

They looked after the sick. They saw the dying. They didn't talk about politics or Palestine or all these international problems.

'They talked about Mecca.'

He started to change.

The fields were full of Arabs, that was the way it was, where they were in the Domaine Sénéchaux, where they make Châteauneuf-du-Pape. They started to respect him more, with his beard, the Moroccans he worked with. They started to look at him differently, Mahjoub, now he looked different, now he talked differently. They listened to him. They looked up to him as someone respectable. The fields were full of their song and their prayer.

Mr Roux, said Mahjoub one day to his boss.

I don't want to steal from you, but I'm praying, five times a day . . . it only takes five minutes and I'll pay you back for every one of those minutes.

Mr Roux laughed and waved him away.

Of course, make your prayers.

And so he would pray, with the Moroccans, out in the sun, at the edge of the vines.

And if you want to go early on Friday, said Mr Roux.

Take that as my gift but make sure you're available on Saturday.

He looked at pictures of Mecca. Stuck up, like posters, on the walls of the mosque. Everybody, moving around that one point. He watched videos of Mecca. *What would it feel like, if only I could feel it?* he began to ask. And the ones who had been, they told him.

It feels like everything.

One day he went back to Mr Roux.

Mr Roux, said Mahjoub.

I'm going to accomplish my pilgrimage to Mecca.

What's that? said Mr Roux.

It's Mecca, it's the fifth pillar of Islam.

Mr Roux looked totally confused.

I have to accomplish it, it's my duty.

The old man shrugged.

No problem, said Mr Roux.

Just tell me when you're leaving.

Mahjoub left for Mecca in 1998, the year the World Cup came to France and the year Zinedine Zidane scored twice before halftime in the Stade de France. Before he left Mr Roux called him in to see him.

Mahjoub, this is for you.

It was an envelope bulging with cash.

For all your loyal services to Châteauneuf-du-Pape.

It was time to go.

Mahjoub's father drove him to drop him off. The organizers, they had arranged everything, the bus, the food, the visas. And there he said goodbye to everyone. His father. His mother. His French wife. And his two sons, Yanis and Karim.

Like he was someone respectable.

'It was a long voyage.'

But he felt nervous.

He felt tense. He felt it in his stomach.

'We didn't know if we were coming back.'

The people on the bus, they were older mostly, white beards, women of a certain age. The bus left. They went to Avignon, to pick up another group. They went to Nice, to pick up another group. And then they really left.

'We were happy, I was content.'

The countryside rolled by the windows.

Then the cities. Then the mountains.

'I was desperate to see Mecca.'

The bus crossed Italy, it got on a boat and crossed Greece, it crossed Turkey, then the bus crossed Syria, it crossed Jordan, and then it entered Saudi. There was excitement now. There was wonder. They were almost there.

They drove through the desert. And they reached Medina.

They saw the great mosque. They saw the domes and the plazas and the minarets and the fading red light in the evening, when night comes quickly, when it comes suddenly, in these lands in the south, and it breathes cool. But they were agitated. They wanted to leave.

They were there for almost a week.

This was not it. They were not there.

'We were obsessed, haunted . . . we only wanted to be in Mecca.'

And they arrived. The pilgrims were carefully organized. They all had the tags of their nations. Algeria. Nigeria. India. France. And from the moment they arrived all they wanted was to see it. Only one thing. The Kaaba, that holy house, that sits like a little black box, at the heart of the Great Mosque.

It was time to go.

They left quickly.

'There were thousands of people, there were millions of people, it was a flow that I felt would never end. There were so many people.'

Mahjoub was there with those people.

'I was frightened that I would drown, that I'd be lost . . . there was the whole world. I was frightened I would be crushed.'

Mahjoub followed. Mahjoub let himself be led.

'There was the whole of humanity . . . I think there was not one country which was not represented. There was every colour and every size. There were women mixed with men . . . there was pushing and shoving.'

And then you see it.

The Kaaba.

'That everything revolves round.'

'And you say it's not possible.'

'You see people crying . . . You see people imploring God.'

When you build your whole life around something, when you think it stands outside of time and space, it beams things back to you like a screen. Things you didn't remember. Things you didn't know you knew.

Faces. Verses. Peace.

Mahjoub was there. In this swirling humanity. In this mass that makes you realize just how black and brown humanity really is. He felt everything.

He knew who he was. He knew his path. Who he had to be.

He would become a new person. He would marry again. A real Muslim woman.

He would correct all his mistakes.

'I pulled him out of myself . . .'

'The old Mahjoub who sinned, who looked at girls, who danced, who sang, who flirted, who maybe scoffed and lied.'

They swirled and swirled, three times fast and four times slowly, around the Kaaba, black people, white people, Arab people, Asian people, young people, old people, reaching to it, touching it. They were together. They were one.

This was it. It flowed in. It filled him. It was there before him.

And Mahjoub, he began to cry.

19 RUCKLA

When they took German back to his cell, everyone who had been in the bunks the night before was gone. There were seven new faces – six of them politicals and one of them criminal. That was Nikolai, the tramp. He stank deeply, was always muttering about how life was hard for him and when they came to toss him out – he was a regular – he didn't want to go, as it was cold and life was better in the cell, where they fed them three times a day.

Sometimes, they took them out for a breath of fresh air in this tiny courtyard whose sky was barred against any dreams of escape.

The first time they pulled German out to be interrogated, a hulking lawyer from the state was there. *I don't want you*, German said.

My wife will arrange a real lawyer for me.

He didn't wait around. And then this young woman, who was handling his case, his investigator, ran him through it until he got a chance to speak.

How can you sleep at night? he said.

How can you do this?

She avoided eye contact, like she was ashamed, until they took him away.

The longer he spent in jail the better he got to know his cell mates: it was like the whole of Belarus was in there. There was the dotty professor who taught IT, hunched reading his own self-published sci-fi. The garden-variety criminals – burglars, traffickers, thieves – and the radio journalist, who sat there, vacant-eyed, saying how he'd just been promoted to anchor some state airwaves, when he'd been arrested on his very first day.

That's probably for the best, he sighed.

I don't think the state and I are going to be working together again.

After a while, he asked to read the mad professor's so-called book. It was unreadable. Just nonsense of the purest kind. But it passed the time.

Guards came and went.

One day they took German to a smaller cell, with just the two criminals and the radio man. Then he found himself in solitary. That's when they came to him again. This time there was another lawyer, one the volunteers had organized, who in the brief moment he had with him before the woman handling his case turned up, gestured forcefully at German – *they could be recording in here* – then scribbled something down on a piece of paper.

your wife and children have already fled the country from criminal prosecution

they are safe in lithuania

Then, quickly, the lawyer grabbed the paper back and ripped it up.

You know those moments.

You feel like you've been hit. Like you've lost your balance.

Like the whole world is moulding into something terrifying around you.

I thought they were at home.

That they were waiting for me . . . at home.

German's mind was racing now, racing with the thought they weren't there. His head was ringing. Ringing in that dark room with the thought it was empty, his home, his family home was empty – *who knows what's happened to my animals* – his heart pounding now. He'd thought all along it was just him they were after with the prosecution.

Not his wife. Not his children.

That night he was alone in his cell. It felt so horribly hard being there. He felt the walls of that narrow space closing in on him. Like they could crush him. Now he finally understood how easy it was for so many to go mad in prison, as he ached with loneliness and fear.

What's going to happen to me?

Where is she . . . my Natasha?

How horrible is it not to have a phone.

What's happened to my children?

—

They did let him out. They gave him some papers to sign, letting him wait at home whilst his case advanced, and he wondered whether the shame in the eyes of the young woman handling his case had anything to do with it.

He stepped out of the gates into the light.

The volunteers were there. Then he saw them: his firstborn Pavel and Uncle Vladimir. They drove him home, to that empty house; the foster dog had been rehomed and there was a cat in the gloom.

Pippa!

She was normally such a shy cat, minding her own business when guests came over, really Natasha's cat, who only ever sat on her lap, but the moment she saw him, she scampered towards him, rubbing herself between his legs and onto his beard, purring, when he picked her up and held her.

Like she'd thought her family had disappeared.

Through those days Pippa never left his side.

That night, the first time he heard Natasha's voice, on the phone, on the new phone and the encrypted app Pavel had shown him how to use, that first time it calmed him like a pill. It soothed him like a balm. Even though he could hardly believe what she was telling him about their escape. But it didn't last.

As the days dragged, the phone became full of stress. The police called: another interrogation. His lawyer called: telling him, when they met, that he was strongly advising him not to flee. Then Natasha: begging him, pleading with him to run away, to cross into Lithuania while he still had the chance. They were going to build a wall, a fence to stop migrants, she said.

I strongly urge you not to flee, his lawyer repeated.

He was a short, slim man in glasses, in his forties, his name was Vasily, and each and every time they met he kept telling German he would either see no jail time or the lightest, open air, community service regime.

She's being emotional about it, he said of Natasha.

It's best to proceed with caution.

By now she had stopped trying to force him.

You make your own decision, she said.

So with an anxious and a heavy heart, German fed the pigs in the morning, he drove in and tended the shop, he came back to Pippa and, at night, he ate alone in the rooms where he'd raised a family.

He walked around, as though in a darkness, struggling with himself. *This has not come from nowhere; it could only have come from Him, from above, this punishment.* And if he left, if he fled, it would be to turn away from the path of righteousness. The icons in every room would catch his eye, their thin, meek and wood-carved faces, faces that had suffered greatly. And as he prayed he said he would accept whatever path they had for him.

Even the path of suffering.

No, said Natasha.

This isn't what's happening.

You don't have to accept everything so meekly.

This isn't a just punishment. It's evil.

It was already winter. The rain was getting heavier. The first snows fell and the wind, which blew from the east, came with them.

Then something changed.

The calls from his lawyer had a new tone in them. German knew Vasily's voice by now and when he called him telling him to come in and speak to him urgently, he knew it was serious. When he arrived, his lawyer was already waiting for him by the door of his office and he flicked his wrist as if to say, *Let's go for a walk.* Things weren't going as planned, Vasily told him; all along German was supposed to have been charged under the administrative code but suddenly there was talk of the criminal one.

Things had suddenly jumped in severity, somehow.

They wanted to make an example of him, somehow.

In that moment all thoughts of accepting their injustice meekly suddenly snapped. Natasha was right. *Of course she was right. She was always right.*

So there's only one thing left for me to do, he said.

Vasily looked at him.

This time I'm not going to encourage you to stay.

They both knew the criminal code meant jail time.

Potentially years of jail time.

—

Is that you, Mr Snezhkov?

He was sitting in the investigative committee, with Vasily, when the operatives presented a video. *No that couldn't be.* That couldn't be him. But who else could it be? That really was him, on the street, on the night it had all gone wrong, pulling an officer from the OMON – four, five metres – and away from the march. Then that was Natasha, running after him, hitting that man, screaming at him.

Is that you?

Is that your wife participating in the assault?

They played it again and again.

It was like his memory was wiped. That really was him. But he had no recollection of it. No conception of it. Like it had never happened. His body felt tight. Like he was learning something new and unsettling about himself. Like he was about to break.

You know when there's no way out.

Then they charged him under the criminal code.

Let's go for a walk.

They were walking away. He felt cold and trembly.

You know, German, said Vasily. *It's good to remember 1917 . . . when the people of the Russian Empire, who were not communists, of course, split into two camps. One didn't want to leave and thought that somehow it was going to be OK, it was going to settle down and they were going to be able to survive. And we know what happened to those people. And those who decided to go. It was very difficult for them as they had to decide to emigrate, whilst breaking off all ties, whilst leaving their property behind. They had a really hard time – but they survived.*

They were still walking.

And that proved to be the right choice, sighed Vasily.

So let's start to talk about that.

It was then they began with the plans and the schemes, coming up with them in the morning and planning them by night; how to get him out, how to get him across the border.

Every night with Natasha.

Do you think I can still just cross into Ukraine, like Tanya?

Maybe there was a slim chance he wasn't on the database. That's why Uncle Vladimir took their car and drove it towards the Russian border, that one's that open, with no border guards or controls, to find out. But they flagged him down and stopped him, asking for German, the moment he got close to the frontier zone.

Maybe there's a way through the forest?

That's when Uncle Vladimir said that he would hunt down the old bootleggers he knew who slipped in and out to the south. But when he found them, they told him – *No chance. Don't even try*, they said.

There were armies and patrol camps massing at the edge of Ukraine. There were drones and thermo visors and sentries now. They'd fortified everything and every day the political situation was worse. Like something terrible was about to happen.

Then there were the marshes.

They knew an old forest inspector, who – they didn't know why – had spent time inside, maybe for smuggling, maybe for stealing, but one night German went drinking with him. And then he asked him.

Will you help me cross the marshes?

Sure, he said, *I can do that.*

And then they downed another one, almost in celebration, so many he could still feel them the next day when he came back, all happy and free, to work it all out.

The man's face had gone dark.

It's very dangerous, he said.

And I'm very sober.

They are patrolling everything.

It's like they're planning something. There are soldiers everywhere. They are sitting in these observation posts and it's really, really incredibly hard.

Then the inspector told German about the marshes, that even if you got to the river, on all the dry paths that he knew, that even if you managed to ford it, through all the currents and the rapids, then you needed to find dry land there, that one false step and you could drown, you could be sucked into these brown-green bogs.

German was looking at the maps he showed him.

Nothing – not one safe place to cross – and he was becoming desperate. That's when they started to talk to their friend in Moldova, that maybe when he drove his truck through Belarus and back again, he could take him as a stowaway, but they lost their nerve when they found out that customs used X-rays to catch them.

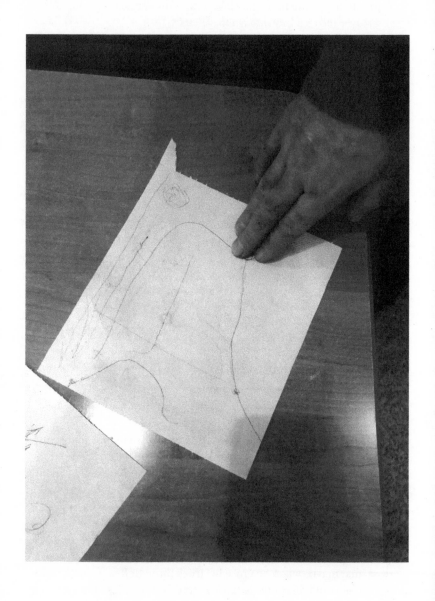

He was panicking now, when Natasha phoned her relative, who, in Moscow, was one of the President's personal bodyguards, who secure the perimeters of his palaces, asking what would happen to German if they got him across.

Is there a chance you can just get lost in Russia? she said.

Not today, he said.

Only if you don't use any cards, you don't set foot in cities where there are CCTV networks and you only live in the villages, maybe. But take one false step and they'll extradite you immediately.

Time was ticking away and German was so anxious he could barely contain it. But there was still that friend in Russia, that dear friend; he had been like a brother to him, he even looked exactly like him, so much so he could certainly use his passport to cross the border to finally reach Natasha and the children.

I'll just say I stole your passport if I get caught.

It was crushing to him when he said no.

On some level it felt like being betrayed.

It felt like now there was no way out.

You find yourself still in these moments. You find yourself hurt.

It was in Vilnius that a strange series of things began to happen one after the other.

Natasha was now in the half-online half-volunteer community of Belarusian exiles there and floating through this world she met this pretty young couple who'd screwed up renewing their humanitarian visa. The slots had run out in the city, so they had to go to Kaunas, a hundred or so kilometres to the north. It was not as though she thought much about them, or they thought much about her, but they knew each other's stories – the whole ordeal with German – and they had each other's numbers.

Can you help us out on this?

Everybody was constantly being asked that and everybody would without fail say yes. It was December now and there were a few Belarusians in a detention centre for border crossers at Ruckla, halfway to Kaunas, who needed a delivery of warm clothes.

Of course, the young couple said.

Of course they'd stop on the drive up.

The camp was full of the people you'd expect: Africans, Kurds, Iranians. People sunken or wide-eyed, bedraggled, from far away. The people the new fence was going to stop. Or people who'd only yesterday decided to flee, people like them. In the camp, the young couple found the Belarusians.

And they started chatting with this big, broad-chested guy, sitting on the porch of one of the barracks, smoking. They said a little about themselves, where they came from in Belarus, and then he did the same. Alexander was in his fifties, he'd been a border guard, he'd finished his commission and he'd been kicking his heels in this five-year cooling period where men from the service were banned from leaving the country. And then his wife couldn't take it any more, how things were, and left for Poland. That's when he'd decided to flee, using everything he knew, as a border guard.

You might have moments like this in your life.

You know those moments where they might never have thought of you. There was no reason for them to. But they suddenly did and it set everything in motion. This was that moment for German.

The young couple were listening to Alexander.

Then suddenly they remembered that woman in Vilnius – *Natasha, yes that was her name* – and the whole horrible story about her husband who couldn't escape the country and now, right in front of them, was this border guard turned escapee, telling them how he knew all the installations and every twist and turn of the patrol root.

Could we put you in touch with our friend?

And that's when Natasha's phone began to buzz and a few seconds later she was talking to Alexander, still smoking, still sitting on that porch.

Of course I'll help you, he said.

That's when they started talking, all three of them, all by secured apps, about what they should do. It didn't take long for Alexander to pull through. One day it simply arrived in their phones: a full escape plan. They opened it and there it was: a screenshot of a Google Map with all the GPS coordinates of every turn to take, every path to follow, every point to cross. They looked closer: there were the pins for the guard towers and the gun points and dashes for the fences and the patrol routes.

And then Alexander told them that wasn't quite it.

You couldn't just walk into a border zone. You needed to either be registered in one of the villages there, be heading on one of the routes out of the country or have a legitimate purpose for trade there. But his father was right there, in one of the villages, where he kept bees. This would be German's legend: he'd come to buy them.

Bees for sale. Alexander made his father post that online.

Then German dropped him an email and printed it out.

The old border guard kept telling him that this wasn't going to be easy: he'd have to walk for miles at night, he'd have to trudge through snow and push through the forests. It wasn't the way he'd used. It was a harder one.

And Natasha kept telling him he'd see her soon.

That morning began like any other. Dawn light through the curtains. That flick in his heart that it was time to feed the animals. And after he fed Pippa for the last time he picked her up and cuddled her, whispering, *We'll get you over, don't worry, I'm not leaving you, we'll find a way to smuggle you out too.*

That was when Pavel arrived. There was no ceremony to that hug; a man's hug and goodbye. It was all very simple. And they had no idea for how long. Uncle Vladimir was waiting in the car for him and then they set off; his house, his bonsai, the scenes of almost everything he'd ever lived vanishing through the windows.

He had nothing on him. Nothing, because he'd need to run. Nothing, because he was only buying bees. They chit-chatted like nothing much was happening. And then they drew closer to the zone as the sun went down, until they reached the village on Alexander's GPS, where he had to continue alone.

Is this it?

It was already dark.

This doesn't look like it at all.

German pulled out the burner phone he'd brought just for this. Alexander picked up in Ruckla.

You're in the wrong place, guys!

And then by memory he told them to turn around, to get out of there, to go in this direction and then follow that road until they were at the right point.

The GPS wasn't working at all.

There's a fork in the road and if you go to the right you go straight into the trap of the border patrol, but if you go left you'll get to the place.

It was dusk. German's heart was beating as they turned onto those little forest roads, Uncle Vladimir's swollen eyes fixed ahead: trying as hard as possible not to fail.

And then the trees disappeared.

Is that it?

The dirt tracks ran through fields now.

I think so, said Uncle Vladimir.

They stopped and got out, the both of them.

And they embraced, one last time.

Thank you, said German. That was all.

And then Uncle Vladimir smiled simply, and left.

Like he was a taxi driver in a rush.

That was when German started to walk, slowly, not too fast, on this uneven, snowy ground he'd looked at so many times on Google Maps, he'd burnt it into his brain. There was the wind, a strong wind, that began to bite the tips of his fingers and the side of his face until he saw the spotlight, spinning through the sky, rushing towards him over the field.

German fell to the ground. It was gone.

I'm supposed to be invisible here, he thought.

Here between the folds of the valley. That's what Alexander had told him. But when the light came rushing back he threw himself down again. Then every half-minute he kept diving and picking himself up until he got to an irrigation trench, thinking, *This is not supposed to be here.* As quietly as he could, his face pinned to the snow, he phoned the old border guard. *There's no way around it*, Alexander said.

But if you've gone too far, it's five metres deep.

The black water hadn't frozen. It came up to German's waist as he waded through. Then he threw himself down from the spotlight again.

The wind was really stinging now.

There was the road. There were the trees, the line of forest, just where it was supposed to be. Then after – there would be the border.

As he got closer, he froze.

Like a terrified animal, he went still, stunned, then lowered himself to the snow. There were lights, just ahead, in the trees. Right in the spot that Alexander said was supposed to be invisible between the watchtowers. They were the screens of mobile phones. His eyes, all pupils in the night, fixed on that point. Then there was a flashlight. It flew to the side, then it swept up, until it caught the bottom of the low flying clouds, so low they were practically fog. There was somebody there.

So I simply lie down and I'm thinking . . .

What do I do? I don't know what to do.

It's too late to go back. It's too late to claim I was here for the bees. So I lie there. Knowing there's no way back.

He stilled his breath, then his body.

He lay there, limp, like a dead man in the snow.

I was really praying to God.

Not a real prayer, from a book, but the words inside his head, the words he needed Him to answer. Like a child's prayer in the dark.

Then nothing.

There were no more lights, there was no more rustling, no more signs of life or soldiers and, after half an hour, snow caked on his half-frozen sleeves, he pulled himself up and dashed over the road into the forest.

German tried to see, he tried to look forward. But he couldn't. He couldn't make out a thing in this darkness, he was so plunged into, so deep, he felt like his eyes had stopped working. He could hardly move forward, feeling branches to push them aside, pushing up against trees to go around them, scrambling, constantly being cut or cramped in the undergrowth, like a blind man lost in a maze.

It's like a fairy tale, he thought. *It's so thick.*

No. It couldn't be.

That was the breath of a dog he felt behind him.

Shallow and fast. That was a dog's breath coming closer.

That was when Natasha started to panic.

She was sitting in a car, on the other side of the border, the young couple who'd made it happen in the front seat.

He's not moving.

The dot on the tracking app sat frozen.

Ten minutes. Twenty minutes. An hour.

Natasha began to fill with fear.

A fear so strong she could see their whole life as it happened.

How has it ended up like this?

We had a shop and chickens and pigs and pets and we went to church every Sunday and we looked after our kids and now we're at an illegal border crossing like it's Mission Impossible *and he's stopped moving.*

His dot's stopped moving.

And she sat there holding the phone until her body couldn't stay in that state of terror any longer, looking at the frozen dot.

Let's drive closer.

And the car drove, towards the forest, then into it, on the Lithuanian side, until they realized they were being followed. Blue blinkers were flashing. A patrol car signalled at them to stop. And then Lithuanian border guards rapped at their window.

Natasha looked at them.

And decided not to lie.

I'm a refugee, she said.

I've escaped from Belarus and my husband, he's trying to escape too and that's him, that his dot on my screen and he's not moving.

They were stunned.

Their eyes softened, then they spoke all together; they would stay with them and then they started rooting for him, full of concern.

He's still not moving.

In the forest, the wolf – *yes, that's what it had to be* – finally passed.

German looked up, out of the darkness that was so dense it could have been at the bottom of a deep pit, and a few stars shone between the trees.

It couldn't be far.

On Natasha's phone the dot had begun to move.

German moved forward. Fumbling blind between the thickets and the branches until, at first, it almost stung his eyes, he could see bright moonlight, and there it was. Right through the forest, freshly ploughed, like a road of soil to catch their footprints, the border. Running right down the middle were these tiny poles, holding the ancient crest of Lithuania and the one the dictator preferred for Belarus on the other.

This is it, he thought.

Those were the crests. The ones Alexander had told him that until you got across them the border guards are told they can shoot.

And then he ran. He ran with his whole body.

Faster than he ever thought he could.

Breathing, gasping, German leant on a tree. He'd crossed. It took a moment to fully feel it. But then a feeling big and powerful, rising like a wave from a sea inside him, swept up and through him. It was euphoria.

I've done it. I've done it.

He grabbed his phone.

WELCOME TO LITHUANIA

And then, with this phone light like a torch, he began to stride forward, his eyes, like his mind, overcome like a headrush. Then it began to buzz.

Natasha?

Idiot – you've crossed back into Belarus!

You're walking right into the watchtower.

German shuddered.

Like he'd been thrown into cold water.

He could see the ploughed soil behind him.

WELCOME TO BELARUS

And then he sprang up and ran again.

With no thoughts and no doubts.

His pocket was buzzing.

Just stay where you are!

It all happened very quickly, like fragments in a dream. There were headlamps.

Then Lithuanian guards.

He's warm in the back of the patrol car.

A man in uniform turns to him.

We can make one stop before the detention centre.

They stop. Then the door opens. There's Natasha in the moonlight, the car behind her, its lights blazing white. Then he's holding her, his old love, his only love, his whole world, his face wet with tears.

I'm here.

I'm here.

Freedom is a process, she thinks, as she's lifting boxes. *It doesn't happen all at once. I can't have it all at once. I'm getting there. But I'm not there yet.*

They are full of olives, those boxes. They nub at her hands and leave them red. And they are so heavy they pull right at her back. *I'm doing this to survive*, she thinks. *It's not that the destination is out of reach. It's that I have to work to get there. And at home, they never would have let me work.*

Then more boxes arrive at the gates.

This is the worst part of the job, the heaviest, the one she knows best. And these are the moments when Nazneen really feels it: that feeling that, *I'm not happy in this country, that I didn't come all the way here to live like this, to wake up at 5:45 a.m., packing olives, in the middle of nowhere for next to nothing. England, Sweden – not Greece. That's where I'm going – that's why I left Tehran. No. I'm not staying here. It'll get better than this.*

Then she stops dreaming. There's a commotion in the yard. There's always a commotion. And there's always too much to do. The trucks are bleeping and the men – a bunch of Pakistanis, sometimes a few Greeks – keep shouting. Yelling directions and curses she hardly understands.

That is morning at the olive plant.

The men do the hard work, getting those boxes, those crates full of olives, right there to the door. Or at least they think they do the hard work, because someone still has to heave it onto the line. *Funny that. That's the way it is in life*, she thinks, *not just in the factory.* And here, like everywhere, the final push is left to the women.

And that woman is mostly Nazneen.

Boxes. One after the other after the other. Heat rising. The morning passing. Unpacking olives. Tossing them out. It's at moments like this her failures start to flash before her eyes. Three times. That was how many times.

They told her it would be easy.

That she would get to the real Europe this way.

You just go to the dealers on Omonia Square.

You follow our advice and you'll find them there.

You tell them what you want.

She could hear them now. On mornings like this, the olives running past her on the line, she feels far away. Like she is right in front of him.

It's the dealer. She's found him.

There's traffic. A bright morning in Athens.

You're Afghan or Iranian? he's asking.

I was born in Afghanistan, but my family . . .

She tries to explain quickly what can't be explained simply. She's Afghan but she's never lived in Afghanistan. Her family fled as refugees when she was a baby. So she's Iranian but not Iranian. Really she's just a refugee.

The dealer nods.

That makes sense. He's not Greek, he's something else. This man rifles through his stash. He shows Nazneen the passport.

That's a hundred euro. This one looks like you, the man says. She's nervous. She doesn't quite trust him. It's just a woman with black hair.

Or what about this one?

That's better. A closer fit.

It's an Italian one this time. The dealer insists. Nazneen feels worried. She doesn't believe him. It looks nothing like her. She tries to say that. But he waves it away.

You see they never check. It's just one glance at your face.

The olives are running through her hands.

She keeps remembering bits of the same moment.

She's at departures. She's reached the end of the line. Her heart is pounding. *That isn't you.* Nazneen looks up at the border guard. He's holding the fake passport. He starts swearing. He calls security. They're escorting her now: *Out – get out.* It's over.

She's in tears outside the terminal.

The memories aren't distinct. Three times the passport fails. Three tickets she's blown. That's it. That's how she got stuck in Greece.

The boxes are done by noon.

Summer work feels longer than eight hours. Her hands sweat in those gloves. Her face runs behind that mask. Nazneen sweats until she starts to smell herself in the pounding heat. The heat that everyone is shocked by. The Greek ladies, who talk sometimes, say it has never happened before. *It's global warming,* they mutter. Everyone on the line knows about that. Sometimes they talk about it on the line. The seasons, they're out of joint.

The temperatures are all wrong.

The *slap-slap-slap* of the stickering machine.

The work is mechanical. It makes you mechanical. The low-quality bin. The high-quality bin. Her hands are moving as if automatically as she remembers how she ended up here. On an island hours from Athens.

You run out of money.

You have to make decisions.

That's what happened to Nazneen. She'd blown it all on those three failed tickets. She needs to eat. She needs a job. And she can't go back to the refugee camp. Not back to living in the container with those old ladies she doesn't know. To those soup lines, frightened to be alone, where the men look at you, where they speak to you – a single woman – like they might do something terrible. It isn't safe.

Everybody knows it happens.

Nazneen doesn't want to be raped.

The camp is just over an hour from the city.

You learn how to live in Athens when you're a refugee. You see the Kurdish graffiti on the wall. You start to find the other Afghans: they tell you about clinics, about hotels, about squats. You spend the night there. They give you numbers to call. You might find an address to sleep. And you start to find the Middle Eastern city – the Syrians, the Iraqis, the Pakistanis – sleeping on the roofs, or sometimes the basements, of this concrete place, that sometimes you forget, really is Europe and not somewhere in between.

Athens seems far away now on Evia.

The island where she works.

Here the cockerels crow in the morning.

You find people in the city. People who want to help.

Mr Mirzaei has been helping her. He's a teacher. He's also Afghan. She can see him now: his tired-eyed face. She can hear him.

I've found a job for you, says Mr Mirzaei.

It's not in Athens, it's on an island to the north.

It's an olive factory with a woman-only production line.

You need the money and I think you should take it.

That's how she ended up on Evia.

Memory fuses with smell.

The whole factory stinks of food. Women at one end stuff garlic, bits of cheese and tomatoes into the olives. And at the other end they sort them. They wash them. They check them for issues. Throw the bad olives here and the good olives there. And then they dunk them in olive oil. She looks up. They are mostly Greek women. And then about ten Afghans who have come in on this scheme. A woman-only production line, she thinks.

She can hear them now.

Sorting. Canning. Labelling.

They wake up before dawn, the Afghan women, in this little house they've put them in, not too far away. This is the only time of day, Nazneen realizes, that it doesn't feel too hot. A car picks them up for the plant.

Then the lifting, then the weighing begins.

And Nazneen's mind begins to drift.

You don't control how you remember things.

There are some things you only seem to remember when they come at you like flashes: when you're tired, when you're sick. There are some things you want to remember: that you pull up, that you look at, until they dissolve in your mind's eye. It's that way with faces: you see them crystal clear when they're ones you've hated; but when you try and hold up the ones you've loved, and picture them, you can't do it. It's not there.

They move Nazneen around.

She learns fast. Most of them don't. The stickers, the simplest tasks, keep giving them problems. Nazneen finds herself stuffing olives one day, labelling them the next; hour after hour until her hair stinks of garlic. Sometimes, in between things, she starts remembering why she ran away.

Reza, that was her brother's name, he was a carpenter and she lived in his house.

That was what the family expected.

She can remember the fear.

The fear when Reza went out, when she told his wife, *I'm going shopping*, and she smiled, *Oh, I'll come with you.*

She can hear that voice now.

Packing olives on the line.

Oh, don't worry, I'm fine.

They smiled like sisters as she moved to the door.

She remembered the fear when she let herself out and walked as calmly as she could, like she was just walking to the shops.

She kept on seeing them.

Flashes of that day she fled. That day she left and cut contact with her family. The day she never spoke to them again. Her heart was beating. *They could kill me*, she knew, because an Afghan woman was not allowed to escape. *They came after girls like me.* She knew her brothers had it in them.

Nazneen went to her friend.

She threw away her SIM card. She found work, she was so lucky, caring for a very old lady. When she wasn't working, she hid. Nazneen knew they were looking for her. And that if Reza didn't find her, if he didn't kill her, he would take all her freedom away. He would make her a prisoner and the little life she had would be gone.

I'm going to leave, she told herself. *I'm going to London, to Stockholm. I don't belong here. I've never belonged here. In this place that hates women.*

The shifts feel longer in the evening. And the longer the shifts drag on the more memories she has. Reza would beat her.

This is how an Afghan should behave.

She shouldn't sing. She shouldn't do that.

She should follow what I say – what men say.

Sometimes, Nazneen touches her head. She can feel the scar where her brother had beaten her with a stick. Then she can see him. The kicking. His eyes as his fist hit her face.

She can see it all.

Another day ends.

Most of the women are so tired after working so hard they eat dinner silently and they seem to simply collapse and immediately sleep. They are crowded together in that room with bunk beds and here, after dark, she sits and she talks with Nigar. Sometimes they listen to music. Maybe a film. But mostly they talk about how they got here.

Nazneen tells her how she was arrested at the border.

She'd saved for two years in Tehran, a lot, $3,000. *Can you imagine?* Every time she slipped out of work – her hijab tight, her sunglasses on – her heart would skip a beat. *That man. I recognize that face. He has to have seen me.* And she would begin to panic: *Now they can find me.* That it was only a matter of time.

The day she left Tehran the smuggler took her to the edge of town. The edge she'd grown up in, where the Afghans lived, in that nasty slum. Then they drove her to the border.

Walk, they snapped, when they got there.

Nazneen tells Nigar how she failed.

The other women are snoring as she tells her about the arrest on the border, about prison, about how she had been deported to Afghanistan; a country she had left when she was a baby. Nigar sighs, amazed, as she tells her the danger she has been in. The family there; they were looking for her too.

Nigar gasps as she tells her about how she had made it back, despite everything. And this time she'd crossed. She'd made it over the jagged mountains and she'd made it to İstanbul, that huge city, with the huge mosques, with so many strange foods, and there she'd spent months ironing clothes for a tailor to get the last bit of money.

And she told her about that night.

There had been ten hours on the water. On that winding river, where Greece touches Turkey. A dark beach. That was where they landed. She would never forget it, that was what she told Nigar, that feeling of victory, that feeling of joy, that feeling that she was very powerful, that she was moving closer to her dream, to her freedom, maybe, in the end, to Stockholm, to London.

At night they hug and they giggle.

And Nigar tells Nazneen about her crossing.

And then the lights go out. It's time to sleep.

Everybody talks to themselves as they go. Often, when she lies there, long after the lights are out, long after Nigar has drifted off, she thinks of herself. And when Nazneen thinks of herself she thinks of a bird. She sees a bird in a cage like the ones she used to see in the markets of Tehran. She knows she was born in that cage. And that tiny bird, trying to sing, that is her dream. The one she'd been carrying inside her whole life.

The bars of the cage are men.

The mornings are hotter. It keeps getting hotter.

There isn't a moment in the day when she doesn't feel it: slowing her down, exhausting her, before she's even got to the line. It's about noon. Her boss comes over with a message. *There are more Afghan women coming*, says her boss. She can see her now, Eleni, sunk into her fifties.

We've got a house by the beach for you.

Three of you. It'll be nice. But it'll fill up fast.

Mohadasse and Zahre. Those are their names. They're also on the line. And in their twenties too. They find it fun at first being in the house. They can see the water. They feel like they are on holiday. They film little videos for their friends on WhatsApp of the waves and at night they tell each other secrets. Nazneen wants to be a singer. She's been singing in Athens, she tells them. And everything her brothers told her not to.

She's sung so powerfully she's made men cry.

At night, the lights go off. Sometimes she feels content.

It's a new day. But that morning they wake up and they smell something. *Yes, that's smoke*. They can't see it. But they know that smell. Everybody knows that smell.

Instinctively.

That morning the car comes to pick them up. Something isn't right.

It is the light. *Is it overcast? Is it clouds?*

No. Nazneen realizes it's smoke.

The bosses say nothing. The trucks keep unloading. The Pakistanis are busy. The boxes are mounting. The Afghan women are

heaving. The machines are whirring. And then at around 8:30 a.m. there's a scream. Nazneen looks up. It's the Greek women. They know something's wrong.

For a moment she leaves the olives.

It's a fire. Their houses are on fire.

The Afghan women watch as about eight Greek women leave. *It's in the villages*, they say. Their houses are on fire out there. They look at each other, Mohadasse, Nazneen and Zahre. But they keep on working. They all keep on working. And the bosses say nothing.

She feels it in the pit of her stomach.

Something's not right.

The smell is getting stronger. They swipe their cards to leave. The car comes to pick them up and when they are back by the little house by the beach she tells Mohadasse and Zahre: *We have to leave. I think something's not right. I don't like it. I think it's not right.*

No. Mohadasse won't listen.

Let's just wait until Friday.

Then we can go back to Athens.

I can't lose this job, it's too important, I just can't.

That evening they see the fires for the first time. Dancing on the horizon. And the smoke. They can see it now in the air around them. But she sleeps.

The next day they start working again.

The smoke is thicker. There is more of it. But there is no word. Eleni, the boss on the line, still, she says nothing. Mid-morning there's another scream. Then a rush to leave as another eight or so Greek women get out as fast as they can. Nazneen can hear their voices and see their tears. *Their houses are burning.* She looks around, and she looks at her friends.

There is no sign to stop working.

There is no word about the fires. Nothing.

That evening the car comes to take them back to the little house by the beach. It's like a small paradise: like they're rich people, here, on holiday, in Greece. But they can see them closer now: the flames, red and yellow, glowing on the horizon. This time she says nothing.

They eat and they sleep.

They would tell them if it was coming close.

Yes, of course they would.

The morning feels different. They feel it in their lungs. They are coughing. The smoke is thick now. You can bat it with your hand. And when the car comes to pick them up – Nazneen, Mohadasse and Zahre – the road is covered in smoke, so close and so thick, they can't make out the horizon.

She feels shocked by what she sees. The factory is half empty. But no one tells them to stop. They swipe in, the Afghan women, and they start to work, next to each other, until there is another set of screams and another rush from the women. Almost all the Greek ladies have left now: half the machines are empty, the stuffing has stopped. Where there were ninety people there are only ten.

Then there's a call. It's Eleni, it's their boss. She wants them outside.

The fire is very close now, she says.

Your lives are in danger.

Then she points at the boxes. *These have just arrived*, says Eleni. *The fire is coming close*, she goes on. *You'll have to leave. But first you need to move these boxes inside so they are not destroyed by the fire.*

There are less than a dozen of them left in that yard. The three Afghan women, a few Greek women, and four Pakistani men. They don't protest. They don't know what to do, so they just do it. They rush and they pick up their boxes as the smoke gets so thick they can hardly stop coughing.

You feel fear. You don't think it.

You feel it in your body, in your hands. You feel it spreading down your spine until you can't feel anything else. This is how she feels. Panting over the boxes.

You can see the fires now.

Is it done? The Afghan women are out of breath.

If it's done then get in the car to where you live.

They first see it squatting over the road. The fire. Crackling and spitting. Stinging their eyes and breathing its heat. The driver reverses. But the road is blocked. Their phones go off one by one. 112. *Leave immediately.* The emergency text messages trill. *Your lives are in danger.*

There's another way, shouts the driver.

Five minutes, ten minutes, winding roads, twenty minutes, and they are there. They are at the house. There is smoke but no fire.

There is the sound of water on the sand. And as fast as he can the driver leaves.

The fear is beating through her. Shaking her.

We can't stay here, Nazneen calls her boss.

You've got to send us a car. We have to leave.

Eleni is on the phone. *You're not in danger. Just stay there.*

The fire is not coming there, she says. *It's not.*

They can see the water and they can see the beach. There are trees right up around them. But they do nothing. Mohadasse and Zahre are coughing. They are coughing so much they close the windows and draw the blinds and there in that darkness by the beach, she feels sleepy, so do they, and they sleep suddenly.

The boxes must have exhausted them.

They wake up with the text messages again.

Leave immediately. Your lives are in danger.

Again they call and again the boss says to stay.

Please send us a car, Nazneen is pleading.

But it's no. *No and don't be ridiculous.*

It's the middle of the afternoon. But with the smoke it looks like evening. They are nervous and they switch on a movie. Something Indian she can't remember if she's seen before. And then it's time for dinner.

It feels like a strange away day.

They chat. They wonder what has happened to the others. And Nazneen makes them all a lamb stew after the Bollywood. It's about 10 p.m. when the electricity snaps. They've just finished eating. They rush to open the windows and as the smoke gushes in that's when they realize they've made a terrible mistake. All around, the trees are aflame.

When you see a forest on fire you don't just see the fires.

You see black tree skeletons in those waving red flames. You see the birds on fire. Trying to escape. You see the animals. You see the deer trying to get out. And you see the people. Screaming. Running with pails of water. Then just running. Their cars on both the sides of the road. Like refugees.

Nazneen steps out and sees the worst.

Even the road is now cut off. There is a wall of fire encircling them. They are trapped. There is no way out. Then she sees the cats.

They are dead on the road beside them. Like they've been burnt or they've passed out from the smoke. And then a little further away she sees there's a dog. And it's dead too.

That's what makes her panic.

You panic and you try and call.

You hit the button and you want to speak to someone.

And there's suddenly no one. They've stopped answering. Eleni. The bosses. The company. Nazneen keeps phoning but nothing. And then her phone dies. She's forgotten to charge it. *No. No.* She swears but Mohadasse thrusts her phone at her. *Mr Mirzaei, let's call your friend Mr Mirzaei, who sent you here.*

He answers immediately.

His tone makes them more frightened.

Get out of the house right away.

Please. Grab your passports and the most important documents. And run to the beach. If the fire hits the house there could be an explosion.

It takes longer than it should to find these pieces of paper. And then they run to the beach, out close by the water. This is when she looks back. It's almost midnight. There is a red band of fire creeping closer, eating houses, eating trees, between the black sky and the black earth. But she can't look for long.

You can't stare straight into the fire. There are winds carrying sparks and embers towards her. They crackle and they sting and they scare her. One of those things might end up in her eye. They huddle on the beach.

There is only one working phone now.

Mr Mirzaei texts: *i'm trying to get coastguards*

And then just like that it loses signal.

The smoke is so thick now they can hardly see anything. There's something there: *Is it a dog? Is it a wolf?* She can't make it out, writhing in pain a bit further away, until it falls still. Mohadasse is sobbing, waving and shaking her phone at the sky.

It's gone. It's gone. It's got no signal.

And then Zahre begins to sob too.

It begins as an itch and a cough. And then she realizes. She can't breathe. The girls are coughing too and gasping – so much so they stop crying – but Mohadasse doesn't stop shaking the phone. How long they've been clutching each other, choking, she hardly knows. Then she hears a voice.

There's a light and a man waving.

Come in here and breathe.

It's that little beach bar with a fridge and some tables. *Just sit for a few minutes and then go*, says the male owner. There are old women in there, with this odd couple. The people who refused to leave.

Can you let us use the phone?

The coastguard, the coastguard, she's begging.

The owner shakes his head.

There's no signal, no landline and nobody's coming.

The owner is drinking beer, slurring, *I'm not gonna die.* The three Afghan women watch him. He blinks. He seems so still, so carefree. And then they realize he's drunk. Surrounded by scores of beer bottles. After ten minutes, after twenty minutes, she begs him again. *No you can't use my phone*, the man snaps.

There's no signal, no landline and nobody's coming.

They crouch on the floor, holding hands.

You hear cracks and explosions as fire eats a village.

Beams snapping. Boilers exploding. Alarms as cars are hit and turn melted and twisted by the heat. You hear the last dogs barking. And then their howls. Then more heaving cracks.

Go. The drunk owner is standing over them.

The fire is coming to this place now.

You'll be safer on the beach.

The old women walk off, silent, into the sand. The Afghan women, for a moment, they waver; the owner behind them slurring over and over again – *I'm just going to stay here and drink beer* – then they leave.

They find themselves back where they were. The fire rearing over them, lapping over them, like a monster. Their faces beaded with sweat. Hiding from it. Burying into each other.

It's then that she feels it.

The feeling that she is going to die.

Mohadasse is sobbing: *I wish we'd gone.*

I wish I'd listened. I wish we'd gone.

Zahre cries like a little girl.

Mummy, Mummy . . .

The fire is so close now.

The fire is so close she wants to wade into the water. But she knows they can't swim. The smoke is thick like fog. It feels like everything is on fire; that it's so hot the air itself might burn. Like the whole island is burning. Like this is the end of the world.

You really do see your life flash before your eyes. When you think you're about to die. That's what Nazneen can see now. She can see herself but she's not sure where. She's almost a baby. She's playing with toys her mother made her from scrap in Tehran. She's very little. She's in her bed and she can hear her mother singing. Songs she makes up as she cradles her, about migration, about the hard road, about love, about refugees. She's crossing the border. She's being beaten by the police.

She's wishing it wouldn't be like this.

That she wouldn't die so soon.

That life hadn't been so hard and so short.

That she hadn't died for a job she did just to survive.

The girls are sobbing next to her. But she doesn't cry, Nazneen. In front of her eyes she sees everything she ever wanted – London, Stockholm – or how she imagined them. Singing, once, to a full house. Motherhood. Love. Her family, her own.

And that none of it was going to happen now.

It's not fair, it's not fair, she thinks.

Then she sees her mother, that one last time. She's dead. She's seven years old. She died in a car accident, an Afghan refugee in Tehran. She's been brought home one last time to say goodbye. She's on a stretcher. And she sees her face. It's puffy. It's swollen. It's not her mother's beautiful face. It has yellowed. There are white cotton balls shoved up her nostrils and inside her ears as she's been bleeding.

Nazneen screams.

Mummy, Mummy . . .

She throws herself on top of the dead body. And then a hand grabs her. It's her father. He throws her and then he kicks her. And that's when all her troubles, when all her beatings, began.

The fire is so close now. It feels like hell.

No, she says, *no*. I didn't come all this way to die so easily.

I'm not. I'm not going to die.

The girls are sobbing but she has not cried. She holds them like a mother. She wants them to be ready if it comes. Ready for the one who knows everything. *Let's say it together,* she says. *Let's say the Shahada,* she says. Like Muslims are supposed to when they need Him. Or when they are about to die.

Ashadu ala,
La Ilaha illa-Ilahu,
Wa-Ashadu anna Muhammadan rasulu-Ilah.

There is no God but Allah,
And Mohammed is His Messenger.

They say it once. They say it again.

There are burning umbrellas and chairs on the beach, she thinks. There are burning houses. The smog is so thick she can barely open her eyes.

La Ilaha illa-Ilahu,
Wa-Ashadu anna Muhammadan rasulu-Ilah.

My life has been so lonely, she thinks. *My life has been so hard. There has never really been anyone there for me. Not since Mummy. Not for a very, very long time. But you, you have always been there for me,* she prays, as she holds the girls, like they are much, much younger than her.

If we are going to die, let's not die separately, says Zahre.

And they wait and they huddle.

They hold each other. They bury into one another.

And then suddenly Mohadasse screams.

Signal! Signal!

Nazneen jumps.

Call him! Call Mr Mirzaei!

There are more missed calls than you can imagine. He's very brief.

This number. This number.

On WhatsApp. It's the coastguards. Drop them a pin. Now. *Hang up!*

Pop. It takes one second. It's blue. It's dropped.

It passes slowly, it passes so slowly, the time that comes afterwards. She's shaking them. *Don't sleep. Don't sleep.* It's carbon monoxide. *You could never wake up again. They might be here any minute.*

She shakes them. Hours slip away.

Are they coming? Are they not?

The phone is on 2 per cent.

They make out in the distance the old woman sitting alone.

The water is hot, almost boiling beneath them.

Mohadasse keeps crying.

I wish I'd never come . . .

I wish I'd never come . . .

Zahre is crying.

I wish I'd left . . .

I wish I'd left . . .

But Nazneen holds them.

A light: round, distant like the moon in the fog. A motor. A voice. It happens fast. Hands lifting them onto the boat. Men passing them water. Wrapping them in towels. The coastguards pulling away.

All the beautiful nature.

It's all gone, she looks, as the boat pulls away.

It's the animals, they're all burnt, she thinks, as she looks back into the fire. There is more and more water between them but as she looks back she feels something else. She feels angry. She feels anger.

They made her pack up their boxes.

Then they told her to stay.

After that they stopped answering her calls.

She thinks of the olive line and she feels rage. There is more water now. She feels safe now. The fire is far away, she can breathe, she can breathe deeply. And suddenly, uncontrollably, she begins to cry.

21 NORRKÖPING

It had been a long time coming.

It had been a long time that Mummy hadn't been able to wash herself, that she hadn't been able to toilet herself, that she'd been in pain.

That's what Maria thought as she went upstairs.

The floorboards creaking as she passed the stairlift.

Is there anything you want for dinner?

There she was wrapped in the sheets – that colour, that smell – of the very old. The carer had already tucked her in. Her wheelchair was in the corner.

Then she stirred.

Can I have my favourite sausage?

Maria was almost taken aback. Mummy was awake. She was smiling, like she hadn't in a very long time. Something in her blue eyes. Something alive.

I haven't got it, said Maria, stunned.

But let me run out and get it for you.

And she rushed downstairs, to her car, to grab that Scandinavian sausage.

Maria's heart sang as she pulled out the drive; the guest house behind her – the Swedish guest house she had always lived in – with her mother and father and all those endless tourists, and now just Mummy and their visitors that kept coming; its paint peeling, its white stained by the rain, silent now in the rear-view mirror to Norrköping.

It made her so happy to buy that thing.

Because it meant it wasn't going to happen tonight.

That evening Mummy sat up and ate. She ate with a very good appetite. The sausage was gone and then she asked for what she

always loved: a shot of Akvavit and a small glass of beer and after that she slept, Kitha her St Bernard at her feet.

They look so peaceful, she thought, and stepped outside.

There were only the sounds of the motorway rushing beneath the guest house. The one they had cut through their land. The one she remembered walking on before they opened it as a little girl. The one they'd got compensation for and travelled the world: Los Angeles – Tahiti – Australia – Thailand – India – the Soviet Union – and home.

Her parents taking her out of school to see all this.

That was how she remembered them.

Laughing on the Trans-Siberian.

The souvenirs that were now in the basement.

Those days when she loved grown-ups more than kids.

Always letting her be older than her age.

That next morning Maria woke up fresh. She did what she had to do fixing the rooms, fixing the breakfast – and then she went upstairs.

A daughter standing at the door.

Do you want to listen to your music?

But there was no reply and Maria asked again, louder and tenser this time.

What about your music today?

Every morning, Mummy always listened to the same thing, she always listened to a *dansband*. The music of her youth. That sound of Sweden decades ago: because she really was – it felt impossible to say it – *ninety-four years old*. But today she shook her head.

Then she refused her food.

Everything in her room went still, her body all curled up in pain, still except for Kitha, whining, refusing her walk, refusing to leave her. That's when Maria knew, in the pit of her stomach, she knew, it was going to happen.

You know this feeling.

You know this feeling is dread.

Fifty-four years. She'd never lived without her.

She'd never left home. And now Mummy was leaving her.

Can you drive yourself to the hospital?

That's what the paramedics said a few hours later. They had

carried Mummy downstairs, past the posters and the guest book, her face white on the stretcher, in pain.

Of course, said Maria, with a thin voice.

The dog barking. The ambulance at the door.

It was really happening. They'd always had dinner together. From when Maria was very little to when Mummy was very sick. They'd always shared this place together. Helped the guests together. Made the sandwiches together. Until she'd got like this.

I knew this day would come, she thought.

But, right then, she felt like she was dreaming as she followed the ambulance over the gravel down the drive. The forest passed, then the lakes, then the town. And when she got to the hospital, they took her into a special room, not to the ward. Maria waited. Not wanting to know. Until the doctor came, his eyes averted from hers, wearing a sombre face.

Your mother's heart stopped, he said.

It happened in the ambulance.

At first it didn't come through.

I'm so sorry.

Everything felt muddled.

Like her head was made of glue.

You can start it again . . . can't you?

Her voice was shriller now.

Can't y-y-you start it again? Isn't it like a motor?

No, he said, slowly, firmly. *I'm sorry*, like he'd said it before. *She's dead.*

Maria froze. The hospital spun around her, the nurses dashing where they had to, the phones ringing, the doctor telling her he had to go, the woman taking her by the arm.

Her eyes were wet with tears.

So it had been her last meal . . . that little sausage.

And there she was, gone.

Not moving. Not breathing.

Like her face was turning to wax.

Shaking, Maria had called her best friend.

Elizabet-t-th?

Her voice was cracking.

Can you h-h-help me get Mummy's clothes?

Trembling, they drove out of Norrköping. Kitha barking wildly when they got home. And they went upstairs, Maria and her best friend. Mummy's bed still smelt of her and her perfume. As they opened her wardrobe, for her Sunday best, it felt as though she'd only just stepped out of the room.

Calm, Kitha.

It was like she knew what had happened.

Calm. I'll be back, I promise.

It didn't take long. Her body was still warm when they dressed her in the hospital.

That night Elizabeth stayed. She even slept in Mummy's bed, the one in which she had almost died. It was only the next night that Maria found herself alone.

The guest house creaked. The dog clung to her.

'I have this little fear, about the spirits.'

'That if you change too much they don't like it. So you have to be careful.'

She walked through the rooms as her mother had decorated them – the gold-framed portraits, the blue china plates on the walls, the gilt chandeliers, promising – *I won't change anything, Mummy, I'll leave it how you like it.* Hoping, somehow, she was listening.

Feelings of shock and sadness turning to guilty relief.

It had moved so slowly. She had withered so gradually. And then the thread of life had just snapped. Maria, slumped in the living-room gloom, couldn't sleep, thinking – *Is there any way Mummy is still here* – telling herself that she shouldn't be afraid – *If she is* – she'd only ever been good to her.

Are you all right, Maria?

The doors opened to the mortuary.

Elizabeth had come with her to hold her hand. When they pulled her out, Mummy's face was cold in the bright light. She was hard and she was almost blue, the way all bodies get, when it's gone, when there's nothing left. And when the men weren't looking, they tucked behind her a little bottle of Akvavit. It was then she kissed Mummy goodbye.

They didn't have to wait long for the funeral.

They held it in the little yellow chapel on her grounds.

They laid the coffin in there and before the priest came, Maria took in Kitha, to sniff for a long time the coffin of the one she felt was her mother too. Then she left her outside.

You stay here during the ceremony.

Then it was time.

The men had arrived to take the body away. But the St Bernard blocked them. All of a sudden Kitha was growling, trying to stop them taking her away. Like she was yelling.

This is my mother . . .

You cannot take her away.

Those men looked almost scared at the angry dog.

Like she might bite them. Like she might leap up and hurt them.

Now you leave her here, Maria said to them. *She has to say her goodbye too.*

And nervously, they lifted her down for Kitha to sniff. Because she knew what was in the coffin. A minute passed. Then another. It was time.

Come, Kitha, come.

And Maria leashed her up, led her into the guest house, before gathering herself for the crematorium. Staying with the coffin until she had to pull herself away.

It had been years.

The paint was peeling. The draught was coming in.

They had not been good years. Ones where she'd struggled to pick herself up again, where she'd failed to think of herself and where she'd stuck to her routines. First dark. Letting Kitha out at the end of the night. Then dawn. Pale light coming into the kitchen. Making breakfast. Setting the plates. Arranging the cutlery. Just like her mother had.

The same brands. The same recipes.

Never throwing anything away.

So many used things, piling up, until it smelt like a damp junk shop.

And the colours around her were faded and dull.

My friends think I'm very strange living like this.

But this is all I've ever known.

The morning rush would trail off.

She'd be there by herself with the newspaper.

And then the afternoon would come and they'd be gone – the guests, for long walks in the woods, or wherever they went – and Maria would be passing the vacuum cleaner round the drawing room, under the piano, over the rugs, the brown floral wallpaper, all around her, until she found herself again. Back in her earliest memories.

The weddings they used to throw.

The rich farmers and their brides, twirling, in those black suits and long dresses, all patterns and colours people didn't seem to like any more; the toasts; the rice being thrown over the couple; and she's there, just four or five years old, brushing it up afterwards. It made her smile how embarrassed her parents had been if the groom found her – such a little girl, staying up so late to do this – but she'd wanted to do it, she'd wanted to be just like them. The room was exactly as they'd left it.

The aristocrat's bust. The wicker chairs. It looked so out of time.

'If you change too much they don't like it.'

The political situation was always fraught, she thought. Then she'd put down the newspaper and step into the hall – the wheel still hanging from the ceiling, the Thai prayer cloth, still there, still framed on the table – then into the dining room. Her mother's oil portrait, still facing her father's. Still in her blue dress, still in his cream cardigan. Watching her serve the guests those same thick supper sauces they'd taught her.

It had been so many years.

But it could make her think of Christmas, this room.

That had been sacred for them. The weeks running up to it, there'd been such a Christmas tree, here in the corner, and a Christmas table for the guests: all smoked herrings and hams, special meatballs, sherries, ports and their favourite little sweets. The guests bustling around, bursting with hugs and cheers until they finally closed up on Christmas Eve. Her father laughing – funny for a Swede – that they should watch the Pope in Rome.

The three of them eating crayfish in their own little tradition.

They'd left her childhood bedroom intact, her dolls and baby bed, and now she couldn't touch it. She couldn't bear to throw her pram out of the attic. Or to touch her father's maps and bookcases.

It was here, upstairs, she'd think of him. How he'd always been so fascinated by life after death. How he'd once gone to a seance and come back exhausted from the effort, he said, you have to muster to talk to spirits. How he claimed to see things in his dreams. He'd been a Buddhist at the end.

As it ended – he'd been so weak – he'd looked at her and he'd said, *If I can help you after my death, I'll help you, but I don't know what I'll be able to do.*

She didn't want to let him go.

Even at the cremation, she insisted on watching.

Until the flames overtook her father's head and it splintered.

'At that moment it was terrifying. I saw his head . . . burst. It's not a nice sight. But I had decided I wanted to do it. And I don't regret it. I think that more children should do it when their parents die. But the people at that place. They thought I was weird.'

The men looking at her like she was a witch.

And then time slipped on.

A cancer came and Elizabeth died too.

The friend who'd really been there for her.

And it built slowly. The feeling that she wasn't alone. Maria would smell her father's cologne on the landing and then she'd find herself in the office, all the documents he'd always handled, all the paperwork she hated doing, unable to find the right form for the tax office, until she put her hands together and asked – *Help me.*

And then she could feel him.

Like he was helping her.

In her dreams, she'd see her parents, but not as they were.

Her father would be screaming:

You stupid bitch. You whore . . . You come back here!

He'd be awful to her mother; things he'd never been when he was alive. And then she'd see Mummy. They would be travelling. On the bus down the motorway. Through the airport. Then terrible things would happen. And she'd wake up, like they were trying to warn her.

You feel it when somebody's watching.

Like a creep on the shoulder. Like a presence in the room.

You know when you have to turn.

It had been in the kitchen, she'd begun to see things.

It was one of those heavy days. One of those days where she had so many guests, so much food to fix, so much to do, she'd find herself flagging, thinking, *I want to go to bed, I don't want to deal with the guests. To do all these things Mummy used to do.* It was one of those days she felt she was not alone. That there was something right behind her. That was when she saw the woman in the window. It was just an instant.

And then she'd look again and she'd be gone.

I think it could be my mother.

And she kept appearing. Again and again.

Each time giving her the strength to continue.

It happened slowly that the guests started to feel something too. They felt cold air, then heat, in their rooms, like there was energy passing through. They felt that somebody was peering at them. That there was a presence. That there was something there.

Then they started to see things. A man in epaulettes on the landing, like one of the old Swedish aristocrats who had lived here long before it became a guest house. Then a woman in the drawing room, hunched over in the corner, like a bride married here long ago.

They said others walked beside her.

It's your father, said one woman – a guest who said she could feel these things, who said she could speak to them – as they were in the armchairs, one night.

He's trying to say something to you.

He's trying to say not to work yourself to death.

The lights went out on the landing.

Maria went upstairs. She left them to the guests.

You know this feeling.

You think there are no haunted places. Only haunted people. You know everything they say about suggestibility. You know it all and you still can't sleep; oil paintings, with strange smiles, peering down at you.

The guests would go. Then more of them would come who had no idea. But it only grew stronger, that feeling that people who were here before – *were here*. And she found herself in the barn, feeding

Crumb the cat, wondering – *Why? Am I just older? Am I more emotional? So I can now feel these things children bat away? Or is there something else?*

'I'm not quite sure.'

'I don't think that we just disappear. I think that something inside lives on. I think something happens with the soul. But I'm not quite sure what.'

It was around then that the guests started to change. The old families she knew from her parents started to fade away and people who had heard about her and the house arrived. People who wanted to see the ghosts. People who wanted to write about them in the paper. People wanting to bring electro-magnetic machines to prove something.

'Those, I always said no. They live here and I do too.'

'You have to leave them alone otherwise something bad will happen.'

But aren't you frightened, they asked, *that this is a haunted house?*

And she would try and explain that, no, she wasn't.

That it was nice not to be alone.

Then one evening something inside her cracked.

It was the daughter who made the reservation. They had no idea.

It's for my mother, she said, *it's her eightieth birthday.*

And she won't travel anywhere without her boyfriend.

Then they arrived. There were eight of them. Her children had all clubbed together so she could stay in this place. And there he was, the old boyfriend, about the mother's age, always talking over her and deciding things for her so much that Maria snapped at him.

No, it's not you that's going to decide when you're having breakfast.

When does she want to have breakfast?

And the little old lady was suddenly smiling at her.

Then it was check-out time. The bags were in the hall.

The old lady turned to Maria, and said, *Oh, isn't it lonely to live here?*

Her sweet little voice so soft and pitying.

It felt like teeth gnashing inside her as she opened the front door.

She's an eighty-year-old woman, she thought.
If she can have a boyfriend, then I can too.
She felt something strong, like envy.
That kept coming back to her.
That was the night Maria made a dating profile.
Thinking, *Why haven't I done this before?*
Why was I so hurt for so long?
Then her phone started to ping.
hallo, said the man in her pocket.
He was a technician, he said. He worked in the iron-ore factory.
i've got a guest house, she typed.
just off the E4 motorway . . . you might have seen it
And then she went back to her chores. The notifications building up.

A few days later there was a ring on the reception phone.
Hallo, he said, *are you Maria? It's Arne from the website.*
Yes . . . how did you find me?
Oh, I was just researching . . .
He was in his fifties. He came, nervously holding flowers, to the guest house. Maria had invited him for dinner and they ate, chatting about life, under her parents' portraits. They kissed, but it felt like nothing special. They made appointments, coming and going for a few years, him bringing her vegetables he grew for her in his garden.

'But it fizzled out.'

And she got back on the websites.

They would ping her as she made the beds but she would leave them to stew.

Dusting her father's porcelain. Adjusting her mother's doilies.

The men came and went.

There was Svante, who'd been so impatient to meet her he'd come on the Monday with a bottle of red wine instead of waiting till the Sunday, then took her out for tea the following week down in Norrköping, always talking about his terrible divorce and his battles with his ex-wife over a boat, until she dumped him. He was fine but the truth was he stood her up one too many times for dinner because of his bad days.

Then there was Stinget, like her in his mid-sixties, who she'd

clearly told on chat she didn't much care for sparkling wine then turned up with it anyway, to serenade her on the piano. But he was a total bore. Just like the next two men that came – and who came with nothing – parking their cars outside the guest house, then sitting half in silence inside.

The two of them so dry – dry even for Swedes.

I can feel the spirits, she would tell them sometimes.

But these men would make a sound like – *p-f-f-t* – with their mouths and ignore her. Like she was mad and soft-headed or both.

I'm not frightened of the spirits, she would think.

I'm only frightened of those with skin and blood.

I'm only frightened of the world I live in.

There was only one time she thought it was going wrong, scarily wrong, and that was when she picked up the weirdo in Norrköping at the train station. He recognized her and waved and the very moment he got in the car she went cold – his face wasn't the same as the one on the profile. And as she drove he nattered about how when they got back to the guest house they could do it. *Oh God*, she thought, *I don't want to have sex with him.*

It was winter and it was hard to steer.

Swirl and ice and everything on the forest road.

The man still talking about it as she tried not to skid.

She served him dinner on her mother's tablecloth. This ugly man sitting there, with a small box of very cheap white wine, he poured for himself and never offered her. The pretence of a conversation petering out into silence Maria wouldn't cover for.

The family portraits muted and stern.

Remembering he lived so far away she'd already said he could stay over.

Do you have any wires?

He was standing on the landing, outside the room she'd shown him to.

His tone grumpy, Maria had made it clear she would sleep elsewhere.

I really need some electric wires . . .

It was something about him – his eyes, his mouth, his little box of very cheap white wine – that made her mind race unpleasantly, picturing things horribly and instantly.

Is he going to tie me to the bed?

What is he going to do with me?

Then she pulled herself together.

What do you need them for?

Oh, he said, *just my snoring machine,* pointing to a mask-like device.

You see otherwise . . . I snore.

That night she couldn't sleep. Maria kept on having visions that he might have died. That he might have some serious health problem. That he might be playing a trick. Night thoughts sticking together, playing with her and refusing to come apart, until she crept onto the landing to see if she could see his face, in a tubed muzzle, through the door.

The next morning he hadn't slept and neither had she.

Instead he was sitting there waiting for breakfast, in a gown.

And his face said it – above all he was waiting for sex.

I've got to walk the dog, she said.

And when she came back he was still there. Fiddling with his phone.

The way he was sitting, the way he was smiling, expecting it.

The guests are going to come early, she said, *you need to go and get ready.*

And he slipped upstairs in his gown, grinning.

Then after ten minutes she called.

Are you ready?

Oh I certainly am, he called back, like he was licking his lips.

No, she yelled from the bottom of the stairs, suddenly angry.

Ready for the train station. You have to leave.

The last she saw of him was him walking away in the snow.

You think it will never be you.

You think it's only you and your ghosts.

You and the things you mourn.

Then something happens.

hello

She hated his profile when he messaged her. Baseball cap turned back to front. Sunglasses so you could barely see what he looked like. And anyway, it said he was forty. That was much too young for her. Then a month later he messaged again.

hello

You find yourself talking.

You find yourself saying things that surprise you.

You find yourself not wanting to get off the phone.

To keep talking. To keep them close.

Gustaf came, soon enough, for a week. He was a truck driver, he explained. He'd dropped out of law school and then out of an office job and it worked better for him, the open road. The 5 a.m. starts and the days when his truck was empty by lunch.

He felt more free.

The young man in the old house.

I'd have married you directly, he said, smiling.

If you were younger.

You find yourself in Sweden, in the high summer.

You drive out into the forest and you find a lake where it's just you alone and you sit on a rock or a bench and you eat a sandwich and watch the dog go for a swim in the silvery light. It's very late and you're not alone. You've someone to talk to.

You realize this moment will never happen again.

It was then that Maria felt something. It wasn't love. It wasn't loss.

It was something else. She saw herself. Shimmering in the water.

She felt at peace. At peace with her living and her dead.

22 CORRUBEDO

Graña hated the tourists. But now he was cowering behind the rocks on the beach with Josephine, he almost missed them. The dog panted. Not that long ago she'd been a stray. Saving her from the pound had been one of the best decisions he'd ever made. At least he was with somebody in the lockdown.

Even if she was a dog.

This is what he did every night. Graña slipped out, even though he wasn't supposed to, and made it to the beach. Corrubedo was empty. There was hardly anybody who lived here and those who did were all cowering at home. *Absurd*, he thought. But still, he didn't want to get caught. They were fining people now.

What a strange feeling.

For years he'd hated it here. He felt like an alien here. In the village, there used to be just fifteen families. Every family had a pig and a little granary. There were four farmers and the rest, they were all at sea. Fishing, that's who they were, that's all they could do. But that was long ago.

'My village . . . it's gone.'

It happened quickly.

First hotels opened, then farms were sold. Holiday homes went up. Buildings sprang up like mushrooms in the night, until his memories of his own home felt like a foreign country. There was even a bar owned by some British architect and, in the summer, when he went down to have a beer in the café, the tourists stared at him. Like he was making them feel uncomfortable. Like he was in their space. And the owners yapped at him about leashing up the dog.

But it was better than this.

Hiding behind the rock, Graña would smoke and think. It had done everything to him, the sea. It was coming to an end, people like him. It was coming to an end, these small places where things passed from father to son. Then he would forget about it and look at the sea. Their world had stopped. But the ocean was still there. Taunting him.

He spent hours there, with Josephine.

Little pieces coming back to him. Of everything he'd seen.

He was in Thailand when they called.

He'd got off after a long time at sea. There's a particular sound at a port like Phuket at night. Mingled voices, laughter, music coming from various bars. Sometimes the patter of rain. That's when they phoned him.

It's The Kunlun, *a good ship. Not much work. Would you look after her engines at anchor? Competitive pay.*

Interesting.

He knew these guys. Galicians. Graña knew all about them. The money they were raking in. The corners they were cutting. If he hadn't been in Thailand he might not have answered. But he was already in port here and hell why not. There wasn't exactly much to hurry back to.

Of course I'll do it.

She wasn't much of a looker, *The Kunlun*. Rusted hull. Small white bridge. You might not even know she was a fishing boat. But when he got into the engine room he found she was in good shape. Good enough for a quiet port stay.

It's just three, four months, Graña, they said.

Just over the winter. Nothing strenuous at all.

Water checks. Engine checks. It was nothing. Morning work. Then he would hit the bars. He loved an anchor like this after months at sea.

'Everything they told you about sailors is true.'

Brothels. Another round at 3 a.m. That was him.

That was the way he had fun.

There was only a skeleton crew on *The Kunlun*. A few Indonesians, hardly any Spaniards. Typical. The World Cup was playing.

It must have been dawn when the knocks came, waking each other up. Then they watched the games. The TV flickering in the dark mess. *Goal.* Then he'd see the sun came up fast in the tropics. The ring of bicycles getting louder on the dock.

'It was all calm. All relaxed. The problems would hit when it set sail . . . but that was supposed to be someone else's problem. I was only looking after it at anchor.'

You might not notice the moment your life turns on. You might have forgotten it by the end of the day. You'll pick it out months later trying to work out what the hell just happened. It was one of those days.

The engine boss got another job. Better ship. Off to Scotland or somewhere. Graña thought nothing of it. The sailors were arriving. His head was already back in Spain.

That's when they called him.

Graña, we've got a proposal. It's the sea job.

You'll be the engine boss.

It was summer in Phuket. The hills were green. The sorting hangars their usual echoing medley. Thousands of fish being thrown into pink and blue baskets. Bright colours rusting on the Thai ships.

We're not going where we say we're going, they said.

But trust us, the pay is good. Very good.

Interesting, Graña thought.

That's when they told him.

It was more like a pirate ship.

It would be very simple. In and out. Everyone knew the seas were emptying. You couldn't get your old catch. But this way they'd get in a month what those suckers were chasing in three. And not any old fish.

This was white gold.

'That's when they said Antarctica.'

Graña hesitated. He was supposed to be going home. But this was money. Serious money. And the second mate they were stepping up to be a fake captain in case they got caught was solid: a Peruvian guy. He knew what he was doing.

'I thought . . . *Why not?*'

You know the moment you've done this. You've evaluated risk.

You cross, you click, you text back. You run through it all really quickly. You smile and you roll the dice.

The Kunlun weighed anchor.

The blue water turned darker as they left the bay. Tendrils of land followed them. Those bright little fishing boats disappeared.

At last. There is a feeling that all sailors have when they set sail: a tingling mixed with dread. The days passed quickly. Through the traffic in the Straits of Malacca. Huge container ships as big as ten *Kunlun*s making their own tides. Then they turned down the coast to Aceh.

They stopped. It was an engine change. He'd forgotten where. Some Muslim place, Graña remembered, no fun with no booze. The women walked behind the men. Another culture. You wondered how they lived.

This was it: the last stop. Graña sat, watching, on the dock. His hands smelled of grease. They always did because that was who he was. Colours, skullcaps, motorbikes. The crowds washed over him. Maybe an hour passed, then another. There was shouting onboard. And then they left. On the bridge, he was told that soon they would make the turn.

You travel the world as a hairdresser, you remember the cuts. You travel the world as an engine man and you remember the engines. Their boats – there were just so many little boats – with an engine taped to a bit of wood bobbing off the back. That was what caught his eye when he went up to smoke and lean over the rail. Incredible.

'They were just so powerful.'

There always seemed to be dozens of them along that great green coast. Engines from buses, or were those cars, strapped onto some oar at the back. And the locals navigated them with amazing grace. Sometimes they passed so close he could hear their voices. Yelling things he couldn't understand.

On the bridge they spoke amongst themselves. Then the message went out to the whole crew. The turn was coming. And when it happened they passed Krakatoa. He saw it. The smoke trailing off it. They talked about it as they passed. Some of the Indonesians said it was holy, like a god. Some of the Spaniards said if it went off again it would be like a nuclear bomb. That it could even destroy our world.

There were six ships out there.

Six heading to Antarctica. The bandit six.

'They were all under those same guys.'

Now the schedule took hold. There were four of them in that dark space with those shuddering machines. His number two; a good Spaniard. And two Indonesian greasers. The rotations were setting in.

'We split the work by watches. Six hours on. Six hours' sleep. But the truth is you never quite sleep that whole six. Just four, five if you're lucky and then you're back down again in the engine.'

The dials. The tremors. That never-ending growl. Graña knew these sounds so well. They followed him into his sleep. The whining. Those thuds. The crackle from the gas. In that space he was a mechanic, technician, blacksmith, carpenter, maybe more.

Quickly, I need you here now.

They had to shout over the mufflers. You got used to the noise but your ears didn't. It was the regulations. But it was too late for him.

Graña was half deaf but he heard the machines perfectly.

Every pipe, every tremor, he knew what it meant.

Change the oil.

Change the cold compressor.

Change the fucking filter.

His face was running with sweat. He was half stripped in the tropics. Sometimes it got so hot the machines were scalding to the touch.

The Kunlun was making knots now out into the ocean.

The plan was simple. When it came to shipping it was always the captain and him, the engine boss, who were criminally liable. That's why they'd stuffed that Peruvian up top. And then the hiding began. Graña smiled. He was taking a risk.

'It's like this . . .'

'If you're going to rob a bank you get your balaclava.'

At night the Indonesians bent over the bows and painted over *The Kunlun*'s name. And they were flying a flag of convenience: Equatorial Guinea, one of those countries he'd heard had not signed up to anything. But there was more. They covered up the windows. They switched off the lights. The ship was in darkness and they worked in darkness.

Six hours on, six hours off.

A week. Two weeks. Engines. Cabins. A moment or two in the mess. He was in the middle of the ocean but he might as well have been underground.

Outside there was no landscape at all.

It hit him one night, where he was. Graña pulled himself up to the deck to smoke. It was late, it had been another six hours, as he fumbled for the door. His eyes stung. The light. It was almost midnight, he never missed the time onboard, but there was the sun.

It was complete day.

Bright silver lapping the waves.

'It rattled me, to see that. Like the world upside down.'

The southern night was as white as noon.

'Something about it disturbed me.'

Then he felt the changes come quickly, even in the engine room. You needed a jumper now or a coat to go outside. It was cold. It bit your nose and your ears and the sea was becoming calm. It had been three weeks.

'We were coming closer . . . they said.'

It was then he began to see the ice, cracked and white, like little bits of enormous destruction. There was more and more of it. Every time he came out of the darkness, there were more pieces. Until they felt surrounded. And there they were. Those little black things. Penguins. Sunbathing on the ice or bobbing along like they were on the bus.

The message went out from the bridge.

They had arrived in Antarctica.

They pulled the levers in the engine room.

They did as the captain said. This was it, where the nets would be thrown out, where the ship would run almost still. The sounds changed. The Indonesians threw the nets. Pirate nets, ones you would never be allowed to use in these protected areas. The engine boys had done their job and now it was time.

Graña stepped onto the deck.

The sea was still, like a mirror, like the water in the Straits of

Magellan, where he'd seen whole mountains and islands perfectly doubled in their silent reflections. The only thing disturbing them – *him*.

Graña stopped and looked as the noise went out around him. That huge wall of ice, staring back at him, behind the wind.

They were fishing now. This was the white gold. He knew it was Patagonian toothfish or Chilean sea bass, with its huge mouth and black scales. Six feet long. But he didn't have the taste for it. They never ate it fresh in the mess. It was for Asians, the whole thing; they paid millions for it. It was an Asian world now. Everything they did was about them. They'd changed the crews too. They used to be all Spaniards on his ships. Then it started to shift.

The bosses, they wanted Indonesians.

'The Indonesians are good workers, but they're not that strong. They don't come from fishing villages. They are just starting out. You can get four of them for one man's pay but the truth is you need four of them to do his work.'

You feel it slowly.

That feeling you're living in somebody else's world.

You notice one thing. Then another. Until one day it clicks.

You're the last of something.

They're the ones who'll be carrying on.

Graña first felt it with the Korean classifier he'd met off the Canaries. He could see him now: an expert on octopus, they called him. Who could just hold one catch and tell you – one kilo, three kilo – blind. But the Indonesians spoke no Spanish and hardly any English. There were some twenty-odd of them but he'd hardly interact with them. He'd nod. They'd smile. But he only ever talked to his engine boys and the Spaniards on the bridge.

'You don't really have friends onboard.'

It was hardly much of a crew. He'd be in the mess. The Indonesians would be around him. But he'd hardly understand a single word.

Sometimes, sitting there, he'd think about Spain. But there was no point hurrying back there. He hardly spoke to his daughter. He was long divorced. None of the young ones in Corrubedo wanted to do anything like this.

'They've got better options.'

But this was all he had.

The smell and the flapping from the fish would flood the deck when the haul came on. The Indonesians would shout and heave and rush it to the huge refrigerators that made it all possible. Graña would come out of the engine room and smoke. His clothes, his hands, his hair stinking of diesel and grease. The light, that bluish light, would colour everything.

It first bleeped on the radar screen. And they froze. It was a ship. It was coming towards them. And it only meant one thing. They'd been caught. They would be radioing in soon demanding to see their permits, checking their nets, assigning them whatever crimes they'd committed.

'We just panicked. We stopped everything. Then we fled.'

There was horror on the bridge and then they heard in the engine room. They had only been fishing for three or four days. Graña felt something. Something he hadn't felt often at sea. He felt fear.

There was shouting.

The Indonesians pulled the nets in. The motors began to whine and thud and growl in the engine room again as his boys powered them up to full speed again. They said it was the Australians, or maybe the New Zealanders, he wasn't sure. That's who was after them. That they'd sailed too close to their waters and they'd picked them up maybe weeks ago on the way down.

Six hours on, six hours off.

The green dot was getting closer.

Six hours and six hours off.

His head was splitting from the darkness, his eyes squinted in the darkness, but Graña pulled himself to the deck.

There, there it is. Can you see it?

You see your own disaster clearer than you've ever seen anything else in your life. You can see every detail, every angle, every way it could have gone so differently. You never forget your first sight of it.

Them. A grey dot on the horizon.

Six hours on, six hours off. They needed to go faster, faster. They couldn't waste a single minute. They were sleeping in the engine room now. Mattresses thrown on the floor between the pipes and the dials. The whine and the thuds and the clatter. He slept lightly there. He hardly slept at all before throwing himself back at the machines. They had to get away. They had to.

This couldn't be it.

'It was horrible, horrible.'

That was when he began to feel it. He didn't feel well.

Court. Policemen. Prison. It kept flashing before his eyes. He could be years in there. He was about to lose everything unless he could make the damn machine go faster. It wasn't fair. It was only his first time. He was only driving the murder vehicle. He didn't pull the trigger. Slumped there on the mattress, mechanical sounds beating into his head, he knew it made no difference. The captain and the head of the engine room were legally liable.

Idiot, I'm an idiot, he kept repeating.

He couldn't sleep. Night or day, they fused together, in the blacked-out engine room. He would jolt from one shift and into another. And they'd still be there, on the horizon, whenever he stepped on deck.

'I could see them every day. You'd navigate for about two hundred, three hundred miles, whatever, and six hours later they were still back there.'

They wouldn't stop. They kept coming. Closer and closer. Graña lay there between the machines in the moments he could breathe, his head filled with fear. He was going to be arrested. He was going to be locked away. It would be dark. He would be alone.

It would be worse than this.

'Yes, I had nightmares.'

'Every time with more and more precision.'

Of them coming onboard. Taking him away. Taking it all from him. Everything he had. For weeks and weeks, they kept coming. Once they got so close they tried to board like it was one of his nightmares. But they kept coming. They got closer and they got further away. But they never left them.

'Every night, I'd repeat.'

'They're gonna catch us, they're gonna catch us.'

It kept going longer and longer like torture. The captain shouting.

Engine room!

We have to outrun them.

We have to outrun them.

It was all up to him. The Indonesians were listless. There was nothing on their faces. They knew if they got caught it meant nothing to them. It would all fall on him. He was the only Spaniard who was legally liable. They had got him in for this. He knew he was the fall guy. He was so exhausted he couldn't sleep. His head was splitting. His eyes were turning pink. They had double fuel, they could outrun them.

Graña was falling apart.

You begin to feel it rising inside it.

You begin to feel it scraping inside you. Getting into every thought and moment. Like a static that you can never tune out.

'I didn't feel well.'

'And began to feel bad, very bad.'

This is a fear you feel differently. Like your fear of falling. You know this feeling. The feeling of looking over an abyss. You can't look. You flinch back. All the time knowing the pleasure in the release if you fell.

'Two months. Three months. Four months.'

The dials whirred in front of his eyes. He was sweating. They were going faster. His life. He could see it all behind this one moment of disaster.

Then the word came down from the bridge. The green dot on the radar. It was pulling away. They'd outrun them. The other ship must have run out of fuel.

A feeling washed over him.

'It was relief . . . pure relief.'

His watch was over.

Graña stood on the deck and smoked. The Antarctic snow blew around his collar. A soft, blustery kind, that caught between his clothes and fingers.

Graña felt old. Graña felt ill.

'I've always thought a year at sea is four on land.'

'I feel like I'm a hundred and nineteen.'

They were fishing again. The Indonesians were yelling. Those deep gill nets, the ones that were completely banned, were down at the bottom. When they were pulled back up they'd be shimmering with life. With hundreds of thousands of dollars of Patagonian toothfish the size of small men. Light still on in the back of their eyes. He didn't care about this. All he cared about was the engine.

He let his eyes follow the ice. There was so much of it, so much flaking and collapsing off the continent, they had to stick a pole out to push the ship between it. He worried about the winter. About dithering too long now and letting the pack ice crush and seal them in. But mostly he thought about nothing.

He just watched.

'It was like a symphony.'

'The quiet, the calm, the stillness.'

His eyes followed the ice. They were hypnotized by the ice. The silence. It didn't sound like he'd imagined silence would sound. It didn't sound like nothing. It sounded like music. Like the spaces between the notes. Like all of this was needed to make our world sing. Like the spaces in Beethoven. Like the pauses any composer knows echo with sound.

'It moved me, it moved me so deeply.'

'As there's no symphony without silence.'

'And every time I stood there, I heard classical music.'

His eyes followed the ice: blues, whites, thousands of shades, some of them almost green. They followed until he felt he was floating with them. Until he felt he was weightless. Like he was floating out in space. Until he felt like he was hallucinating. He was so far away.

And then a feeling came.

It was a feeling of grief.

When you're not well, it's always there, hiding in the moment. When you're not right, you always know it, long before. The ice, it was everywhere. It was all around them. And that's when he began to realize. It was dying.

The world was dying.

'You stand there and you ask yourself: *How can we be so stupid to destroy all of this?* Because you know we're going to end up destroying everything. You've had a lot of time to think in your life. But you've never felt it . . . Now you're seeing a beautiful woman. You're seeing a beautiful mountain. But you're in shock. Because it's disintegrating. You can see it. We're destroying the planet.'

'And there's nothing we can do to stop it. Nothing.'

It made him feel ill, the symphony.

He'd seen so much in his life.

He'd seen dolphins hunting with humans off the coast of Africa. He'd seen humpback whales leaping with seals off the tip of Chile. Their heads in and out of the water, like there was a rhythm only they knew. He didn't want to be the last generation to see all this. Like it had all been for nothing. Like man was only here to write a report on this dying world.

'It's almost exterminated, overexploited.'

'All of it, all of it.'

Those nights he slept in his cabin again.

As the ship rocked he thought about everything he'd seen.

He'd seen the favelas of Peru when it had been swordfish season. He'd seen the inside of half the whorehouses from Punta Arenas to Montevideo. The smiles of escorts. The jokes the men tell on their beds. He'd sat on the back of the truck they used to collect the sailors for the bars in Durban, waiting to get sloshed. He'd seen the flowers on Table Mountain. He'd seen Scotland and Nova Scotia and the Bar of Lost Souls in Vigo, at the moment the people of the night mix with the sailors at dawn.

'The workers coming in off the giant cranes.'

He tried to think about what it all meant.

He wasn't himself any more.

And Spain wasn't Spain. It had made the world. It made all these countries he had spent a lifetime sailing to. But now all that was over. Hardly anybody wanted to work on the water any more. There were hardly any Spanish sailors now. Whatever it was, all that energy, all that hunger, or was it greed, it was gone. Spain was just a normal country.

Just a small part of Europe.

Just another corner of an Asian world.

'I'm a dreamer, you know. I dream a lot.'

'I didn't want to live in this palace and only see one room.'

The word came from the bridge. North. It was time to head north. The six-hour shifts started to fade into one again. The engine whined louder again. They passed icebergs so large it took a day to navigate around them.

The Kunlun was on its way. The water began to change. First the penguins, then the ice, began to disappear. And the word came out they were converging: three other ships on the same course. Half of the Bandit Six.

They drew closer and the news came. They were loading it all on this one. That way it was easier for the others to get away in case they got caught. The smell of fish, the smell that had been everywhere, only got stronger as the ship rocked with the thud of their haul. Then it was done. The illegal nets: they threw them out.

Hiding the murder weapon.

'How did I feel on the way back?'

'It was like if you went on a trip and you had to cross customs hiding a kilo of cocaine. You don't feel normal, you're alert the whole time.'

'It's draining. It's so draining.'

The nights were becoming warmer. Graña no longer needed a coat to smoke after his shift. Sometimes he would think of home.

What it was like to come home. It was always the same. The clothes that he'd worn onboard, the stink, he could never get out. He'd have to throw them away. On those first days he couldn't go out. He'd just sit there on the couch, blinking, trying to acclimatize. Trying to steady himself now it was over, watching TV, trying to work out if Spain was a republic or a monarchy or what currency they now used. And only then would he take small steps. First to the shop, then a little further, a little braver.

'I thought I was building a family.'

'That I needed the money.'

'But now I know you can't have a family and have the sea.'

He remembered the village. He remembered when it was so small there it was like one big family. He remembered his mother. And then he remembered how the cottage door would open. There would be a man standing there he didn't know. Graña would run and hide and try and try and find Mummy as quickly as possible. *That's your daddy*, she'd say, pointing at the stranger in the door. *Go and give him a hug.* He'd hardly know him. With these seven-, eight-month trips.

'We never talked much.'

'I wasn't close with him.'

'And then I felt it happening again.'

He remembered the date: June 16th.

Graña was married and that was the date he realized he'd spent a year at sea. His daughter, she hardly recognized him. And standing in the door, she'd grown so much, he hardly recognized her. She used to come for Christmas to the village, but now that hadn't happened for many years.

'It's all I know, the sea. It's harsh, it takes you with it.'

'But if you asked me, I would . . . I would do it all again.'

All this floated through his mind in the engine room. They headed north. The pipes grew hot, the sweat returned, they had to strip down again to work. The seas changed. The light changed. And on watch he didn't feel well. He'd been on the ship too long. He'd been at sea too long. Too long.

Graña had nobody to call from the satellite phone on the bridge.

Nobody to say: *I miss you.*

He didn't feel well.

The ice was far away but it was still in him.

They changed the flags over at night. Down came the African flag and up went the flag of Indonesia. Then they changed the name. The Indonesians bent over the side and painted it over. The alias disappeared.

It was now *The Taishan*.

The word went through right down to the engine room. First land. The Indonesians, they shouted with joy, when they first saw their homeland. Their green world. They grew closer. The Spaniards, they began to speak about it, what they'd do when they got to land. The bars. The girls. That feeling of being so pent up. The younger ones said their dicks were ready to explode. They ran through the plan. Tell nobody about the white gold. Any word about Patagonian toothfish and it could land us all in jail.

Arrival. That sudden feeling. They were still.

Phuket. Laughter. They'd done it. The sound of fish falling away. The feel of the ship getting lighter. The sight of women. The feeling of dry land, still shaking for you, like you were still at sea. Graña laughed. He was almost home. Engine checks. The shifts were over. It was back to morning work.

'I felt . . . At last I felt calm.'

Yelling. That's how he knew.

It only took him a moment, once he heard, to know. Then it all came at once. Police. Dogs. Documents. Warrants. Requests.

The authorities had got them.

'They took everything. Everything.'

'They said we were sealed. We were stuck.'

They'd tricked them the whole time. They'd known exactly where they were and they'd planned the whole time to catch them red-handed back in port.

'The sailors and the cook, they didn't care. But it was me and the fake captain who were on the line for the whole thing.'

You know you're falling when you can't hold on.

You know you're falling when you know you can't turn back.

'I had to get off.'

'I just had to get off.'

It had all been for nothing, nothing. The chase. The journeys. The money. It had all been for nothing but prison.

Graña was shaking. He was collapsing.

You know you're spiralling when there's no way out. You know there's no way out when you look at your life and you realize you lost the game.

'I was the only one who got out.'

'I just had to get off. I just had to get off the ship. I took a knife and I slit both my wrists . . . and then I slit both my arms.'

He went up to the deck and cut himself. He wasn't sure who bandaged him. He wasn't sure who took him off or where he was when he woke up in that Thai hospital. He didn't remember anything of the flight back to Spain. When the hammer fell in the Galician court it was only a €3,000 fine for environmental crimes.

'It had all been for nothing, nothing.'

Graña woke up late. Then he fed the cats. The lockdown was still going on. The village, or what there was left of it, felt miles away as he scooped out tins of food into their bowls. Nothing. He'd thought he'd been building a family.

But instead this was all there is.

'And now I've got no family, no money and no job.'

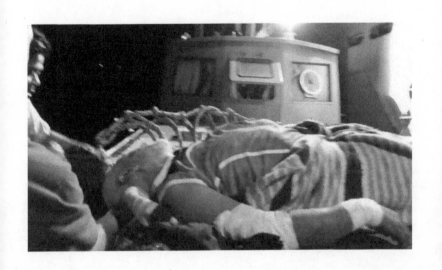

Graña waited for it to get dark before he wandered outside. Summer was coming. The sun disappeared slowly. His days were all the same. He walked on the beach. He picked up cigarette butts on the street. He took a few sausages out to feed to the strays. He spoke to nobody. He'd pass a holiday home that had been a farm.

He'd pass a ruin that had been a taverna.

He'd notice even the dunes looked different.

They'd ransacked them for all this construction.

Then he would remember Antarctica.

'You know what Covid is? This is a warning from nature telling us who's in charge. That we're just her guests. That's all.'

'And we don't even notice.'

Graña walked on the beach.

Sometimes his mind filled with melting ice.

With goodbye meals of ray fish and potatoes.

With half-remembered things about extinction and polar bears.

'It's coming, I think . . .'

He knew the old-timers around here. He knew where they lived. The bigs, those guys who had called him in Phuket. The bigs would be fine, in their big houses by the water, nothing would ever happen to them. *What a joke.* It was people like him who would get fucked. Some things never change.

He never went to sea again.

The sky had gone a dark blue by the time he slipped outside.

It was time to walk the dog.

23 CASTLETOWNROCHE

It had been such a week.

They'd had Henrik and Lisa, her stepkids, down at the castle from Germany.

It had been quite the year. They'd got married, she'd got pregnant and then they'd moved into Patrick's family estate. *Maybe, it's all been a little too much*, thought Sheila, as she wheeled the baby over Dublin cobbles, chills and a cold sweat creeping over her.

There was an ugly scraping sound. *Shit*, she thought, flinching. The pram tyre had popped. Now the thing could hardly move.

There, there, Moya.

The baby bawled as she carried her back to the hotel.

Shoving the buggy along with one hand.

I don't have a sling or anything.

The whole day she'd planned – Grafton Street, St Stephen's Green, the post office – was disintegrating into a screaming baby and a broken pram.

My husband's up in the air, she sighed.

Her stepkids were so small he had to fly with them to their mum. *At least Patrick is coming right back tonight*, she thought, her head filled with an unusual anxiety.

And I'm not feeling myself, she thought.

This was odd because she never felt ill.

She was one of the healthiest thirty-six-year-olds she knew.

I can't stay cooped up inside. Stuck in a hotel bedroom. I need a new wheel so I can walk my baby . . . so we're not locked inside for seven hours.

That wasn't supposed to be a very long time. But now it really felt like that.

We were supposed to have fun in Dublin.

It was a hot sweat now, coming over her. Then she was shivering again.

Maybe they should fix it just for a short walk.

All she needed was a new wheel.

Are you sure you can't help me? she asked the man.

Sheila, with the seven-month-old on her hip, was holding the wheel in a garage. suddenly trembling. The guy just shook his head. *I don't . . . do . . . buggy wheels,* he scoffed. Every inch of his face saying, *I'm not interested in helping you. Could you please leave.*

You annoying woman.

She stuttered.

Are you s-s-sure?

Sheila was feeling nauseous now – cold, vulnerable – like the confident solicitor she was no longer existed, like she'd completely lost her footing.

He's not going to be back for hours.

Looking at her watch. Counting how many left.

The little hand hardly moving.

It had all happened so fast, since she met Patrick. It had been at the Cork Jazz Fest, they'd got talking, then they'd got emailing. At first they didn't ask too many questions. Not even knowing what each other did. She'd phoned him one day – *I'm up on a roof* – he'd said – and she'd assumed he must be a builder. And she didn't like talking about work.

I work in an office, she'd say.

She'd always thought like this.

If you told men too much – *I'm a solicitor* – they often started to treat you a little funny. Like you might be a difficult woman. Or you attracted the wrong types.

An office. *That's all they needed to know.*

That wasn't even that long ago.

In the hotel room, she thought she was going to be sick. It was exhausting even to stand up. These waves rolling over her.

It shocked her to be feeling like this.

I really need you, Patrick, she kept thinking.

The baby finally falling asleep.

The one she'd not expected.

You tell yourself you'll never get married.

You tell yourself you know what love looks like.

You don't expect it to look like a divorced Swedish Finn, who has spent most of his life in Germany, older, with two children over there, giving it a go in Ireland. You also don't expect them to be called Patrick. Or to be living with his mother in a castle in County Cork.

This was a rather eccentric purchase of my father, is how he put it.

You never know what love will look like.

I'm not feeling right at all.

They couldn't quite believe it when she got married, her friends, her sisters. They'd always expected her to stay single, like she had been for most of her life. They'd never expected her to leave Limerick, to move down there, let alone into a place like that.

They couldn't believe her luck.

I'm really feeling terrible, she thought.

Feeding the baby on the hotel bed.

It hadn't got any better by the time he landed.

Patrick texted saying he was coming as fast as he could. They'd hoped to get back to the castle tomorrow, but from the way she was feeling, she wasn't so sure.

It was winter when she first saw it.

Glinting frost. That grey haired sky.

The car passed the gate and turned down the avenue.

Oh my God, it is a real castle, gasped Sheila.

The keep. The turrets. The battlements.

Patrick laughed, *Well, you could say that.*

Even the village was named after it: Castletownroche.

Sheila was retching by the time he arrived. Vomiting these horrible colours. Like clockwork every fifteen minutes. That was when she called NurseLine.

You need to go to the hospital, went some man's voice.

Because from what I can tell your colon is not working.

Sheila left Patrick with the baby.

The taxi didn't take long.

Dashing between the bathroom cubicles she saw so many sick people that night, under those bright lights, with so many different

kinds of ailments – cuts, drunks, falls, pallors. It made her feel worse.

Here's a laxative, said the doctor, at last, at 3 a.m.

His face as worn down as the patients'.

I think that'll do the trick.

The next morning she was vomiting less.

I'm fine, I'm sure, she told Patrick. *Let's just go.*

Sheila normally loved pointing things out on the way: battle-fields, country homes, county lines. Telling Patrick bits of their history he didn't yet know.

But it had started: this horrible pain that meant she could hardly sit still, she couldn't think, let alone feel anything, between clenching her teeth.

No, no . . . it's just a stomach ache.

They were hardly back at the castle.

Their dreams of turning the place into a wedding venue, of making it pay for itself, the thoughts that normally crowded in on her, nowhere, as the hurt ached through her.

Patrick was looking down at her on the sofa.

I don't think this is what's happening, he said.

His accent making the words fuzzy round the edge.

His mouth pinched with worry.

I'm going to call your mother.

It was a few hours before Sheila's parents got there, supposedly to mind the baby, but it only took one look at her to decide to leave.

We're taking you back to Limerick, said Mam.

And you're going straight to hospital.

They left Patrick with Moya. The keep and the courtyard vanished behind the trees. The lawns and the walls were gone. The acres where they'd started a little life.

Are you all right back there?

I'm fine, she said. *I'm fine.*

The farms and the hedgerows rolled past, that brilliant green, the kind there is nowhere else in the world, the kind that made her so happy, all of it blotted out by pain. It was getting worse. It was maddening now. The kind of stabbing that takes over everything. That makes you want to whimper. That fixes all of you on it and into it.

Until there's nothing else.

I think we're going to be admitting you, said the tired nurse.

Finally the painkillers started to work, dulling it, almost taking it away. The agony becoming distant. Until it was hard to feel it had been that bad. They'd been there for hours. The doctor, somehow, she came to know he was new, kept screwing up her admittance, then the forms she needed to get a bed, until a nurse hit him over the head with a biro.

I'm sure it's fine, Mam, you can go home, it's just a stomach thing.

You don't know why it's taking so long.

You're in the ward but you've got to wait.

You keep asking. You keep getting told, *I'm so sorry, not today.*

I've got to get back to Moya, she fretted, the nurse walking away.

You start to lose your sense of time in the hospital.

Your days stretched but tiny.

Sorry, it's a Sunday.

Sorry, we couldn't fit you in today.

It kept repeating. The instructions to fast, leaving her hungry all day. Then telling her the CT scans were done for now and that the kitchen was closed. Then again. And again.

Like a bad joke.

I've got to get out of here, she muttered.

This is ridiculous, I'm not an invalid.

Taking a bite of this cold piece of toast, a hard clump of butter wedged into it, that was all they had for her, after hours. Sighing at least Patrick's mother had given her a framed picture of Moya to keep her company. The low hum, the occasional rush of feet. Repetitive sounds filling the ward around her. Unnerving her. She looked at the frame.

Mammy will be home soon, Moya, this is all just crazy.

You don't want to worry the people that love you.

Her mother was standing in front of her.

I've had an X-ray and they say it's not cancer or anything.

You don't want to worry yourself.

Oh, stop it, won't you, her mother said, tutting at her.

They were putting cannulas into her when she first felt surprised. *This is very medicalized*, she thought, as the nurse crouched down, injecting dye into her body.

It's just for the contrast, you see?

Then there was a hot flush that started in her head and ran all the way down into her bladder, until it started to get really hot, like she was urinating herself.

You're not. That's just a side effect.

Then the staff seemed to huddle together.

Right, Sheila. The doctor was back.

It was like it wasn't her life.

That was running half-marathons.

That was being someone who never got flu.

That was rebuilding the castle with Patrick.

Always chiding her husband not to eat that – *Or I'll be a widow when I'm older.*

We're going to get you to a colonoscopy right away.

The trolley rattled uncomfortably beneath her.

It seemed only moments later the injection went in and she was gone.

You wake up very suddenly from sedation.

Not like in the morning. You flinch and you're back.

You feel groggy. Your speech slightly slurred.

It was some sort of public area where she came to. A small corner, where she could see from her trolley that there were a few people sitting around, having tea.

What's wrong with you?

There was something wrong with Patrick's face.

The tension in it. The colour of it.

Almost the same as the wall.

What is it?

There was an old man nearby nibbling his toast.

You have cancer in your colon and it's spread to your liver, said Patrick.

That moment, there was a sudden hush. The other's faces, they were blurs, quietened and pulled away. They'd all heard. There and then she might have smiled. For Sheila felt like time had slowed down, like her sight was watery, like her body was tingling with shock. You feel suddenly distant. Like you're suspended in space.

Her own voice felt like somebody else talking.

There was some talk about seeing the consultant.

Then the nurses told her she was heading back to the ward.

They turned the corridor. The windows forming a wall of light.

Then it came rushing in like water.

I have cancer. I have cancer. I have cancer.

It was like her mind was running very fast.

Whole thoughts – hundreds of them – here and gone in a series of instants.

Then rage.

Why are they wheeling me like this?

I can still walk.

Liver and colon cancer.

It was like two moons in the night.

It was like nothing Sheila thought possible.

I'm in my thirties. I'm never sick.

This can't be happening to me. I'm not an old woman.

The sedatives had worn off by the time they let her walk again, the nurses taking her and Patrick, holding her hand, into what felt like a store room, to see the consultant, paperwork and boxes stacked everywhere around this exhausted man at the desk.

This is quite serious, he said.

The way he's looking at me, she thought, *I must be in the soup.*

And you must be Patrick, he said.

You never know quite what it is when you recognize someone from when you were young. Is it the smile? Is it how the eyes still squint between the wrinkles?

How do I spell your name? she said.

He hadn't finished spelling Eoghan when she saw him.

Just a little boy at school in Limerick with her.

Eoghan . . . are you the butcher's son?

It did help, that it was someone she knew, telling her that she'd probably been sick for a long time, that this had probably been there for ten years. It did soothe, when he told her he was going to remove one third of her colon and then another surgeon would take one third of her liver. And it did calm, when he'd gone over it – the two operations she needed – when she had to call her mam, not telling her about her liver, not all of it, as she was with Moya. The consultant was talking calmly and firmly now.

You're first on the list in the morning.

I'm going to come in and operate on you.

There's nothing more to discuss, you need to prepare now.

You need to shower and you need to sleep.

It was then they tried to be practical – they both shook his hand – he said all the best to her mam and they stepped out of his office, like it was nothing, trying quickly to make it to the store for a few things before it closed. Thinking on autopilot.

I need some boiled sweets for nausea.

It was on the pavement that the sunset caught her. Orange, diffuse in the clouds, pink, gliding in gold. The blue turning sombre. Sheila hovered for a moment outside the shop. It wasn't that meeting, where they told her the five-year survival rate was twenty per cent, where they said it would be irresponsible to have any more children, because she wouldn't be there to care for them. But looking at the rose-bronze light she already knew.

How many of these am I going to see?

Even seeing it made her feel fragile.

Like her firm place in all this had gone.

Then she followed Patrick inside.

Not mentioning any of that to him.

Trying just to focus on what had to be done until she took a sleeping pill.

She had no other way to rest: the feeling of this thing inside, that every twinge. It must be puckering her, puncturing her, too much to face alone. The thoughts of her baby. That – she'd done too much medical litigation not to know this – she might never see her baby again, too much to let her sleep. That was why she took it.

That morning, getting into the shower, putting on the gown, suddenly remembering she hadn't updated her will since Moya was born, she kept trying to focus. *I've got to get this out of me.* She kept trying to be herself. To be Sheila – the serious solicitor – who got things done. *This is my only way through.* Not to let it get to her, when she had to ask these matter-of-fact old nurses to witness it, their tears blotting those handwritten pages, she made them sign as she told them what was happening. *I've got to get this done.*

The trolley rattling underneath her.

Her last glimpse of her husband's face.

You'll feel much better when this is out.

The doctor smiled. Then the anaesthetist bent over.

The cold gas coming out of the mask.

Count back from ten for me now.

You never make it to seven.

It was a yellow room she woke up in.

There were these voices around her. Then suddenly she began to be sick. A flurry of people in white around her. Then it happened again. The burn in her throat.

That feeling she'd lost control.

It was then the pain started to build. Scalding, piercing, searing pain. Like a hand being slammed in a car door, like a knife twisting into her, like she was on fire – all at once, unceasing – as she writhed and sweated, through this sheet, onto the plastic mattress, soaking it, until it started to squeak. Tossing and turning, trying to find a way to ease into it, any way of contorting herself, just to dim it. But it wasn't there. It only seemed to get worse, the nurses saying – *I'm sorry, you've had everything we can give you* – until finally, hours later, it started to dull, it started to fade for a few seconds. Just enough to think. There it all was, between the throbs and the agony. The only thing that mattered.

The love in Patrick's smile.

The smile in her baby's eyes.

I can't die now, Moya.

It was like she was bargaining, but not with a higher power. It wasn't clear who or what she was talking to, even to her.

Just give me five more years, she pleaded.

Her mind felt broken.

Sheila was squinting at the framed picture of Moya. Like it was from another life, another world, when she'd thought she'd live to ninety-two.

Five years, that's all I need.
Just to get her to preschool.
Just to form her.
Please.

The noise wakes her every day.

There are feet on the landing, a thud, then the whine of the shower.

It's Moya getting ready for school.

Sheila is still in bed when she hears the door close behind her.

You feel cloudy, those first moments in the morning, old memories and new, clumped together from dreams. You can see yourself clearly, sometimes.

Your milestones. When Sheila thinks of hers, they're all about her. Her baby birthdays. Her first day at nursery. They're not about the chemos and the MRIs. Not about the twenty scars she has from five resections. Not about being told it has spread to her lungs. It's at moments like this, she hears herself think.

I can't believe I'm still here.
I can't believe she's in secondary school now.
My baby's thirteen years old.

The moments cling to her as she stirs.

Choosing Moya's school subjects together.

Harry Potter, at a London theatre, together.

I couldn't have hung on like this without you.

There's birdsong. Something clears in her head. It's been a few minutes now and Sheila heads downstairs to *The Irish Times*. The markets, the scandals, the fighting. She follows it as closely as ever. A look on Twitter. Then she attends to the castle. Not the place. But the bookings. Another wedding party. More emails that haven't been answered. A fiddle on the website. She's got it all in a folder – *Sheila's Tips* – for Moya when she's gone.

It's then she goes outside.

It's late summer, a great blue sky over her.

Through the courtyard, she enters the walled garden.

The bricks in the wall, as mysterious as old books.

Her husband must be somewhere tinkering with an old tractor.

This is where she spends most of her day.

She starts in the greenhouse, with the little things she's grown from seed, then on to the flower garden, the fruit garden and the orchard. She sometimes thinks how her world has shrunk: she hardly goes to Limerick any more, into pubs, or restaurants. She's here.

It's been a few years since they told her it was terminal.

And that they would do what they could with palliative care.

It's so different from when this first started, when she studied every scan and sat there with a notebook, trying to get it all down to search up on her own, later.

Could you repeat that? she would ask.

Are you sure about that? she'd ask specialists.

Now Sheila only asks for the essential.

Tell me what I need to know and don't go beyond that.

They leave the one question she asks.

'I don't need to know how long I have left.'

'I don't want to know that. I never ask that.'

Now she thinks of it, she can see herself with Dr Power, in his consulting room in Cork, telling him, *I don't ever want to know that.* This is how she wants to live.

'I know he will never say that to me.'

'Unless we get to the point it has to be said.'

The bees are over the redwort, lingering and pulling away.

The ferns are shaking in the breeze. There's a cry overhead and she sees the buzzards, circling over the keep, until one falls, then another, behind the walls.

I just want to know . . . Is it stable?

They talk on the phone, mostly.

She doesn't like to go down there, to the hospital, to see him. It upsets her. It makes her feel tense for days. Being in those waiting rooms. Sick faces all around her.

Grand, she says, when the doctor says – *Nothing much.*

'That's all I need to know.'

You're not in denial.

You know perfectly well what's going to happen.

You're here and you just want to be here, while you can.

The peas have grown so big this year.

'I no longer have that kind of panic. *Oh, I'm dying.* I don't have that any more. Because I am dying. But I've been living with it for so long that the mind has to accept that. You move through the stages almost like grief. And here I am at the acceptance stage.'

The breeze rustles through the trees. In the winter it will wail, they'll hear cracks from ripped branches in the gale. But not at the end of the summer. Not today.

The snapdragons are taller than ever.

Her mind wanders, round the castle, through the nettles, to the glassy stream. It's all been here, from the beginning. Someone's always been here: the flints from the ancients, the earthworks, from the beginning. Sheila's thoughts wrap themselves around their well of St Patrick. They dwell in the tower on the face of the Sheela-na-Gig: that carved stone woman, squatting like she is about to give birth to a whole world. They've all been here: the knights and the rebels. They've all passed like flowers.

Brilliant. Then gone.

'I don't think there's an afterlife, you see . . .'

'Which is paradoxically comforting. Because what kind of after-life would offer comfort to a person who's entering it? I mean, eternity as what? As a broken body . . . as they say around here . . . *riddled with cancer?* What state is your body in if you pass into an afterlife? Is there no body? If there's no body, you're a soul wandering around.'

'What kind of existence is that?'

'I don't believe in any of it. Haven't for forty years.'

'It comforts me that I'll be ashes in the wind.'

'Just a speck in nature's cycle.'

She's in the garden.

You watch the swallows.

You wonder where they go.

Why they leave for the deserts.

When it will be, they've gone.

It's easy to feel drowsy here, almost evening, her eyes on the vermilion in the rose. It's easy – she coughs, she wheezes – to run out of breath, if she carries on too long. They took a third of her lung. So she sits for a moment. The colours in the blooms, the long ones and the little ones, the whites and the blues, she empties her

mind and stares at them, chattering voices of a podcast fading away. The petals glow in passing sun.

It's then she notices that some of them have started to turn.

Mother – there's a shout from the courtyard.

Moya has come back from school.

I'm coming, she calls.

Give me just a second.

AUTHOR'S NOTE

You might be curious about how *This Is Europe* was written.

I wanted to write about the lived Europe, not the Europe of memory or political systems. I didn't want to write a travel book because I wasn't interested in my impressions. Rather, I was drawn to other people's impressions, those of old and new Europeans alike, each at their own point on the arc of life. What they saw and how they felt about a very changed place felt important.

This concept of exploring narratives from the start of adult life to facing death – and the geography of those stories – was how I selected voices. But many were self-selecting because they belonged to storytellers.

It took over five years to meet everyone and then write up their tales.

Travelling, calling, Zooming.

Most of the time, I thought I'd gone mad and would never finish.

Things happened. A pandemic. A war.

With every person included in the book, I first recorded then transcribed their interviews, after which I wrote up the story from their perspective. The quotes in quotation marks are taken directly from those conversations. The quotes in italics are what they told me they were thinking or what was said at that moment.

The storytelling – what happened, and when – is their own.

Behind every chapter is me as a listener, trying to catch their flow.

I chose the third person – *She did, then she thought* – as novelists have found for generations that it creates the greatest intimacy with a character, the closest feeling to being inside their head. I'm not sure why, but books of first-person interviews – *I did, then I thought* – have the opposite effect. They create distance. I tried other techniques – I hope successfully – to make you feel that any one of these people could be you, or at the very least that you are there alongside them.

Once I'd done that I returned to each person's story at least several times until I got it right, sharing the manuscript with them and correcting what I'd written, reading it aloud to them or getting it translated if the language was a problem for them. Several times I had to track people down again across Europe.

I have changed names or other details when it matters for their security.

The photos are almost all mine or theirs.

Any mistakes, of course, are mine alone.

— Ben Judah, London, January 2023

ACKNOWLEDGEMENTS

Text to follow

PICTURE ACKNOWLEDGEMENTS

Text to follow